ENDORSEMENTS

"A seed, by itself, remains alone. A seed that dies, upon being planted in the ground, produces a plentiful harvest of new lives. Jamie Stewart tells the beautifully redemptive story of her beloved son, Logan, in *Walk With Me*. If you have ever felt the ache of loving, then losing a child before having the chance to watch dreams unfold, you will find great comfort within the pages of this book. The captivating stories and tender lessons provide life-breathing messages of purpose and hope. You will quickly see that you are not alone. Your story is not over. Your child's story is not over. Jamie's journey builds courage to believe that it's truly possible for loss to bring forth a wealth of new life."

—JILL JOHNSON,
Co-Founder & Pastor of Red Rocks Church

"*Walk With Me* provides hope for those suffering from the heartbreaking loss of an infant. Through the power of engaging stories, covered in wisdom gained from personal experience, Jamie Stewart offers courage to believe that healing is possible."

—SHAWN JOHNSON,
Co-Founder & Senior Pastor of Red Rocks Church,
Best-Selling Author of *Attacking Anxiety*

"God clearly spoke to Jamie in writing this book and sharing her story. As bereaved parents of two boys in heaven, we know the pain that loss-parents feel. Jamie and her husband, Andy, walked with us through our losses, and without them, we would not have the community and hope to move forward. God will move in mighty ways to those who spend time in this book. There is something in here for all."

—CILE & CASEY FISHER,
WWM beneficiaries &
Parents to heavenly sons, Plum & Boone

"Once in a while, you run across a book that immediately captures your attention and curiosity and ultimately grips your heart. *Walk With Me* is so much more than just another book. It is a powerful testament to recapturing lost hope, trust, and faith after experiencing great loss WHILE being spirit-led through the difficult and very painful grieving process. IT IS A MUST-READ!"

—GARY BRUEGMAN,
Family Life Therapist,
Ordained Minister of 50 years

"Jamie Stewart's book, *Walk With Me*, is truly a gift to the infant loss community. This book is a love story, taking the reader on an intimate journey of love between a mother and her child, as it converges with unfathomable loss and heartbreak. Jamie's willingness to share her personal story with raw vulnerability, exposing her innermost thoughts and feelings will bless and comfort anyone who has faced the devastation of infant loss. This book is a 'must read' for family and friends of those walking this path—an honest guide on how to support and come alongside those you love as they walk through grief."

—KELLY ZIBELL,
Loss-Mom

"Jamie's gift for words brought me deep into this heartbreaking love story. Her letters to her sweet little Logan are so beautiful! I appreciated her raw honesty and how this gives the reader permission to go to our Heavenly Father with ALL our emotions, knowing He can handle it. The perspective she and her sister, Kelley, share on how to walk alongside someone going through tragedy and loss was EYE-OPENING. It's a perspective we all need to hear and learn from."

—LORI BRUEGMAN,
Human Resource Director of Red Rocks Church

Walk With Me

Walk With Me

A Journey of
Infant Loss, Grief & Hope

JAMIE STEWART

Contributions by Kelley Kuhn

XULON ELITE

Xulon Press Elite
2301 Lucien Way #415
Maitland, FL 32751
407.339.4217
www.xulonpress.com

Contributor: Kelley Kuhn

Editors: Daniel "DJ" Martin and Deb Hall

Cover Design: Emily Lennon and Kristin Van Lieshout

Paperback ISBN-13: 978-1-66285-400-2
Ebook ISBN-13: 978-1-66285-401-9

How we walk with the broken speaks louder
than how we sit with the great.

—BILL BENNOT

To my heaven-side, world-changing little boy, Logan. You are extraordinary, and one of my life's greatest honors is the ability to call you mine. Not to be where you are will forever be my greatest sorrow, but with immense hope and anticipation, I look forward to the day I will find you in my arms once again.

And to the two who helped mend a very bruised and broken heart—my son, Sullivan, and my daughter, Emersyn. You are the delight of my world, and you fill the darkest of days with sunshine, the stillness of sorrow with music, and all that is muted with vibrant color once again. I pray that you don't spend your life searching for what the world deems great or spend your time in its pursuit. I pray you would use your talents and gifts, not in search of status or title, but with those who would benefit from them the most. May you walk with the broken, stand for the oppressed, uphold the weak, embrace the excluded, and love people with a passion and zeal that matches your King's. May your lives be loud, but in the quietest way.

Sweet children of mine, I love you to the moon and back.

—Mommy

CONTENTS

Preface xiii

PART I: IN THE STORM. 1

1 — Searching for a Testimony 3
2 — Popcorn Boy 7
3 — Expecting Miracles 13
4 — "Something's Wrong with the Baby" 19
5 — Broken 27
6 — "A Person's A Person, No Matter How Small". 36
7 — Amidst Immovable Mountains 44
8 — In My Shoes 51
9 — Let Go and Let God 64
10 — Into the Water 68
11 — Broken Together 79
12 — The Beginning of the End 83
13 — Run to Jesus 92
14 — The Sorrow May Last Through the Night. 107
15 — Someone Else's Miracle 113
16 — Until We Meet Again. 117
17 — A Matter of the Heart 126
18 — Before I Die. 134
19 — An Unexpected Filter. 139
20 — Small Talk. 149
21 — Remember Me 155
22 — It Is Well with My Soul 162
23 — Letters to Heaven: A Walk through the Years 172

PART II: IN THE WAITING 187

24 — Walk With Me.......................................189
25 — The "Sickness" Called Grief.........................199
26 — Loss Support 101 202
27 — In Sickness and in Health 210
28 — Unnecessary Wounds...............................220
29 — The Hierarchy of Loss 224
30 — Anticipated Good-byes 231
31 — You Did Not "Miss" Carry..........................236
32 — The Shore 240
33 — Six Plates 243
34 — Proof of Life.......................................246
35 — Sticks and Stones...................................250
36 — Fear and Anger.....................................256
37 — Weeds and Wildflowers.............................262
38 — Battle Wounds 267
39 — Sympathy Cards and What Not to Say 274
40 — If Not Us, Then Who?..............................280
41 — Love Remains.......................................285
42 — An Unfathomable Gift..............................288
43 — Forsaken?..291
44 — Choose Hope.......................................296
45 — Earth Has No Sorrow Heaven Can't Heal 299

A Special Thank-You 303
About the Author.......................................305

PREFACE

> *If I speak with human eloquence and angelic ecstasy but don't love,*
> *I'm nothing but the creaking of a rusty gate. If I speak God's Word*
> *with power, revealing all his mysteries and making everything plain*
> *as day, and if I have faith that says to a mountain, "Jump," and it*
> *jumps, but I don't love, I'm nothing. If I give everything I own to the*
> *poor and even go to the stake to be burned as a martyr, but I don't*
> *love, I've gotten nowhere. So, no matter what I say, what I believe,*
> *and what I do, I'm bankrupt without love.*
> —1 Corinthians 13:1–3 (MSG)

You are about to read a love story. It's a story not only about love but about loss and, ultimately, the hope we have in Christ *even* when we find our hearts in the deepest and darkest pits of sorrow.

I believe God wants me to share my journey—even the messy and ugly parts—to help *someone, somewhere,* who has found themselves (or someone they love) where I once was. It would be a disservice to you if I did not stay transparent and honest in the pages ahead. A surface-level and sugarcoated story where I didn't share the things others would prefer to hide would be beneficial to no one. I am about to give you a window into one of the most delicate, sacred, and tragic seasons of my life. So just pretend you are having a cup of coffee with your friend who constantly overshares, and you should be good to read on.

I am sharing my story because I want those who have experienced sorrow and pain in ways I have to know *hope is not lost.* I know your future feels uncertain, foreign, and so scary. I know you are probably wondering if you will ever know joy again or if you are going to feel smothered under a blanket of grief forever. A piece of your heart *is* gone, and I would be lying to say its absence ever goes unnoticed. However, the intensity of the pain and the frequency of its visits *will* lessen in time. Hope may feel impossibly far away right now—but it *is* on the horizon. It's just hard to see through all the rain. For now, just *survive* one minute at a time. Let your heart rest when it needs to rest, and let it seep tears when it needs to cry. Lean into your grief, and take a deep breath when you find those (few-and-far-between) pockets of peace.

If you are the person I have written this for, I want you to know *you are not alone*. There is a community out there that understands the brokenness of your heart. Many of us have gone through a similar season in life, and many, despite the pain, have made it through the most treacherous parts of the journey. Find that community. Find those people. Reach out for help—*even* if it feels uncomfortable. The only thing harder than grieving is grieving *alone*. You already have so much weight to carry, new friend of mine, so please, let those who have walked the road before you carry that weight *with* you.

Lastly, and I wish we really *were* having a cup of coffee for this one so I could hold your hands and look you in the eyes as I told you, there is a God who has counted your every tear and wants desperately to pick up the pieces of your heart and tenderly put it back together. Yes, the new you may be full of cracks and holes and missing pieces, but broken is *still* beautiful. Broken is not worthless. It's not inferior, and it's certainly not unusable. I would argue the more cracks we have, the easier it is for love and compassion to shine through us. I personally am *full* of them. It is *because* of those very cracks this book is in your hands.

This book is broken into two parts. The first part is my story. It's the storm I suddenly found myself in. It's the story I never would have picked for myself but, nonetheless, the one that is mine. The second part is full of the lessons I learned *from* that storm—it's my life as I navigated blindly through the hills and valleys of deep pain and unanswered questions. It's what my world looked like *after* all color had been removed, and the delicate and painful process of learning how to see in color once again.

The wake from the loss I suffered still trails behind me, and in ways, it always will. My hope is to share that wake with you—so you may learn from my missteps. I hope you can walk away from these pages with lessons that took me *years* to understand—but hopefully with fewer scrapes, bruises, and scars than I did.

This book was written over *ten years*. Yes, you read that right. A full decade. There will be pages where you bounce around in time with me a bit, and not all chapters are structured exactly the same. I could have made the layout and flow more predictable, but I decided to share what I felt I should share when I felt I should share it. Like my journey, this book doesn't always take the expected route, but there's purpose in every step. It may be messy—but so is grief.

Throughout these pages, you will find journal entries I wrote in the thick of my chaos. You will find prayers—many for my family and even some for you. You will find times where I am sharing the raw details of my journey, and you will even find times where my big sister, Kelley, tells what she saw as she walked with me through my grief *and* hers.

I prayed for you when God quickened me to, and I stopped my narrative to explain things further at His prompting. So moving forward, expect a story, because that's exactly what this is—it's just one with lots of layers.

The words you are about to read have cost me and my family an *immeasurable* amount. These words were not easy to write, which is one of the reasons why they took so long to compose. The number of times I had to close my computer due to tears blocking my vision, my heart pounding too loudly to think, or my hands shaking too much to type, are far too many to count. The truth is, I have poured my heart and soul into the pages that follow.

You are holding one of the *only* things I have left of my son. *You* will get as much of him as I did. As unfair as that is being his mother, I know it would be selfish to keep him to myself. He is just too special not to share with the world. So here you go, world—*walk with me* on this journey, and I will walk with you on yours. I hope and pray that by the end of these pages my sweet boy will have impacted your life as much as he has impacted mine.

PART I:

IN THE STORM

When the storms of life are so turbulent that we cannot see ahead of us, God's truths *still* remain. In the most hopeless of situations, God's mercy can be found. Even in the worst places imaginable, a single light can displace absolute and consuming darkness.

The following chapters hold my story. From the early days of meeting my husband, to our walk through infant loss, this is your front row seat to it all. We certainly may cry together, but my prayer is that somehow, through the tears, you won't feel so alone. Together, and by God's grace, we *will* find the light, but first we must walk through the storm.

1 — SEARCHING FOR A TESTIMONY

Whoever believes in the Son of God has the testimony in himself.
Whoever does not believe God has made him a liar, because he has
not believed in the testimony that God has borne concerning his
Son. And this is the testimony, that God gave us eternal life, and
this life is in his Son.

—1 John 5:10–11 (ESV)

Photo by Jessica Fox

I used to wish I had a testimony. Little did I know that many testimonies—especially the ones that hit you square in the chest and change your life forever—are born from trials. I didn't understand, in order to have the testimony I hoped for, I would have to endure a test.

I grew up in a loving Christian home. From childhood into my twenties, life was good and I was incredibly grateful for all I had been given. I was the youngest of three, had amazing parents, and grew up in the beautiful Rocky Mountains of Colorado. Of course, I had my ups and downs, and experienced pain and loss, but I never faced anything that shook my faith to the core. I gave my life to Christ at a very young age and always had Him by my side. Sometimes I would feel His presence close to me, and sometimes I felt distant from Him. But nonetheless, He was my constant and *always* my foundation.

At one point in my early twenties, I remember thinking, *I don't have a testimony.* God had always been a part of my life, and I didn't know what it felt like to be without Him. I had nothing profound to say, no inspirational story of how God had drastically changed my world. I had been a believer for as long as I could remember, and I had nothing life-altering to share with the world. I didn't *want* to endure tragedy or difficulty to inspire others. I just believed because I didn't have a "story" that I had nothing to offer people who didn't know Christ. I felt unusable, stagnant, and invisible. I often saw others living what my heart so badly desired, but I could never seem to get where they were.

I remember sitting in church one Sunday morning and watching a video of a girl similar in age to me. She had walked through such darkness, and in the end, despite her pain, she gave her life to Jesus. She didn't turn from Him or blame Him for the abuse she had endured, but instead, she used it as a platform to draw people *to* Him. I left church that day feeling inspired by her. Inspiration, however, quickly turned to shame, as Satan seized the opportunity to tell me God loved her more.

What would you share if you had the chance? I heard the enemy say. *You have no value, no story, no impact. You, Jamie, are nothing.* I believed his words and cowered back into a very familiar corner. In those shadows I succumbed to his lies and whispers, truly believing I would *never* be enough and would *always* be useless in God's eyes.

Looking back, I just wanted God to be proud of me. I didn't want to waste my life, but I felt like I had nothing to give Him in return for what He had given me. I didn't understand all God wanted was my love. I didn't understand *His love* was nothing I needed to earn. And so, throughout my early twenties, Jesus took a backseat in my life. My relationship with Him was a piece of my story, but it was stagnant and lukewarm. I went to church on Sundays, and I prayed and read my Bible from time to time. I loved God and lived my life *for* Him, but not *with* Him (and, oh my goodness, is there a big difference between the two).

Well, I have lived a lot since then. I *now* understand those feelings were built on a foundation of lies. I *now* understand that even though I wasn't an alcoholic set free from addiction, a child saved from a broken home, or a cancer survivor healed by the hands of our Creator, I, too, had something to offer. I *now* realize one of the *greatest* testimonies a person can have is a lifelong relationship with Jesus. Being able to say He had been a part of my life from the start was my story *and* my testimony. God can use *anyone* and *any* story for His kingdom and His glory. It took me over thirty years—and a lot of trauma—to learn such a simple truth.

Had I known then what I know now—had I known I was walking into one of the greatest tribulations of my life, I think I would have spent less time worrying about my testimony, or lack thereof, and more time embracing the calm and beautiful season of summer God had kept me in. But seasons *always* change —and *mine* was about to.

─────

As I look back at that timid and insecure twenty-year-old version of myself, I wish I could cradle her face in my hands and give her a gentle, yet authoritative, hug. I would prefer to grab her shoulders with both hands in an attempt to shake some sense into her, but I'm certain it wouldn't yield much of a response. I wish I could stare into her eyes and help her see something she has overlooked for so long. She has been so focused on what she *isn't* that she has become completely blind to what she *is*. She's missed so much of the innocence and joy found in youth and created a burden she was not meant to carry. I wish I could force her eyes open to see the peace and beauty that surrounds her.

Then I see the twenty-six-year-old version of myself. I want to run toward her with my arms waving back and forth in a desperate warning. She's still looking back, full of insecurity, and has no idea what is about to collide with her. Even though she still has baggage from her past, she has finally started to settle and find a rhythm in her life. But she is living in a bubble that is about to pop, and I want to yell for her to brace for impact. I want to warn her that she is about to be blindsided. Soon, the color will disappear from her world. Soon, she will feel as though she is trapped in a never-ending winter.

Next, I see the twenty-seven-year-old version of myself. She's muted, exhausted, and drained of all energy. Her frame is whittled, and her core is empty. She is laden in grief and keeps her head down. I wish I could wipe the tears from her cheeks and tell her that one day it won't hurt so bad. I wish I could tell her I am proud of her and that she is doing a good job, even though she feels like she is drowning. I wish I could pull her close and give her a big motherly squeeze (we call these "ten-second hugs" in my family now). You see, God was walking with her down a road that would change and redefine her life in too many ways to count. He was starting the long and tedious process of sifting through the rubble to recover pieces of her heart so He could ever-so-lovingly stitch it back together.

Now in my mid-thirties, my life looks nothing like I ever would have dreamed. I am still me, just a different version. Do I *now* have the type of testimony I felt I was missing earlier in life? Yes. Would I change it if I could? With every fiber within me—*yes*. I trust God and know He has a detailed plan and purpose for my life, but I'm still human, so I naturally question Him on that plan from time to time. I am now on a very different path than I ever would have imagined—but I am nonetheless *still on God's path.* He is the author of my story, and regardless of where He takes me, I will choose to trust Him fully.

I must admit, though, I wish I could have a moment with the forty-year-old version of myself. I have learned so much in the last ten years, yet I know I could still benefit from her wisdom and grace. I need her to remind me this will all be okay someday. Even now, I could use a ten-second hug. The problem is, I cannot gain her knowledge and insight, and I cannot learn what she would know, without first walking the road between where I am and where she waits.

I am already getting too far ahead of myself, so before I explain more, I want to tell you a story about my son. Actually, scratch that. *First,* I need to tell you about his dad.

2 — POPCORN BOY

"For I know the plans I have for you," declares the Lord, "plans to prosper you and not to harm you, plans to give you hope and a future."

—Jeremiah 29:11 (NIV)

I t's strange to look back on the decisions made in my youth that seemed small and inconsequential at the time, only later to watch those *small* decisions become *life-altering*.

After high school I made the *seemingly* small decision to go to a community college rather than follow suit with my friends and attend a university. I had no idea what I wanted to do with my life, I was responsible to cover the cost of my education, and I didn't want to rack up thousands of dollars of unnecessary debt.

The college I chose was quaint. It was close enough to home that I still felt under the reach of my parents' wings, yet distant enough that I could still spread mine. I knew I would not have the typical college experience people always talk about. Like the wide variety of students who would soon surround me, I was there simply for the education. I expected to leave in two years with my associate's degree complete—and nothing else.

The social scene at the school was lacking. And by lacking I mean it was *nonexistent*. As I walked through the many corridors of the old building each day, I saw a hodgepodge of middle-agers who refused to make eye contact, exhausted and overworked parents who couldn't make eye contact even if they tried, and awkward twenty-somethings who would beeline to their cars as quickly as possible after class. There were no dorms, no parties, no sports—heck, we didn't even have a mascot. Well, maybe we did. But not one I knew of.

After getting through a semester and literally having only a handful of interactions with my peers, loneliness started to sink in. I missed my friends. I missed feeling part of a group, and I missed feeling like I had *any* social life.

Then, on the first day of my second semester, as I sat in my American History class and stared down at my desk, something unexpected happened. I looked up, and a tall, blond, curly-haired boy, with a backward hat and beautiful blue eyes, walked through the door. He was late, most likely due to the never-ending line in the lobby to get the free popcorn he was unashamedly carrying in his hands.

It wasn't love at first sight, but I suddenly found myself very aware of what I was wearing and counting the days since I had last washed my hair. He looked at me as he walked past my seat and paused for a split second. My heart skipped a beat. I have no idea what the professor said for the next hour because I was too busy staring at the new kid's curls and trying my best to look cute and noticeable—but in the most effortless way, *of course*.

It was no coincidence that, from that moment on, I spent a bit more time getting ready for school on Mondays and Wednesdays. The additional efforts repeatedly left a trail of evidence in my apartment, where a flat iron was more often left to cool in the sink and half the contents of my closet were more often emptied on my bed in search of the perfect outfit.

But after three months of exchanging shy stares, I started losing interest. He came to class late *every day* with popcorn in hand (which started to really bother my very punctual upbringing), and still, I would think, *Maybe this is the day he will speak to me,* only to realize that once again, it was not. He had gone, ever so slowly, from the tall, cute guy in class to the strange (but still cute) guy who stares. Eventually, I stopped caring about what I wore on the days I went to history class, and my flat iron found a more permanent home in my drawer—well, for the most part.

Then, to my surprise, as the end of the semester was nearing, Popcorn Boy finally said hello. To be more accurate, he came up to me and, in a teasing manner, asked why my pants had holes in them. They were my comfy jeans (again, I had stopped caring so much about my outfit choices), and my love for them was evident in their condition. His approach was so third grade that it caught me off guard. I raised an eyebrow in return. He apparently hadn't gotten the memo that being mean wasn't considered flirting once you passed the age of ten. But in all honesty, I was mostly shocked he could actually speak. Luckily, the "I'm gonna make fun of you because I don't know what else to say" approach apparently works well after *three months* of waiting. A few days later, we went on a very romantic date to . . . Panda Express.

It was awkward—for me. I didn't know his name, though he clearly knew mine. You are likely asking, how in the world is it possible to go on a date with a nameless man? Touché. I don't have an answer. My only defense? He was cute, and crazier things have happened.

I couldn't believe in all the months of class together I never learned his name. Believe me, I was listening. I hoped I would hear someone else say it—but I never did. His best friend always called him by his nickname, but I most certainly wasn't going to call him Stew, and I don't think our professor knew any of our names. Yet somehow, he knew mine. And he unknowingly rubbed it in all afternoon by saying it a thousand times. Later that day, as we were sitting on the couch in his apartment and watching a movie in a nervous first-date cuddle, I couldn't take it anymore. I grimaced, covered my face with my hands, and popped the question.

It still makes me laugh remembering the way he shot up off the couch like a startled little prairie dog popping up from its burrow, looking completely shocked and completely insulted. I kindly reminded him that he never actually introduced himself to me, but that didn't ease the tension as quickly as I had hoped. *If only I had some popcorn . . .*

Finally, as the shock settled and he sat back down on the couch next to me, I learned his name. Andy—Popcorn Boy's name was Andy.

If you think that's bad on my part, it was easily trumped. I may not have known Andy's *name* on our first date, but *Andy* had a *girlfriend* (of sorts) . . . on our first date. To this day he argues they weren't "official." But I'll let you be the judge of that.

Our first day together came to a brief pause after the name incident. I had a job at the mall, and my shift was fast approaching. It was a "saved by the bell" type of moment for me.

Later that evening I was in the middle of creating the most perfectly folded jean wall at a clothing store I will *never* admit to working at. Imagine a library with a giant, stuffed bookcase that reaches to the ceiling, but instead of books, we used jeans (side note, my manager told me he hadn't seen a wall as exceptionally crafted as mine in years).

I was gazing up at a job well done when, out of the corner of my eye, I saw familiar curls sticking out of a backward baseball hat. Andy was at the entrance of the store, wearing a white hoodie covered in . . . *chocolate?* Hot chocolate, to be exact.

Andy decided to surprise me at work with Starbucks but with nervous hands had spilled half the contents on his shirt as he walked into the mall. He looked at me with a sheepish grin and held out the cup that looked as if he'd found it at the bottom of a trash can. I thought the gesture was adorable, even though poorly executed. Andy didn't hang around long, but after I got off work that night, our first date continued as if it had never been interrupted.

Andy had long forgotten his name-debacle grievances as he sat at my desk. Out of nowhere, and sporting a clean shirt, he popped a very peculiar question: "So . . . do you have a boyfriend?"

Huh? I am pretty sure if I had a boyfriend, you would not be in my apartment. I raised my brow (once again) and responded, "Noooo . . . do *you* have a girlfriend?" I figured at that point it was just a formality we had to get out of the way. "Wellll . . . "

This time *I* was the one who popped up from my seat like a startled prairie dog. Before I could even begin to voice my protest, Andy continued, "Don't worry! I will break it off with her for you!"

"How flattering!" I lashed back. "You have a girlfriend and you are in *my* apartment, sitting in *my* room?"

Not Single Boy reassured me it wasn't "official" and that he would end *whatever it was* in the morning. I was still less than amused. I looked at my watch, said it was getting late, and headed toward the front door.

As we walked through the living room, my open balcony revealed a moon bigger and brighter than either of us had ever seen. Like two little kids distracted by something shiny, we ran to the balcony for further investigation. Andy closed the door behind us and we heard a big *thump!*

The locking bar that had never once caught my attention before suddenly had the power and authority of a prison guard.

We spent the next four hours locked on my balcony with that big moon. No phones. No jackets. Freezing temps. A conversation with a very strange drunk man in the parking lot below. A first kiss (what can I say? It was cold, and I succumbed). A chivalrous second-story, barefooted jump into the bushes. And, finally, freedom and a sunrise.

Later that day, Andy broke up with his not-girlfriend (as promised), and I claimed the title. I felt sad for her, but it turns out she didn't like popcorn, so it never would have worked out anyway.

And just like that, Andy and I had our first date, first embarrassing moments, our second date, our first fight, first kiss, and first trial—all in twenty-four hours. We were on the fast track and were soon *inseparable*. He was my person, and I was his.

Five years later, our family and friends watched as we made a promise to God and one another that we would love and support each other no matter what this life would throw our way.

Andy and I both wanted children but decided to push the "when to start trying" discussion out a few years. We were constantly surrounded by tiny nieces and nephews, and we witnessed firsthand that kids weren't all sunshine and rainbows. I loved when the herd of crazy toddlers visited, but they were a *ton* of work. They never stopped moving, fighting, talking, and eating. Oh my goodness, the eating. No amount of food could satisfy their little animalistic appetites. Sometimes I worried I could lose a finger if it had recently been in contact with a Goldfish and still smelled of its crackery delight. They needed something from me at every turn, and I couldn't even go pee without their little hands creepily finding their way underneath the bathroom door. They were more volatile than any human being I had ever known and shifted gears faster than I could adjust. They managed to find items in my house I never knew we had, and had an uncanny ability to break only the most valuable things we owned.

But then they would fall asleep, and suddenly all memories of their monstrous behavior would disappear. There is nothing quite as angelic as a sleeping child, and in *those* moments I would stare at their perfect, chubby, and beautiful faces and feel a tug on my heart.

I wanted kids of my own. I knew they would destroy my house, my sleep routine, and possibly my sanity, but I wanted to be a mom. I wanted to experience the miracle of life and one of the greatest gifts we could be given. I wanted a mini-Andy or a mini-Jamie running amuck in the house. I wanted to snuggle on the couch and feel their little hearts beating on mine. I wanted the beautiful disaster that only a home full of children could bring.

3 — EXPECTING MIRACLES

For you created my inmost being; you knit me together in my mother's womb. I praise you because I am fearfully and wonderfully made; your works are wonderful, I know that full well.

—Psalm 139:13–14 (NIV)

Photo by Ken Papaleo

As we approached our third wedding anniversary, the baby bug hit. Well, truth be told, I had to go off birth control for medical reasons, but we had been discussing starting a family and decided it was a good time to start trying. By default, we walked head-on into a season of expecting miracles.

A few months passed, and on a whim I decided to take a pregnancy test. I had finally reached the time where a positive could possibly show, but I didn't think I was pregnant. *There's no way*, I thought. *After all, we really haven't been trying very long.*

I watched the little window, anxiously waiting to see two blue lines appear. To my disappointment, there was only one. I shrugged it off, jumped in the shower, and didn't give it a second thought. When I got out, I picked up the test to throw it away and just happened to notice a

13

very faint second blue line. *What in the . . . Is that thing positive?* I immediately researched whether a very weak line meant I could still be pregnant.

Turns out the only reason even traces of the pregnancy hormone
would be in your body is if you were indeed—pregnant. I couldn't believe
it! *That thing tricked me!* I couldn't stop smiling, although I was still convinced it had to be some sort of fluke.

Coincidentally, my annual physical at the doctor's office was scheduled for that very morning. While I was getting my labs drawn, I decided
I might as well ask them to double-check.

I sat on a chair in an empty hall and waited for the nurse to come
back with the results. So many things were going through my head. I was
excited but still doubtful—and a tad terrified. I could feel myself trying to
subdue the tremble in my hands. Finally, the nurse came out of a nearby
room with a big smile and said, "Congratulations!"

"Wait—your test came back positive too?" I said.

She looked at me and laughed. "Yes, honey. You are going to
have a baby."

It just was too hard to believe. For nearly five minutes I sat on that
chair with my knees pulled up to my chest, unable to move or process what
I had just been told. Baffled and walking with a slight stagger, I made my
way out to the car. My eyes were wide, but my smile was wider.

With fumbling hands I called Andy to tell him the shocking news. In
hindsight I probably should have waited to tell him in person, but I was
too excited to wait. I could tell by his voice he was slightly annoyed that I
had called him at work so early in the day and demanded he drop everything and go somewhere private. His first response was, "You're pregnant?!
How did that happen?" I remember laughing and responding, "Um, you
should know—you were there."

We were both surprised, to say the least, but also ecstatic in anticipation of the blessing ahead of us. It was hard to imagine that by Thanksgiving,
our lives would forever change, and we would be parents.

As I look back at that day, I wasn't wrong in the way I envisioned my
world would change come fall. I just had no idea how much change was
coming my way and how drastically different it would be from the picture
I had created in my mind.

I hate to admit it, but I am a worrier at heart. So, of course, after the exciting news of being pregnant settled, the reality of everything that *could* go wrong began to take over. Worrier or not, I can almost guarantee every expectant mom goes through stages of anxiety during pregnancy. *What if I miscarry? What if my baby is sick?* I remember praying every day, "Please God, protect my baby. Please let my child be healthy and whole—ten fingers . . . ten toes . . . ten fingers . . . ten toes." Every cramp, twinge, and pain triggered the thought that *something* could be wrong.

Being the one to carry a life comes with an incredible sense of responsibility. It is something only a mother could ever understand. I knew if something were to go wrong (whether I could control it or not), I couldn't help but feel responsible. Like my body had failed me, and I had failed my baby.

Only one week had passed since my positive test when I started spotting. It stole my joy in an instant, as I was convinced a miscarriage was on its way. In addition, I started having constant, and sometimes severe, pain in my lower right abdomen. Since the pain was isolated and not subsiding, there was concern of a possible ectopic pregnancy. It was too early to see anything on an ultrasound, so I was told to wait a week and given a list of warning signs that would warrant a visit to the ER.

A week of waiting felt like an *eternity*. Time moved at a glacial pace, and I spent the entire week completely terrified. We finally went in for our ultrasound, and I openly cried when the technician confirmed our baby was exactly where it should be. The blood they took that day, however, showed that my progesterone levels were very low, and I was immediately put on hormone pills.

In light of the new information, I did what I thought any sensible person would do in my situation—a Google search. The ever-pessimistic wisdom of the internet told me I was probably going to miscarry—if I didn't die first. Regardless of the symptoms, Dr. Google will somehow always lead you to something terminal. Runny nose? Tell your family you love them because you're dying. Achy leg? Update your will because you're dying. Stomach pain during pregnancy? You're going to miscarry, and then (shocker here) you're definitely dying.

Once again, I was scared to death and lived the next few weeks on pins and needles waiting to lose the life within me. I never thought every trip to the bathroom would instantly cause heart palpitations in anticipation of seeing *anything* red. Then it happened. I woke up one morning, went to the bathroom, and lost my breath when blood appeared.

I know there are many women reading this right now who can relate to a moment similar to the one I was going through. In fact, if that is you, there is a good chance you've just relived that painful memory. In my story, thankfully I was just spotting and our pregnancy continued. However, I know all too well that is not true for all of you. If you are a parent who has suffered a miscarriage (or many), please know my heart breaks for you. Please don't let anyone belittle what you have gone through. A loss is a loss regardless of gestation, and you have every right to grieve. The moment I found out I was pregnant, believe me, I was attached. It is an instantaneous bond. The instinct to protect, provide, and love is conceived the moment your child is. So today, if that is your story, I would be honored if you would let me take a moment to pray for you.

Heavenly Father,

I pray for every person reading this who has suffered a miscarriage, or maybe even many. I ask, in your gracious name, that you would comfort them, give them your peace, and fill them with the hope and joy that can only come from you. Please draw near right now. Let them feel you wrap your loving arms around them. Cover their pain in a peace that can only come from you. Remind them of how much you love them and how much you love their unborn child. I pray they would find comfort in knowing they will see their child again, fully restored and covered from head to toe in your glory. I thank you, Jesus, for the cross and the promise of eternal life for those who follow you. "He will wipe away every tear from their eyes, and death shall be no more, neither shall there be mourning, nor crying, nor pain anymore, for the former things have passed away" (Revelation 21:4 ESV). I thank you, God, that you know our pain, have counted our tears, and have a plan of redemption for each and every one of us. Amen.

For the next couple of months, I continued to take progesterone to help maintain my pregnancy and lived in a constant state of anxiety. However, as every week passed, I would begin to feel a bit more at ease, and the weight of my fear would lighten. All I wanted was someone to tell me I would get to bring home my baby. It was a request no doctor could possibly grant.

I checked my pregnancy app every day. Well, let's be honest: I had three apps, and I checked them all. I loved seeing what my little one was up to and how big he or she was getting. I watched the daily countdown to delivery decrease at a painfully slow rate due to all the discomfort, reflux, and nausea—oh my goodness, the nausea. As many pregnant women know, it is really hard to keep pace with life when it feels like you have the flu 24/7.

I am a hairstylist by trade and had a very hard time with the physical demands of the job coupled with the physical demands of my body. My clients kept giving me the clichéd "Oh, you're just glowing!" I would smile and thank them but laugh to myself because I was hot and nauseous and the "glow" was just sweat.

Despite all the challenges, I was getting through it. I knew the blessing of being a mom would far outweigh the struggles of being pregnant. In the end, my arms would have a child to hold. I had finally reached the point in my pregnancy where I felt like I could take a deep breath. We were past the "scary" part. I, like most people, assumed that once you got past the first trimester, all would be okay. I had a precious life within me, and for the first time, I allowed myself to believe I would be able to keep it. I was going to be a mommy. Andy was going to be a daddy. We were well into the second trimester, and everything looked good.

Thankfully, the next few months were uneventful. Well, except for a quick trip to the ER to check on the baby after a porch swing I was sitting on collapsed. And no, it was not my weight alone that did the swing in (just in case you pictured a poor swing succumbing to the weight of a lone, huge pregnant woman. However, I have to admit that is a much funnier scenario). It actually took the weight of three adults to do the old, rickety swing in. Thank goodness, after spending a couple of hours attached to a monitor at the hospital, all looked okay.

My mind was continually going in a thousand directions all at once. *What are we having? How are we ever going to agree on a name? Why can't*

I have a hot dog? I really want one. I need to pick a date for the baby shower. What the heck is a NoseFrida and must I actually use one?

The weeks kept coming and going: 19, 20, 21. Finally I found myself days away from the appointment I had been looking forward to since March: the gender reveal ultrasound.

I told Andy I thought it was a girl. I was pretty convinced, and for the most part, so was the majority of my family. My three-year-old niece, Sydney, wanted a girl cousin so desperately that when I told her there was of course the possibility it was a boy, she fell on her face and cried herself into a puddle of tears.

Unknown to Andy, I had been calling the baby "Logan" for a couple of weeks. In my mind I had already named "her," and getting Andy on board was a detail I would worry about later. Luckily, just days before our appointment, Andy agreed that, if the baby was a girl, we would name her Logan. But we would just have to wait and see. After all, it still could be a boy.

4 — "SOMETHING'S WRONG WITH THE BABY"

These things I have spoken to you, that in Me you may have peace. In the world you will have tribulation; but be of good cheer, I have overcome the world.

—John 16:33 (NKJV)

Photo by Ken Papaleo

I don't like doctor's offices and probably never will. They give me anxiety, regardless of if I'm being seen for a physical or a broken toe. Sitting in the waiting room always gives me the jitters. It starts in my chest where my heart begins to quicken and works its way to my hands where I feel a subtle shake.

Nothing was different the day Andy and I went in for our anatomy ultrasound. It was June 28, 2012. The day will forever be etched into my heart because it's the day my life was split into two epochs: life *before* and life *after*. It's almost as if that day drew a thick black permanent line on the calendar of my life. Even now, it's hard to believe how one moment can shatter your world.

As I sat in my chair, nervously flipping through a magazine that could have been blank for all I cared, I couldn't get the beats of my heart to calm. My nerves were more pronounced than usual, and I could see the shaking of my hands mirrored in the pages they were clutching. I looked up at the clock and saw we still had a grueling ten-minute wait—*if* they were on time. In moments like this, I found my own punctuality highly annoying. If it had been up to Andy, we probably would have stopped for popcorn on the way in, and I wouldn't have had to wait so long.

I kept thinking, *Something just feels different today. Something is wrong.* A quiet but resilient voice played on repeat in my mind. I shoved the thought as far down as it could go.

I closed my eyes, wrapped my hands around the baby wiggling in my belly, and rested my head on the wall behind me. Images of the last months flashed through my mind. Clients in my chair asking my gender preference. My response always being, "A healthy baby." Private moments where my excitement was suddenly subdued by the thought of a health issue arising. I realized that the upcoming anatomy scan would either be the moment I could finally take a breath or the moment it would be stolen away.

We were so excited about having the gender mystery solved, but were uneasy with the fine-tooth-comb nature of the ultrasound. If there was an issue, many times that is where it would be detected. We didn't talk about it, but behind the smiles, we were both thinking the same thing. *Please, God, just let our child be healthy.*

We had arranged a party for that evening to reveal the sex to our families. I couldn't sit still, thinking about the special menu I'd planned and constantly questioned, driven by my need to overachieve and make way too much food. I was excited to bake a pink or blue cake hidden under a layer of white frosting. When the time was right, both grandmas would cut into the cake and reveal the sex to everyone. I could see the moment as clear as day in my mind. I could see, in slow motion, the slice of cake being pulled out and family and friends clapping their hands and jumping in joy.

Pink or blue? Pink or blue?! I almost couldn't stand it anymore. I had so much to do after the appointment: grocery shop, clean the house, make the cake, prep for dinner. I had never been that thrilled about anything in my entire life (sorry, Andy, our wedding is a *very* close second). But that would all have to wait. First, I needed to get this appointment out of the way.

"Jamie Stewart."

I was jolted back to reality and sat straight up in my chair. Making eye contact with the tech, I smiled and slowly walked behind her, with Andy by my side. With each step, that once-small voice within got louder and bolder in its warning.

The ultrasound tech was young. Her inexperience was clear as day. She was friendly enough but didn't have that warm, fuzzy, and comforting "I've been doing this for decades" feel. The room we entered was small and dark. I hoisted myself up on the exam table, let my head find the pillow behind me, and kept my focus on the ceiling above me. *Soon this will be over, Jamie. Stop letting your worry rob you of beautiful moments like this. You are going to find out the sex of your baby in just a minute—focus on that!* I took a deep breath after the inner pep talk and gave Andy a big smile.

The moment the probe touched my belly, the young tech's face became pale and her demeanor shifted. A room that moments earlier was full of excitement switched to a tension that was palpable. She feverishly retrieved a handful of measurements, and with each input of data, I could see her level of concern rise.

"Is everything okay?" I asked, in as calm a voice as I could muster. She gave an almost nauseated and forced smile in return and said some nonsense about struggling to get a few of her measurements because the baby was in a weird position. A moment later she unexpectedly stood up.

With her head down to ensure her eyes only made contact with the floor beneath her, she removed her gloves and left without a word. Andy and I exchanged nervous glances, and I felt my face flush. My heart began to beat so hard in my chest that it reverberated in my ears and made it hard to focus.

After a few minutes, a more experienced technician came in with the first and started taking measurements of her own. She was focused and quiet, even though she *was* the "I've been doing this for decades" technician. Unfortunately, the much-longed-for (and much-needed) warmth and comfort she typically exuded did not accompany her through the door. What the two women *did* say was purposefully masked in medical terminology. Andy and I tried to make conversation, asking questions and trying to remind them they were dealing with *real* human beings, but we might as well have not been in the room.

I am not just another patient! We are parents with feelings and emotions and fears. This is about my child! My firstborn! Please tell me something!

I knew they were not allowed to give us any information, but something was obviously wrong, and by ignoring us, they were making what was clearly an already bad situation nearly unbearable.

I wanted out of that dimly lit room more than I ever wanted anything in my entire life. I wanted to take my baby *and* my husband and run as far away from that building *and* that moment as we possibly could. I wanted the life we had a mere fifteen minutes earlier. It was so close I could almost touch it, but that permanent black mark was slowly beginning to make itself visible. That line would prevent me from *ever* returning to the life I once knew.

I squeezed my eyes shut and turned my head away from the techs in an ineffective attempt to keep my emerging tears at bay. *Maybe it's not as bad as it seems. This could be anything. Deep breaths, Jamie, deep breaths.* As I looked to my left, I could see Andy's jaw clenched. His hands were in equally tight fists—so much so that his knuckles had lost their normal color. I could see his eyes starting to glimmer.

The ultrasound that was scheduled to last an hour only took twenty minutes. They cleaned off my belly, printed what looked to be about thirty pictures, and walked out the door. Instead of the usual routine of lab work followed by an appointment with our midwives, we were immediately taken by a nurse to a secluded back room and forced to wait *another* grueling twenty minutes. By that point, my whole body was shaking. I couldn't focus, and I felt a nervous energy I had never experienced before. I could feel a scream emerging from my core—a scream that took all the power within me to hold back.

My mind was racing in every direction. *They are hiding us in the back for a reason. This must be bad. What's wrong with our baby?!* I no longer cared whether my child was a boy or girl. I just wanted to know my child was okay. *Down syndrome? Trisomy? Will I have a special needs child? Will I have a child at all?*

With trembling hands I stared at my phone and my list of favorite contacts. *I should text my family. They will be expecting my call soon. I need to tell them what is taking us so long.*

Without hesitation I clicked on the picture of my older sister, Kelley, and wrote, "Something's wrong with the baby." It was all I could get out. With the click of a button, the semi that had just run us over was now on its way to broadside her.

Andy was doing his best to keep me calm, but I knew the strong facade was only for my sake. I kept praying, *Please, God, no. Please, God, no!* I tried to hold on to hope. I tried to tell myself maybe it wasn't as bad as it seemed. I didn't want to succumb to the overwhelming sensation of my heart beginning to crumble—not yet. There was still hope, wasn't there?

Finally, a doctor opened the door. One look at her face and my heart completely shattered. There was a heaviness in her walk, a tell in the sullen positioning of her head, and an obvious discomfort in allowing her eyes to align with mine. Before she ever said a word, I knew. "We found some abnormalities with your baby."

Everything went dark. It felt like I had just been hit by a bomb—disoriented, numb, a loud ringing. *I can't breathe. I can't move. Is this a dream? This has to be a dream! What is happening? I can't understand what she is saying. What exactly is she saying? Are you seriously telling me our baby might die?*

The doctor didn't know what was wrong, but whatever it was, it was bad. The woman staring down at us shut the window on any crack of hope we still had, and also somehow left us confused and completely unsure of what was happening.

Our child was *very* sick; that's all we knew. But the prognosis was grim, and our care was now beyond their capabilities. She offered her condolences, which sunk a freshly placed dagger even deeper into my chest, and handed me a card with the number to a specialist.

I have zero recollection of the minutes that followed. I don't remember leaving that awful room. I don't remember walking to the car. I have no idea what Andy and I said to each other during that time. The next image I can conjure is the front seat of our car. Tears were falling in a way they never had before. Through blurry eyes, I was trying to repeat the number from the card that was shaking in my hands and get it into my phone. Easier said than done. God bless the woman on the other end of that number. I was trying so hard to communicate and gain my composure, but any words that were able to escape my lips between sobs were disjointed and muddled. Somehow, by the end of the conversation, we had an appointment scheduled early the next morning.

There is no book or guideline on how to call your family and tell them the baby we had all been waiting anxiously to meet could potentially die. All the calls blurred into one. Each time the phone would ring, the person on the other end would frantically answer, desperately searching for more information, only to be met with silence and then my incoherent wailing.

June 28, 2012, was a day I will never forget. Walking out those office doors was so very different from walking through them just an hour earlier. In one moment my world was turned upside down. In one moment the innocence, joy, and blissful ignorance I had lived with much of my life vanished.

So many of the details of that afternoon have become blurry, as if it's my mind's way of trying to protect itself. I remember feeling numb and empty, yet uncontrollably panicked at the same time. *Is this really my life? Is this all just a dream?*

THROUGH KELLEY'S EYES

"Something's wrong with the baby." Looking back, it's amazing how much confusion, disbelief, sorrow, and anguish were created by such a short text message from my sister. I sometimes think of the moments before I received that message from Jamie, jealous of how blissfully unaware I was that my whole world was about to be rocked to its core so quickly and completely. You never see tragedy coming—but it shows up all the same.

I was busy getting myself and my two little girls ready for my sister's gender reveal party set for that evening. I remembered how exciting that ultrasound had been for my husband and me during my pregnancies. I remembered how long we had looked forward to it and all the fun activities it set in motion preparing for our babies' arrivals. Baby showers, gift registries, nursery decorations, arguments over names—you know, the good stuff. I was so excited it was now my little sister's turn to do all of those things and equally excited that I was going to help every step of the way. As much as we love all of our kids, there is something almost magical about your first.

But on June 28, 2012, tragedy entered my life with the familiar chime of a text message. As soon as I heard it, I knew the message was from my sister, and I nearly fell over myself trying to reach the phone. Her appointment should have just ended, and while I knew she wouldn't be sharing any hints with me, I was excited to be getting a message from her all the same.

The moments that followed reading it are still a big jumble of extreme haziness, yet also a painful clarity. I could never forget the words I read: "Something's wrong with the baby." I sat there and stared at my phone for the longest time, not knowing what to think and desperately trying to figure out what it meant. I know that sounds ridiculous since Jamie's text was pretty straightforward, but it just couldn't be right. I had to be missing something. All of the baby's initial testing came back clear.

I was desperately trying to put a spin on the message that would result in some kind of minor complication. I had to be missing something. How can something be "wrong with the baby"? Like something is slightly off that they'll have to keep an eye on? Maybe an indicator of a mental problem or a growth issue? For the life of me, I couldn't figure out what to make of it, but a large wave of overwhelming panic had begun to swell. Panic that strangely led to *anger*. What the heck was going on? Why in the world did my sister slam me with such a vague, yet terrifying, message?

It felt like an eternity had passed before I was awarded some clarity. Oddly enough, I don't have the foggiest idea how the details I desperately longed for were finally shared with me. I can't remember if Jamie sent me another message or someone else in my family called and explained. Either way, the reality of the situation was much worse than I could have ever imagined.

Jamie's ultrasound showed several drastic abnormalities with their baby, abnormalities that even her OBGYN couldn't explain. She and Andy didn't even discover the sex of their baby that day. They were simply sent home for the evening with a follow-up appointment set for the next morning. All we could do that night was wait. And you can guess how much that completely and totally sucked.

Jamie and Andy only lived a few minutes away from us, so I showed up on their doorstep in no time, prepared to be the epitome of strength and peace I figured they so desperately needed. Instead, I became a blubbering mess upon entering the house and seeing my little sister sitting on her sofa, hugging her sweet baby bump with eyes swollen and red from an onslaught of tears. I still can't wrap my brain around how insane it was to go from the highest high to the lowest low in the blink of an eye. How utterly helpless I felt. Helplessness is such an awful place to camp out.

Before that night my prayers for Jamie and her little one sounded as you might expect: "Please keep baby and mommy safe and strong." But after seeing my sister crying on the sofa, I began to *beg* God with *all* of my strength that the baby would simply *survive*. What a difference a day makes.

I sat in a ball on the couch as family members poured through my front door. I was frozen, unable to remove my hands from my belly and still reeling from the shock of what had just transpired. Tears had emerged from a pool with a bottom I had yet to find. The house felt quiet—but chaotic. A straight shot to my kitchen revealed the pile of cake ingredients I had set out only hours earlier.

We spent the rest of the afternoon cuddled on the couch, surrounded by family and frightened for what the future would hold. The heaviness that rested on our house was ominous, like a dark and threatening cloud had suddenly appeared above our roof and our roof alone.

Later in the evening, I found my dad sitting outside on the front stairs with his hands covering his face. Tears seeped through his palms and made their way down his tan arms. He had a hard upbringing and had already experienced so much loss in life. He was strong on the surface but tenderhearted and delicate in his core. His grandchildren were his "crown and glory," and I had a sinking feeling in my heart that he was about to lose one.

I wrapped my arms tightly around him and told him not to worry. I told him it would be okay and everything would be all right. And for the first time in my life, I lied to my father.

5 — BROKEN

When you go through deep waters, I will be with you.
—Isaiah 43:2 (NLT)

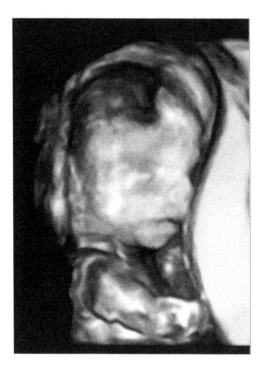

There is a sickening sensation I get after waking from a nightmare. A moment exists where I am not fully awake but no longer asleep, and for an instant, it's hard to distinguish dream from reality. The horrors of the images flooding my mind feel anything but made up, and I am left to sit in a hazy but fleeting limbo of what is real and what is not. Finally, my surroundings become clear, my brain is able to reset, and my body allows a much-needed exhale. *It was just a dream, and all is well.*

I jolted awake the very next morning momentarily locked in such a state. Without warning, I was hit with a giant wave of panic. Eerily familiar, yet incredibly foreign, pictures flashed through my mind. Blurry images fueled my palpitating heart and clammy hands.

Oh, thank you, Jesus, it was just a—a second wave immediately hit me square in the chest. The terrors that haunted my dreams during the night were *not* imagined. The exhale wasn't even complete before it was swiftly sucked back into my lungs. I was trapped in a nightmare. The world I woke up to looked the same, and yet I couldn't recognize it.

I had spent hours the night before praying for a miracle. On my knees, next to my bed, with my head in my hands, I begged God that *somehow* what we had been told was a mistake. Maybe they were wrong. Maybe it wasn't as severe as my OB led us to believe. Maybe this appointment would put an end to the nightmare that consumed me. *Maybe . . .* we would get good news.

Later that morning, I found myself once again lying on a small table and staring at the ceiling of a *new* room with a *new* probe pressed to my belly. Andy was in a chair beside me, cupping one of my hands in both of his. The ultrasound tech looked down at me and said, "I'm glad your parents are in the waiting room. It's going to be a hard day."

My heart sank at her words. *She hasn't even looked yet. How does she already know this is going to be "hard"?* Apparently, my OB had shared more with the specialists than what she had divulged to us. Our ultrasound tech had read our file and was more prepared for the exam than we realized.

After a handful of minutes, the tech looked down at me and asked an unexpected question. "Do you want to know the sex?" Andy and I looked at each other, smiled, and nodded in her direction. She smiled sweetly and said, "You are having a little boy."

Yes, of course we are. The news caused us to laugh and cry simultaneously. I had been so convinced we were having a mini Jamie, but no, we were having a mini Andy. The laughter stopped and the realization cut through me like a dagger. My *son* is sick. My *son* could die.

Moments later, an old doctor with glasses and a gentle demeanor peered his head through the partially closed door. He nodded at his tech and, upon her returned nod, made his way right toward me. His comfort and warmth immediately filled the room. It was almost as if a lifetime of experience and compassion walked through the door with him and surrounded us. The admiration and respect from his peers was tangible. He wasn't just a doctor, he was *the* doctor. He was safe. I could feel it in my heart. But I was still afraid.

The doctor stood at my side and tenderly placed his hand on mine. Everyone in the room had their eyes glued to the ultrasound screen in front of us. Everyone, that is, except me. I kept my eyes glued to *him*—desperately dissecting his every reaction.

The technician effortlessly maneuvered and measured her way through our son's body, and at every turn, it seemed as though the doctor nodded his head, as if in agreement to himself of his earlier, yet unmentioned, suspicions. It was like he had a mental checklist, and as he moved down it, he was able to confirm each and every marker for which he searched. He knew exactly what he was looking for and exactly where to find it. It felt like an eternity, but in reality it only took a handful of minutes to get the answers we were looking for.

He looked down at me with sympathetic eyes. He squeezed my hand and very softly said, "I'm sorry, but your son is not going to make it." It took a moment for the weight of his words to sink in. I stared at him blankly, not knowing how to respond.

The doctor continued to explain that our son had a condition known as Osteogenesis imperfecta (OI) Type II and wasn't going to live. He pointed out that our baby had multiple fractures in both legs, both arms, and throughout the rest of his tiny body. His rib cage and abdomen were underdeveloped, and his skull was not fully calcified. Osteogenesis imperfecta had caused a devastating mutation in his bones, and as a result, they were incredibly fragile. This would, in turn, cause his lungs and other vital organs to be unable to grow and mature as they needed to. Of the many variations of OI that exist, our baby had the most lethal version.

The doctor told us there was a possibility our boy could die at any time. *If* he made it to term, he would very likely not survive the process of delivery. If his delicate body *happened* to make it through both labor and delivery, we would have mere minutes with him, at best.

I held my breath and squeezed my eyes shut as tightly as I could. I had my head turned toward Andy and away from the staff in an attempt to let the surge of pain pass. I didn't yell or scream or cry out. The scream was there, but it was hidden inside.

Within moments, the onslaught of tears was much stronger than my ability to hold them in, and suddenly, my cheeks resembled a riverbed. "Can we still name him Logan?" I opened my eyes and looked down at

Andy. He smiled and nodded in agreement. Logan was *not* a girl, but the name was still a perfect fit. Actually, it was an even better fit.

The bomb had been dropped. Osteogenesis imperfecta would steal the life we planned to share with Logan. There would be no need for a baby shower. No first ride home from the hospital. No sleeping baby in the nursery. No first smile. No first tooth. Like a thief in the night, some horrific disease I couldn't even pronounce would rob us of *everything*.

We hadn't even caught our breath from the explosion when the fallout hit. "How do you want to proceed?" I didn't understand the question. Everyone else had shifted gears, while Andy and I hadn't even found the clutch. My mind had not yet processed what was being asked. I had not moved on to "what's next?" because I was still reeling from "what's now?" In our silence, a nurse took the liberty to explain.

In a nutshell, we could end our pregnancy in one of two ways: induce labor or abort. *Terminate my pregnancy? Terminate Logan? Is that the only option?* In all fairness, the option to continue my pregnancy may have been made clear to me as well, but I simply can't recall it being brought up. Shock seems to be skilled at stealing memories, because these ones are foggy and full of gaps. Some pieces are crystal clear, and some remain completely dark.

Unless my ears were betraying me, abortion was the "easiest" option. Inducing labor at such an early gestational age was, more often than not, a grueling several-day process. It was an avenue, but a complicated one. There was also a question as to whether or not Logan could be delivered without the aid of tools. They were worried his soft skull would not be able to create the pressure needed to be pushed out. If necessary, the use of tools or *any* intervention to aid in delivery would crush him.

We were being bombarded with opinions and scenarios, told there was no chance of survival. This was it. Game over. Better luck next time. In the end, we were given two suggestions and one consistent outcome: the death of our boy.

I was overwhelmed, nauseous, and I couldn't think straight. Our situation seemed too horrific to be real. For a very brief moment, and in the depth of the chaos, a part of me forgot I had another option. I could choose to let God be in control. *I could choose life.*

I had always told myself that, short of my own life being in jeopardy, there was *nothing* a doctor could ever tell me that would make me terminate a pregnancy. But never in a million years would I have pictured a day when I would have to prove it.

THROUGH KELLEY'S EYES

The next morning, I waited at home with my girls while Jamie and Andy went to see the specialist. I called them on the way to their appointment and read them one of my favorite children's books called *You Are Special*, written by Max Lucado.

It's the story of a little wooden fellow named Punchinello who, regardless of how hard he tries, doesn't measure up in the eyes of the other tiny wooden people where he lives. Eventually, he ends up seeking solace with the carpenter who created him. The carpenter proceeds to tell Punchinello that it doesn't matter what *anyone* else thinks about him because the carpenter made him *exactly* how he was meant to be. The carpenter didn't make mistakes. My sister's baby was fearfully and wonderfully made by God, and like the carpenter, God doesn't make mistakes. This sweet child's life had a purpose.

I was (once again) waiting for the results of another ultrasound, but this time I couldn't shake the feeling of despair I was wrestling with. I found myself begging God for good news and waiting for a call from my family. While I did finally get the call, I did not receive the good news for which I had been begging.

I had a nephew, and he had been diagnosed with a *terminal* genetic disorder. A big scary name that came with a whole list of even scarier complications. In a nutshell, it was quickly determined that *if* our Logan even made it to delivery, he would not be able to survive outside of my sister's womb.

Helplessness. I cannot begin to describe to you the overwhelming feeling of helplessness that was my new and constant companion. I often felt like I was suffocating. There is *nothing* in this world like watching the people you love drowning in grief and sorrow.

All I wanted to do was fix it. I wanted to say *all* the right things and do *all* the right things and *somehow* spare Jamie and Andy this nightmare. It took me a long time to realize that, even if I said and did *all* the right things, *I still couldn't fix this.* How could my words or deeds, no matter how loving, mend this broken chapter of Jamie and Andy's life? This was above my pay grade.

I had to remember the Carpenter. He is Jehovah-Rapha, the God who heals. And I? I was Kelley Elizabeth Kuhn, the sister who couldn't—no matter how hard I tried.

I wish there were words that could properly describe the relentless and debilitating pain Andy and I felt driving home that day. Regardless of how hard I try, mine will fall short *every single time*. Our entire life had screeched to a halt. Our hearts shattered into a million unrecognizable pieces. Our world was suddenly foreign and its rotation had been lost. My life turned gray—covered in the ashes of what used to be.

Our baby was sick. He wasn't even out of the womb, yet he had more broken bones than most people experience in a lifetime. My son—*my everything*—was dying. His body was *broken*.

Knowing Logan could be hurting tortured me. My instinct was to protect him, regardless of the cost, but there was *nothing* I could do. I felt paralyzed as I helplessly watched my child drown right in front of me. It was all happening right before my eyes, yet despite my efforts, I could not move an inch. The feeling of helplessness was beyond anything I had ever experienced. I would have given my life for his in an instant if I had only been gifted that power.

※

We had lots of visitors in the following week. The anticipation and joy that had filled our home days earlier were replaced with a sadness that was claustrophobic. There was a weight on my chest and it was going to crush me. I wanted to scream, cry, throw up—*anything* to make the anguish of my soul relent.

My older brother Jordan came over with a Costco-sized package of Kleenex, a box of ice cream bars, and a leather-bound journal. At the time, I had no idea the value of the gift he had just given me in that journal.

Before that day, the written word was a seemingly mundane, but necessary, part of life. But the significance of words and the power they wielded shifted for me in the days that followed. Suddenly, words could reach the core of my heart and provide an avenue for my sorrow to flow freely. I found comfort in their presence—almost as if they could somehow better connect me to God, Logan, and even myself. The world around me was dark, scary, and spinning way too fast, but the ability to put pen to paper gave me solace. Words became a much-needed companion—one that could give my heart refuge and pause the world around me.

My journal became an extension of me—a place where my grief, my anger, my fears, my hopes, and my sorrow could coexist. In the weeks and months ahead, there was no place I went that it did not follow.

Just days after Logan's diagnosis and early enough one morning that the sun hadn't peeked over the horizon, I gained the composure to write for the first time. Curled up in a blanket on my couch, with one hand on my belly and the other holding a pen, I poured out my heart to God. A seemingly endless amount of tears ran down my face—tears I knew He would catch and count on my behalf, but tears I wished had no place in my story.

7/2/12

Dear Heavenly Father,

I give my son to you today. I ask in your holy name that you would strengthen him, take his pain away, put your healing hand upon him and restore his little broken body. I ask that you would give him your peace—that you would speak to him and tell him not to be afraid. I stand in faith today, as your servant and your creation, and ask that you would work a miracle in Logan's life.

I know you understand my pain and anguish, for you, too, had to face the loss of a son. I am so sorry it was my sin that put your son on the cross, but I thank you for the gift of salvation that came as a result. By Jesus's stripes we are healed. Not just eternally but physically too. I am asking for that healing today for my little boy. I know nothing is impossible for you. I know you have a plan and a hope and a future for him. I know you love him more than I ever could. So today I lift him up to you, I dedicate him to you, and I ask in the name of Jesus Christ that you would breathe life into his lungs.

I ask that you would hold Logan in your hands and remove anything from his body that is not of you—and only good and perfect things come from you. I thank you, God, for the greatest gift you have ever given me, and that is your son and my salvation. I accept your gift with every fiber within me. I dedicate myself to you as a living sacrifice and ask that you would use me to bring glory to your name all the days of my life. I also thank you, God, for the second greatest gift you have ever given me, and that is my son. I vow to only speak life to him. I promise I will support him, uplift him, love him, and fight for him just as I would if he were here in my arms.

I will cherish every moment I have with him, and if it is in your will, I ask for more time. I want his father to be able to hold him in his hands. I long to touch his face and marvel at your work. I want to teach him all about you and raise him to be a man after your heart. I want him to bring honor and praise to your name and be a reflection of your glory to the world.

Jesus, please hear my cry! My heart is broken, and you are the only *one who can put it back together. The pain is so severe that I feel as though I can't go on. Please help me trust in your Word! I know when we are weak you are strong. I know we can do all things through Christ who strengthens us. I know if I come to you when I am weary, you will give me rest. I know you draw close to the brokenhearted, and I know you will never forsake me. I can trust your heart, but God, I cannot trace your hand! Please help me understand.*

Make straight our path. Help us to know what to do. Help us to trust in you, to lean not on our own understanding, to acknowledge you in all our ways so you would direct our path. I give you full authority over my son's life. We want what is best for Logan—please help us to know what that is. If it is not in your will for him to be restored, and if he is in pain, then please take him home with you. I want time with him, but not at the cost of his suffering.

I trust you. I know your ways are not ours, and many times we don't understand why things happen. But I also know, regardless, that you are good, that you love us more than we could ever understand,

and that all things work for good to those who love you. Please have mercy on my family today. Give us peace—the peace we read about it your word, which surpasses all understanding. Please help us not to be afraid, because we know your perfect love casts out all fear. Please move your hand today, and give us the strength to get through whatever our future holds.

Help us to praise, honor, and love you no matter what our circumstances may be. May your Holy Spirit radiate out of us and your love shine through us. Through this trial, may you be glorified. I pray the life of my little boy, no matter how brief or long it may be, would make an impact on someone, somewhere—that through your mysterious ways, his story would bring someone to you.

You, Heavenly Father, are the Author and Creator of life. You knew us before we were in our mother's womb, and today, I entrust my son, Logan Andrew Stewart, to your perfect will.

6 — "A PERSON'S A PERSON, NO MATTER HOW SMALL"

My frame was not hidden from you, when I was being made in secret, intricately woven in the depths of the earth. Your eyes saw my unformed substance; in your book were written, every one of them, the days that were formed for me, when as yet there was none of them.

—Psalm 139:15–16 (ESV)

Photo by Ken Papaleo

B eing a couple who decided to carry a terminally ill child was more or less an anomaly—at least that's how it felt to us. The medical world seemed to have no idea where to send us or, quite honestly, what to do with us. It felt as though our son was a lost cause in their eyes, and we quickly found out it wasn't common for a couple with our diagnosis to maintain the course.

Some doctors were kind and sympathetic. Others were calloused and cold. The sweet old doctor who diagnosed Logan and whom I had grown quite fond of turned out to be a pillar of support in a world of doctors who seemed to question our every move. Once he and his team understood termination was not an option, they were compassionate and understanding. On so many occasions, they went above and beyond their professional duties.

To this group of individuals—thank you. You know who you are, and I want to thank you from the bottom of my heart. I wish all those we crossed in the medical community throughout our time with Logan could have been half as compassionate as you all were. You were proof of God's grace in our lives, and the support and love you offered my family will never be forgotten.

Others in the medical world, however, tried to tell us it was cruel and inhumane to continue Logan's life. They explained the process of abortion as "gentle." They dehumanized Logan by calling him a fetus—a fetus that was broken, incompatible with life, and in the end, not worth the emotional and physical pain continuing to carry him would create.

We quickly learned "pro-choice" could be a double standard. I had always associated the term *only* with the right to terminate but never realized the way it should support *any* choice. And yet, it didn't seem to. It meant full support and understanding when ending a pregnancy, but in our situation, when the "choice" was life, it meant questions and doubt. A pro-choice world that, ironically enough, questioned the one we were making—it didn't seem fair.

"He is not just a fetus!" I wanted to scream it at the top of my lungs a thousand times! "His name is Logan—he is my son, a gift from God, and the absolute love of my life." It was God's decision when to call his child home—not mine. No matter how brief Logan's life may be, we knew he had a purpose. After all, "oops" is not in God's vocabulary. For reasons only known to Him, we were picked to be the parents of this amazing little soul. Our only choice was to offer our son a chance to live, to fight for him with all that was within us, to continue on the road ahead of us, and to let God decide the number of days we would get to be together.

We have come to a place in my story where I am walking on immensely volatile soil, and it would be a disservice to us all not to take a moment to pause. For a multitude of reasons, a multitude of opinions, and a multitude of emotions beginning to brew on behalf of the topic we have entered, it is crucial that we all stop for a moment and embrace the tension. For some of you, this may feel new and foreign. Leaning into super uncomfortable conversations is never easy, but it would be naive to think the contents of this book are going to be anything but. In full transparency, this won't be the last time we must sit in a difficult space together.

Sometimes, in a situation like this, there is nothing left to do but rip the Band-Aid off. So that's exactly what we are going to do. My hope and prayer is that God would soften the posture of *all* our hearts in the moments ahead—that, where damaged and open wounds *should* exist by the world's standards, new and healthy skin would emerge by God's grace.

We all have our unique belief systems. Often these systems are birthed from our upbringing, our environment, and our experiences. Our stories have the power to shape the way we see the world. As a result, we all have different eyes. Not to be confused with "bad" eyes or "good" eyes—just "different" eyes. It would do all of us good to remember that from time to time.

A woman's "right to choose" is a delicate topic in our society, and the question "when does life begin?" seems to send people into a tailspin. *Everyone* has an opinion. It's one of those places where there isn't much gray area, and there probably never will be. It's no wonder people put on their boxing gloves when the topic arises.

By now, it's no surprise that I have a Dr. Seuss–type mindset. "A person's a person, no matter how small." *My* eyes see a world that has exchanged the word *baby* for *fetus* to mask what it is that termination is terminating. In my mind, a beating heart should mark the beginning of one's life, just as a still heart marks one's death. In my mind, the length of a life belongs in the hands that created it. My eyes see a culture that has become deceived—but again, those are *my* eyes.

I don't feel threatened or defensive if you see this differently in your world than I do in mine. And I can only hope and pray that you will let down your guard for me *if* you are feeling threatened or defensive on my account. To the best of my ability, I am standing here, vulnerable, exposed, waving a white flag and begging God to create a neutral space for us all. Regardless of where you toe the line, how convicted or justified you feel in your beliefs, or how strongly you may consider it your duty to force the world's eyes to match yours, there is only *one* thing I want you to take away from this moment. This isn't about abortion. This isn't about women's rights or lack thereof. This isn't about pro-choice, pro-life, left, right, blue, red,

CNN, Fox News, or all the outrageous (and sometimes horrific) things people do in solidarity with their "side." This is about *grace*. It's about taking off the boxing gloves, stepping out of the ring, and accepting one another, in true Jesus fashion, regardless of the lens we view this world through.

As we move forward, that is all I ask of you. Grace for me. Grace for you. Grace to hold space where our opinions may differ. Grace to understand the outstretched arms of our King on the cross are big enough to span the differences that may exist between us.

Now that we have (hopefully) cleared the air a bit, we have to enter a conversation where if God's grace isn't front, center, and paramount, we may as well stop right here. There are some decisions a parent should *never* have to make. One of those decisions is the choice to continue or end an unborn child's life amid a terminal or severely life-altering diagnosis.

This book will inevitably find itself in the hands of parents who chose the road of termination in light of such a devastating crossroad. In the medical world, this is known as TFMR (Termination for Medical Reasons).

Now I can assure you any parent who comes face-to-face with such a gut-wrenching decision doesn't make it flippantly. If you are a parent who chose TFMR, I don't think you did it because you didn't view the life within you as anything less than your child. I don't think you made your decision because you viewed the life within you as one with little value. I think you made your decision wrapped in a blanket of mercy. I think you made your decision to put an end to suffering. With all my heart, I believe your decision was just as agonizing as mine.

Opinionated and cruel people may say you killed your baby or didn't give them a chance to live. Opinionated and cruel people said I let mine suffer. At the end of the day, people have too many opinions. And at the end of the day, unless those people found themselves at the same unthinkable crossroad as we did, they have no right to have an opinion. In the end, I believe we both faced an impossible and awful decision. We both hoped for life but instead were handed death. Please know, I have nothing but grace for you in this space.

If you are a TFMR family, some of my story may trigger you, and you deserve a heads-up. Please know, my heart is not to hurt you—it's just my story told through my eyes. Please don't let the different roads we walked put a wedge between our similarities and the strength we can find in each other. The scale is overwhelmingly tipped in our favor.

Take all of this to the King, for whatever feelings or thoughts may flood your mind in the pages ahead, belong at His feet and His feet alone. I encourage you to drown out the voices of the world and let all but His fade away. His is the *only* opinion that matters.

I hope and pray you continue on this journey with me. There is so much more in the pages ahead for you. My eyes may have differed from yours, but my heart, new friend of mine, is 100 percent *for* you.

As I sit here and continue to tread in the turbulent waters of abortion, I can't help but think about those reading this who have had one (or many) for reasons other than a diagnosis. Maybe you were young. Maybe you weren't ready. Maybe you were assaulted. Maybe you were scared. Whatever the reason, please understand the intentions of my heart on this matter. I am in no way trying to condemn or judge those who have terminated a pregnancy. I believe at the end of the day, we all try our hardest to make decisions we believe to be best given our circumstances. I believe we *all* need to be more careful when judging shoes we have never had to wear and a path we have never had to walk.

There are several beloved women in my life who are carrying the painful and heavy burden of past choices. Regardless of what their personal trials were at the time, their decision seems to haunt them. Guilt and conviction are two very different things, but I can promise you, guilt is not from God. He doesn't exist to point out our flaws. In fact, He chooses to love us despite them. It is for that very reason He sent His son to pay the ultimate price—for our debts, for our shortcomings, and for the choices we (sometimes) would give anything to take back. If today your heart is feeling the burden of past choices, I pray you would finally allow yourself to release the weight you have been holding. God doesn't want you to carry this anymore. Give it to Him and walk in the freedom for which He paid such a high price.

As if that was not enough, want to know the beauty in all of this? There is complete hope and peace for you, and you will experience it in its entirety someday. Your child (or children) are happy and whole. They are safe in the arms of their Creator, and you will see them again if you know Jesus as your Savior. No guilt, no shame—just family reunited in the presence of the Most High. I can't picture a more beautiful scene.

We had countless appointments in the week following Logan's diagnosis, and at almost every one, it felt like we had to defend our decision. In the middle of one appointment, in particular, a doctor was trying very hard to convince us we were making the wrong decision. I was actually a bit shocked how hard she was pushing. At one point, Andy asked how she expected us to pick a day on the calendar to end our child's life.

She became quiet with a puzzled look on her face. After tilting her head to the side and pausing briefly, she regained composure and continued to argue that our delivery could be "potentially gruesome" due to the complications of Logan's disorder and that we were taking the "more difficult" path. My blood was boiling by the end of it all.

Why must I fight so hard to justify fighting for the life of my son? Is it not my right to continue the life growing in my body, just like it's another's right to end it? Why does it feel like this doctor is rolling her eyes behind that clipboard of hers? And potentially gruesome? Really?! I am not going to be able to shake those words. But either way, I'm pretty sure termination would also be "potentially gruesome."

A day later, the same doctor gave us a call. I can't say we were thrilled when we realized who was on the other end of the line. It turns out she couldn't stop thinking about Andy's comment. She had never heard anyone put it that way and thanked Andy for giving her a new perspective. It seemed so clear to us, and yet it seemed to be a revelation to her. A baby is a baby, regardless of whether the child is being carried in its mother's arms or its mother's belly.

THROUGH KELLEY'S EYES

So what happens next? The medical world had made its decision and recommendation. Logan was not going to survive, so the solution was to terminate the pregnancy—aka Logan. Why draw out a hopeless situation? If the theme of this story was chivalry and not honesty, I would proudly tell you that I didn't entertain the idea of abortion for even a second. *But* since I'm going for honesty, I'd have to tell you it wasn't the case.

Honestly, I didn't know what to think. This situation was bigger than all of us, and there wasn't a "What to Expect When You're Expecting . . .

Your Baby to Die" book on the shelves. If the doctors recommend "terminate," then I guess we should take their advice, right? I mean, they are the experts in this situation, aren't they? As I was continuing to sort through these thoughts, a new idea quietly presented itself to me in my mind. It went something like this: "If you take Logan's life into your own hands, you are taking it out of mine." God had entered the conversation.

If an end was put to Logan's life, an end was also put to all God was going to do through it. I remembered what I believed: "A person's a person, no matter how small," as Horton so elegantly put it. And if I really did believe in life, I had to continue to believe in it no matter the circumstance. No matter what kind of fancy terminology a doctor might use to justify terminating a fetus, at the end of the day, a fetus wasn't being terminated; Logan was. Remembering that made me feel like I was finally on solid ground again. But I still felt sick to my stomach.

I knew choosing to abort Logan would have destroyed Jamie and Andy in the long run, but I also knew choosing to move forward was going to be heart-wrenching beyond words. How do you carry something so precious and priceless knowing you will have to let it go?

Moving forward, the whole family seemed to be on the same page. Life was chosen. Logan's life was chosen—and we embraced him *every day*. Jamie and Andy did a beautiful job loving Logan and honoring *every* second they were blessed with him, which wasn't shocking. But what *was* shocking was how blatantly so many professionals in the medical community could not honor Jamie and Andy's choice to continue to carry their boy.

The fear tactics were relentless and exhausting. We all had to constantly bring ourselves back to what we believed for Logan. It took the strength of us united not to be shaken, which brings me to this question: if we truly live in such an "enlightened" day and age, where a woman's right to choose termination is respected, then why wasn't my sister's right to choose *life* respected in the same way? Maybe we aren't all that enlightened after all.

Everywhere we went, people would tell us how strong we were and how proud they were of us. But I can promise you this: we were not strong, and we were not brave. We were stuck in an impossible situation. I didn't feel courageous at all. We were absolutely terrified but made a decision to give all our fear, all our questions, and the road in front of us to God.

The truth is, without His help, without Him picking us up and carrying us, we wouldn't have made it a single day. When we found out Logan was sick, it felt like we had been hit by a truck and left for dead. If it wasn't for the mercy of Christ, I promise you, we would have never left that spot on the side of the road.

There were times along the journey where I felt like a helpless infant and would fully allow my Heavenly Father to cradle me in His arms and walk the road *for* me. There were also times when I was angry and would fight the path He was leading me on. These were the moments of my life where, even though I was kicking and screaming like a child in protest, He never gave up on me. He was going to get me through the valley, even if at times He had to drag me.

7 — AMIDST IMMOVABLE MOUNTAINS

Every valley shall be lifted up, and every mountain and hill be made low; the uneven ground shall become level, and the rough places a plain.

—Isaiah 40:4 (ESV)

F or years, Andy and I hosted a big Fourth of July BBQ since we could see our city's firework display from our house. We obviously hadn't anticipated how badly our world would be rocked as we entered the month of July that year.

Our first instinct was to cancel the party. However, after several torturous days hiding in the house, we decided maybe a distraction was exactly what we needed. We hadn't spoken to most of our friends since Logan's diagnosis. Everyone knew what was going on, but we left the majority of the correspondence to our families. We knew people wanted to see us, so we figured we would take the "rip off the Band-Aid" approach. We were in desperate need of some relief from the pain, and maybe some company could be that outlet.

We ended up having a bigger turnout than we ever had before with over fifty people showing up. I don't think it was a coincidence. Everyone came with good intentions. They were loving and supportive, but I found out early in the afternoon it was too much. Brand new babies were *everywhere*. Expectant moms were *everywhere*. I could feel everyone's eyes on me in sideways glances, and could hear my name in hushed conversations. Every set of those eyes that connected with mine were somber, sympathetic, and quick to move on. Head tilts. Halfhearted smiles. I felt like a spectacle. Welcome to the circus. Population: one. There was no way to overlook or ignore my pregnant belly. I was the girl carrying the dying child.

How did I really think this was going to make me feel better? How naïve was I to believe anything could distract me from this pain? I am so stupid.

I wanted to forget for a moment, but instead, I felt like the (pregnant) elephant in the room. I quietly snuck away to a back office in my house and pulled the door shut behind me. I curled up into a tight ball in my papasan chair and cried. Outside the window behind me, I could hear sounds of the celebration continuing. Laughter. Country music. Too many voices to pick out just one. The occasional pop of a firework, followed by the screams and approving claps from a crowd of small children. Even through the window, I could smell smoke off the grill and the hamburgers almost ready to serve. *So* much energy, *so* many people unaffected, unphased, and blind to what was happening just one room away.

Thank goodness it's so crowded. They will never notice I'm missing.

A while passed, and I saw the shadow of someone walk past the door. *Please don't open it. Please don't open it.* It had happened several times before without anyone coming in, but this time it opened, and I was face-to-face with my brother's wife, Andrea. I was at least relieved to see the comforting face of a family member instead of yet another friend full of questions.

Andrea had just found out she was pregnant with her third child. In fact, my brother had called and told me the news just two hours before Andy and I went into our anatomy scan. Unfortunately, the joy of their news had been overshadowed by the tragedy of mine.

Andrea and I hadn't had a private moment together since the anatomy scan. Neither of us wanted to address the new and awkward tension that had suddenly rooted itself in our relationship. Andrea and my brother were obviously excited about their pregnancy, and I . . . well, I was as happy for them as I could be. Of course, a new niece or nephew was exciting and a blessing for our family, but it rubbed gallons of salt in the open and bleeding wound that was my heart.

I knew we both felt the strain between us, and I knew we both wanted it to go away. It wasn't fair they were unable to have the company they deserved in what should have been a wonderful announcement. It also wasn't fair that as they were embracing the hope of new life, I was trying to accept the reality of death.

Without asking permission, grief and sorrow had repositioned my heart. In just days, it had changed so much of me. I didn't recognize who I was. I didn't recognize the jealousy I felt. I didn't recognize my sudden regression to a child-like state, complaining about how unfair it was to watch someone else get what I wanted. All I knew was how much I disliked the new conflict raging in my heart and how much I wanted it to leave.

But now, we were face-to-face and there was no way to avoid an inter-action. Andrea and I looked at each other for a moment, neither of us making a sound. She gently closed the door behind her and walked toward me. I could see big tears filling up her eyes. I looked up at her with the most pathetic smile I could muster, my own tears about to spill. In a moment, and without a word being spoken, the tension gave way.

In that small room of my home, with the sounds of happiness and laughter surrounding us, we sat in a ball on the floor and wept. She was one of the last people in the world I wanted to pull away from me, and in that moment, I got her back. I wish I had known that, in the next week, Andrea would lose the little life within her. Even in the middle of all my sorrow, all I wanted to do after her loss was take her pain away. Sometimes, the weight of this life is just too much.

The massive firework display scheduled for that night was canceled because of the lack of rain and all the horrific wildfires in Colorado at the time. It felt apropos to me. Just like my heart, the night sky was empty and dark when it *should* have been full of something bright and beautiful.

7/6/12

Dear Logan,

I spoke with a pastor this morning, and he prayed with me for your healing. He told me God picked your dad and me to be your parents because he knew we would show you love—even if you weren't here very long, you would at least experience one of His greatest gifts. He said it's not the *length* of your life that matters but the *impact* your life has—and, my son, your life has already made an impact on me. I am forever changed because of you. Thank you for being such an important part in the long journey of becoming the person God wants me to be.

I heard a song today called "Blessings," by Laura's Story, that really hit home. It talks about trials and how God's mercies are often found in the midst of them. *Many* times, I have questioned why God gave you to me if he was just going to take you right back again. But after hearing the song, I felt God gave me a bit more clarity. This is, without question, the most difficult season I have ever endured. But I no longer question God on why He would allow me to become pregnant knowing what would happen because if He hadn't, I would have never known you.

While I may not get to spend this life with you, I know with certainty that I will get to spend eternity with you. Sometimes it's so hard to separate myself from this life and realize this is not ultimately where I belong. This is a drop in the vast ocean of the time we will get to spend together. Right now, I feel as though I am walking amidst immovable mountains, and yet, I know what is impossible for man is possible for God. I am trying to remember this is my temporary home, and even though it seems so dark right now, I know that, because of Him, joy will come in the morning.

Love you to the moon and back,
Mommy

A few days after the BBQ some close friends came over for dinner. While we quickly learned big gatherings were not for us in this season, there were a select few whose company was still welcomed.

After we finished eating, Andy got up to get a drink, and I casually asked him to grab my prenatal vitamins. I caught the ever-so-slight glimpse of confusion from one of our guests. It was brief and unintentional, but it stung, nonetheless. I could feel several sets of eyes on my back as I slowly walked to the counter and took my pills.

It probably would have been a bad time to point out that not only was I *still* taking my prenatal vitamins, but I was taking them with milk—every night. After all, milk makes strong bones, right? The juvenile logic sounded pretty good to me. I knew the reasoning was completely absurd and totally futile. The damage had been done at the genetic level, and I understood that. But maybe, just maybe, if I drank enough milk . . .

It just goes to show the desperate mind of a grieving parent. What I wanted to explain to that set of eyes was how I would do *anything* to protect Logan and make him whole again. I wanted to scream, "Don't you understand? I'm not going to give up on him! I will not stop—until he does!"

And yes, if that meant a gallon of milk a day, then that's exactly what I would do. Maybe I should have casually mentioned my newfound obsession with calcium and vitamin D. It would have *for sure* taken the focus off the prenatal vitamins.

The following week, I went back to work. I was dreading it and wished I worked in a cubicle like Andy, where I would be left alone all day. After all, a cubicle wouldn't ask any questions. Unfortunately, in a salon setting, I wouldn't get that luxury.

My clients knew I was going in for an ultrasound to find out if I was having a boy or a girl, but that's where their knowledge stopped. Now, a seemingly never-ending stream of people continued to sit down in my chair excited to hear all about the big news. I had to prepare myself for the same uncomfortable conversation—multiple times a day.

I was continually bombarded with questions—questions about what Logan had, about what was going to happen, about why we chose to do what we were doing. I tried to keep it vague with the majority of my clients. I would simply say, "We got some bad news, but we are trusting in God and praying for a miracle." Some weren't satisfied with that response and kept pushing. I didn't want to tell them Logan was not expected to live. I hated even giving voice to it. Saying it meant it was true and I was succumbing to the boundaries of modern medicine's opinion. I knew God could change our diagnosis in an instant, and I refused to speak death over my son.

Sometimes, however, I was too tired to give the sugarcoated version, and I would be direct with them. Maybe a little *too* direct, to be honest. Many times, it would end with a crying client in my chair and *me* trying to console *them*.

To make the situation even more uncomfortable, I worked in a salon that had less-than-private workspaces. Everything was in the open, and no conversation was discrete. With every client that sat in my chair, I had to absorb the uncomfortable posture of everyone in my salon. I could feel them cringe right along with me whenever the topic of conversation would transition from hair, spouses, work, the weather, and inevitably, *my pregnancy*. Oh, how I longed for that cubicle.

Every one of my clients had his or her opinion on the situation. Many were kind and gentle, some tried my patience, and some *really* tried my patience. The things people would say were shocking, especially around an emotional pregnant woman who was carrying a dying child and holding a sharp instrument in her hands.

I always did my best to make it through each day as professionally as possible. My boss made it very clear I needed to separate my personal life from my business life, but how exactly was I supposed to do that when I was asked about it *all* day? How was I supposed to go from "Logan is going to die" to "What do you want to do with your hair?" in the same breath? Even when the topic would finally change, Logan would begin wiggling around in my belly. It was nearly impossible to maintain composure. Most days I would do a decent job hiding behind my professional facade, only to completely lose it in the car on the way home.

———⚬⚬⚬———

Visiting the doctor regularly became a new normal in my weekly routine. I appreciated the opportunity to check on Logan, but I loathed going into the office where my life had fallen to pieces in a matter of minutes. I could trace my steps and relive that day so effortlessly. And to top it off, it was *swarming* with babies and pregnant women. I looked just like them, but I wasn't one of them.

I would keep my head down in an attempt to avoid any amount of small talk. "What are you having? When are you due? You must be so excited!" I didn't have the strength to field such comments and became very good at the "don't talk to me" face.

One morning, I was sitting in the waiting room, counting the minutes until I could hopefully leave, when I caught the tail end of a conversation happening behind me. It was between two pregnant women who had just learned the gender of their babies. One of them was furious her baby was a boy. My innocent eavesdropping quickly heated to boiling rage. That *boy* was perfectly healthy, but for nearly five minutes, she openly complained about how she wanted a girl and how annoyed, disappointed, and cheated she felt.

Cheated?! Disappointed?! You feel cheated and disappointed!? Let me tell you a little bit about being cheated...

By nature, I am not a confrontational person, but for one of the first times in my life, I was ready—and willing—to fight. I clenched my teeth, swallowed the rage surging within me, and exhaled deeply in an attempt to subdue my ever-growing need to interject. Tears poured down my cheeks after escaping from my tightly closed eyes. A tug of war was occurring between social etiquette and blinding anger. Just as my anger was about to take over my brain's ability to be rational, I heard the nurse up front call my name.

I couldn't resist the urge to turn around and look at the two women as I stood. When our eyes met, they were greeted with a halfhearted—maybe slightly forced—smile from what looked to be a fellow uncomfortable pregnant woman. Good thing they couldn't read the myriad of thoughts desperately trying to escape my lips. While I would usually endear myself to other women fighting the constant discomfort and emotional swings of being pregnant, I nearly made an exception.

In those moments, I wished moms and dads like me had our very own waiting room, maybe even our very own entrance. Actually, our very own building—someplace where we would never be hurt by other parents with healthy babies or susceptible to unnecessary moments like that one. So maybe somewhere away from *everyone*.

8 — IN MY SHOES

I knew you before I formed you in your mother's womb. Before you were born I set you apart.

—Jeremiah 1:5 (NLT)

Have you ever looked at someone else's life and wondered how you would handle the pain they have endured? So many times we see and hear about people in the middle of tragic situations, but rarely do we attempt to step into their shoes.

Oftentimes, when it comes to grief, we only see the facade of the bereaved. We see the outside of a very shattered inside. Rarely are we privy to the *real* face of grief. It takes courage to go to such a dark and intimate place and allow ourselves to feel pain simply for the sake of understanding. Most of the time, our hearts can only *sympathize* with their stories. We only have the ability to *empathize* when it's a road we have personally walked. It's the difference between saying "I hurt *for* you" versus "I hurt *with* you." Switch *one* word and these two simple statements couldn't be more different.

A few weeks after Logan's diagnosis, a client asked me what it was like being pregnant with a dying child. A pretty bold question, for sure, but it got me thinking, nonetheless. Sitting right in the midst of it, it still felt impossible to answer. For many, it's too much to comprehend, and for a few, you know exactly what it feels like, because your story is like mine.

For those who can't relate, I am going to *attempt* to explain how it feels to carry a child you have been told is going to die, and I am going to do that because there is endless value in empathy. But let me warn you: allowing your heart to truly empathize with another's is a painful process. Sometimes, opening our hearts to feel what others feel and see what others see is uncomfortable—but it's the only way our hearts can grow.

I'm confident this book would not be in your hands if the pregnancy and infant loss world hadn't already somehow touched yours. I'm equally confident some of you are using it as an avenue to understand something foreign to you, so that in turn, you can be a better vessel for support. If that's you, and on behalf of the hurting family you see clearly in your mind right now, let me be the first to say, thank you. Thank you for opening *your* heart to pain for the sake of *theirs*.

———∞———

So, what does it feel like to carry a terminally ill baby? It is a complex dynamic that is impossibly hard to quantify. Hope, fear, sorrow, anxiety, love, anger, faith, agony—all wrapped up in one big, tangled mess.

I struggled with knowing and believing in my heart that God was bigger than *any* diagnosis and could effortlessly heal my son, while simultaneously trying to prepare myself for the heartbreak that was likely coming our way. Miracles happen. I knew they did. But would Andy and I get one? In my core, I don't think I ever really believed we would. I was desperate to walk in faith and feel hope, but I was carrying the weight of death on my shoulders.

Too many times to count, I would start mourning Logan's life, and simultaneously, he would start wiggling around in my belly. I would instantly feel guilty because he was still with me. *How can I mourn something I haven't lost?* I didn't want to waste the little time I had with him. I was grieving a life that had not yet left and then feeling guilty for such a natural emotion. If I let myself mourn, was I giving up hope?

I was terrified of the unavoidable emotional pain speeding toward us. *If it is already this bad and Logan is still here, what will it be like when he is gone?* He had become a part of me, and I didn't want to know who I was without him. Scarier still was the thought of who I might turn into after he was gone. What ugliness was lying beneath the surface, just waiting for the opportunity to devour every piece of who I used to be?

The fears that previously consumed the naive and tender mind of my youth suddenly seemed so small in hindsight. Back then, my focus was value and worth—things that still mattered but seemed so trivial compared to the unknown future I was now facing. Would my core turn bitter? Jealous? Would my heart harden? Would I forever hate the world and lose every piece of what made me, *me*?

The path Andy and I walked daily was uncharted and full of land mines. At times, I would feel slightly encouraged and at peace, while at other times, I would be inconsolable. I had never called out to the Lord with such urgency that my voice would go hoarse. Logan was being pulled away from me. I fought it so hard but could feel the separation happening, and the process was physically tearing me in half.

As terrible as it sounds, it felt like a gun was pointed at Logan, and I had the foresight to know the trigger *would* be pulled. Not a question of *if* but a question of *when*. There was nothing I could do but watch helplessly, hands bound, as my child died before my eyes. Having a glimpse into Logan's future sparked an uncontainable panic. Sometimes I would drop to my knees and start screaming at the top of my lungs. Sometimes my screams were at God. Sometimes I was simply screaming—no words and no direction—just a physical release of sorrow built up in my body. It's what sorrow looks like in its most raw form. It's what sorrow looks like behind closed doors. It was the kind of noise that only arises when your eyes see horror. My eyes couldn't see it, but my mind could imagine it, and to me there was no difference.

There was only one reason I could eventually stop—Logan. I didn't want to scare him. With all energy exhausted, I would fall to my side in a ball on the floor, cradle my belly in my hands, and tell him it would be okay. As tears puddled on the hardwood floor beneath me, I would tell him how sorry I was that I had, yet again, lost control. This back and forth—this constant strain of being both a new mom *and* a mom in mourning—was a tension I lived with and fought *daily*. Who was I supposed to be? Which group did I belong in? Most of the time, I just didn't know.

I believed God was in control, and I knew He had a plan. I just didn't know if His plan was going to include a life on *this* side of heaven with our son. Even when we didn't necessarily feel like it, Andy and I forced ourselves to run *toward* God, not away. He was our *only* hope. No matter what we were going through, we knew He was good, He loved us, and He still had a purpose for our sweet boy.

I didn't believe God gave Logan the horrible sickness. I didn't believe that was His original plan, and I didn't blame Him. I didn't believe He created Logan and then decided to break his body. That would be cruel, and my King is anything but. I knew it was the result of the world we lived in. The fall of man. The birth of sin. The birth of sickness. And yet, at times I felt the pull to turn my back on Him.

Satan is an opportunist, and when little thoughts like, *If God loved you, then how could He let this happen?* popped into my mind, I wasn't ignorant of the source. That being said, I suddenly understood how people could feel the desire to turn away from God. The younger version of myself, the girl whose biggest issue was Popcorn Boy's inability to speak, *never* could have related to such a feeling—for she had never felt *truly* betrayed. But the new version, the heartbroken girl carrying a dying child—could easily relate. I may have questioned my value to God in the past, *but* I always trusted His heart.

After living all my life with Christ as my foundation, I suddenly had to rebuke foreign thoughts that constantly flooded my mind. *This is His fault. He didn't cause it, but He certainly could fix it. Why would He take my child? Did I do something to deserve this? Is He mad at me?*

I would often find myself having to combat these thoughts, because I knew they were not true. I knew they were lies. There were more battles being waged than what my eyes could see. So, I made a promise to myself, and to Logan, that Satan would have no part in our story. I made a promise that I would fight for my faith as hard as I would fight for his healing. In the weeks and months that followed, I would come to learn the battle of my mind was not so easily won.

Everywhere I went, people would ask what I was having and how excited I was. They would look at me with a big smile and want to touch my belly, all the while having *no idea* the pain they were inflicting. Most of the time, I would play along and smile back. After all, it wasn't something I wanted to get into with the woman in line behind me at the grocery store.

"What are you having? Oh, a boy! Get your running shoes on because they have endless energy! How *exciting* for you! You must be thrilled!" The pain in my heart was searing but invisible to her. I swallowed hard, smiled back, and told her we were indeed, *thrilled*.

There were, however, a few times I couldn't contain my emotions when such comments arose. To the woman at Shane Company (if you ever find this book in your hands), I am truly sorry. Instead of lying, I looked her straight in the eyes and, with an unwavering and almost monotone voice, told her my baby was going to die. Just to make sure I had painted a clear picture, I added, "And no, I'm *not* excited." Pretty sure that translated into a rough day at the office for her.

After that day, I pledged *never* to make a comment to a woman about her pregnancy. She could be the most obviously pregnant woman in all of history and giving birth on the sidewalk in front of me. But unless she brought it up, I would completely ignore it. That sounds a tad extreme, but if you knew how it felt to pretend your child is living and thriving every single day, when they are in fact dying, then ignoring the obvious wouldn't sound quite so over the top.

THROUGH KELLEY'S EYES

It's funny how what you don't want to see is suddenly *everywhere*. Places that were once mundane stops on the way home, like the grocery store, somehow morphed into dangerous war zones when Jamie was with me. *Just get in, get out, and don't make any eye contact with anyone that may unknowingly have something stupid to say about Jamie's baby bump.*

Bob and weave as we did, eventually we'd be spotted by some well-meaning person who, for reasons beyond me, needed to ask ten million questions about a stranger's pregnancy.

It wasn't just strangers who made me weary. Many people wanted to come over and visit Jamie and Andy, again bearing good intentions but with such a lack of understanding. Who knew what a painful combination that could be? Time and time again, I'd watch them sit and smile and nod as people would unleash all kinds of platitudes and advice on them. Then I'd watch my sister curl up in a ball and weep as soon as company would leave, because ignorance left them feeling isolated instead of loved.

Very few people understood how to quietly and patiently bear witness to Jamie and Andy's grief. It was something that I, too, had to slowly learn. We were all living in what a good friend of ours often referred to as "the land of *and*." We were trying to soak up every moment we had with Logan *and* wrestling with the inevitability that we were not going to get to keep him. We were delighting in the pure joy that we were blessed to be given him *and* dreading the nearing moment when we knew he would be taken away. We were praying for a miraculous healing *and* living in a reality where miracles of that magnitude seemed few and far between. It was a mix of laughter *and* tears, wailing *and* rejoicing, incredible closeness to the Father *and* a haunting notion that we had been forsaken.

The lens I saw the world through shifted the day I found out Logan was sick. The world I resided in was unchanged—my eyes, however, would never be the same again. I would see certain women staring at me with the same look I had unconsciously given other pregnant moms: envy, longing, pain. I would think to myself, *If only you knew . . . this belly you are longing for, this belly you are envious of, is carrying a child that is going to die. Don't be jealous of me.*

I never recognized that look prior to Logan. It's hard to understand until you have felt the pain of losing a child or being unable to bear one. But I promise, if you know what to look for, it is *clearly* written in their eyes.

I would see other expecting moms and instantly feel like I couldn't breathe. Many times, the very sight of them would make me angry. I never wished my pain on anyone else, but they were everywhere I looked, and no matter how hard I tried, I couldn't escape them. Even TV shows and movies I watched suddenly featured pregnant women, brand-new babies, and even pregnant women *losing* their brand-new babies. My email was bombarded with articles on how far along I was in my pregnancy, what the baby was up to, and what I *should* be doing in preparation for delivery. "It's Time to Get That Nursery Ready" . . . "Make Sure to Have Your Car Seat Properly Installed" . . . "Baby-Proof Your House" . . . "Find Your Pediatrician." Meanwhile, my "Unsubscribe" button was apparently broken.

Places I loved to shop suddenly were no longer safe. I couldn't muster the strength to walk by *any* baby section. In fact, many times I would purposely go out of my way just to avoid it. I couldn't help but think about how excited I was to go shopping once we found out the gender. I had been saving money for months, but Andy had told me I wasn't allowed to buy anything until we knew if our baby was a boy or a girl. He knew once the buying started, the shopping wouldn't stop (probably true). Since we found out we were having a boy on the same day we found out he was sick, I never spent the money I had been saving. So walking by the areas in stores where I should have been shopping was nothing but a slap in the face.

The only time I braved a baby section was at Target one morning with Andy to pick out an outfit and blanket in which to bury Logan. Those were the *only* things we ever bought for him. It was a terrible experience, but if we were going to have to bury him, we wanted him in something from us. *This is supposed to be so different!* I started repeating it over and over to myself. *I should be picking out something to bring him home in, not something to bury him in.*

I remember standing in a daze in the aisle full of adorable, fuzzy baby blankets. A friend had encouraged me to buy two of the same blanket: one to hold him in and keep, and one to put in his casket and bury. I stood and stared at those blankets for ages. Andy was restless by my side and understandably just wanted to leave. But to me, it was a massive decision that needed my time and attention.

Should I bury him in the one with the zoo animals? Or maybe the one with all the stars? I definitely don't like that one with the monkey. Maybe I should just choose the simple green one. Jamie! What are you doing?! Just pick a stupid blanket!

Finally, I begged Andy to pick. Without hesitating, he grabbed two of the monkey blankets and threw them in the basket. I didn't have the energy to voice my protest or even care. At least that part was over. We went around the corner to look for an outfit, and I found myself face-to-face with a young girl, *maybe* sixteen—pregnant and with her mom. She looked about as far along as I was, and she was visibly annoyed as her over-zealous mom dug through stacks of baby clothes.

Really, God?! I have to see this right now? She's a child! She probably doesn't even want her baby. Why would you give a child to a child and take mine away?

I had about as much as my heart could take for one day. I beelined for the cash register and dropped fifty dollars on two blankets I wanted nothing to do with. I felt ashamed of my thoughts and anger toward the teenager on the drive home, but I soon learned thoughts like that would come more often than I liked.

Later that week, while shopping at the grocery store, I saw a mom with a giant pregnant belly, a cart with three children, plus a couple in tow. Genetics were strong within the family. Bright red curls and light eyes were all around, and it was obvious where they all originated.

Do you want to know my first thought? It was nothing nice. I immediately thought she was a tad . . . greedy. Do you want to know my second thought? It was directed to God and had something to do with Him giving her *six* and taking my only *one*.

Moments like that happened to me on a daily basis. They were hard, and they were painful, and they made me feel like a terrible person. I was losing Logan but also pieces of myself. I continued to feel like something ugly and foreign was beginning to wrap itself around me, and I hated it. But I couldn't confess my thoughts to others, because then they, too, would know how terrible I was.

Unknown to me, a tiny seed was being planted. And no, it didn't belong to a flower or an oak. It belonged to a thistle, a weed—something invasive. The type of noxious plant that chokes out all other life. It was intentionally planted in the vulnerable and fertile soil of my heart by the king of lies. The conditions were perfect for deceit to grow and spread like wildfire, and he took full advantage of the opportunity. His tiny thorns began to wrap themselves around my heart like barbed wire, and his whispers that once said, "You are not valued," suddenly changed to "You are not loved."

I was slowly being poisoned but couldn't openly share my fears with the world, because then I would have to share my thoughts too. And if they knew, how could they still love me?

—◦◦◦—

Remember at the beginning of this book how I promised to share even the messy parts of my journey? Well, this is one of those times. If you can relate to my struggle, I promise it doesn't make you as awful as you may feel at the moment. I'm in no way proud of the thoughts that so often ran uncontrolled through my mind, but I'm also human. They were the result of circumstances out of my control, and I was responding in a very natural and normal way.

If you have never been in my shoes and find yourself rolling your eyes or judging my reactions, then I say this to you (as politely as humanly possible): *I don't really care.* Unless you have walked in these shoes, you have no right to judge the dirt that is on them. If you *have* walked in these shoes, I see you. I am you. It's okay. Your grief will not always manifest in anger, envy, and jealousy. Give yourself grace, and know this is not your fault. You are not a monster. You are just carrying a shattered heart, and it's impossible that remnants of it will not fall out wherever you go.

———

7/15/12

Dear Logan,

I've had a couple of rougher days, but I'm trying very hard to stay strong for you. I've been praying for grace and peace and finally today at church got a little bit of both. We had a guest pastor whose sermon was about having strength through life's storms. I felt like he was talking directly to me. While I am not in control of my circumstances, I *am* in control of my reactions. God loves us, and even when the storm is so bad that we can't see ahead of us, that truth remains.

In these times, we must have faith. I don't understand why we are going through this, son, but I know God loves us more than we could ever understand. I know His grace will give us the strength to get through this. I am fighting for you, Logan. It is amazing the amount of people around the world who are praying for you—you are loved so much! Keep pushing through—we are going to make it. I love you so much, son. I hope you know that. I will never give up on you, even if this world thinks I'm crazy.

I will never understand the love of God, but being your mother, I can finally understand a love so radical that nothing could ever cause it to surrender. I think that's the way God loves us too. You are a reflection of His love to me. May our Healer continue to restore you more and more every day, may He strengthen your body, encourage your spirit, and continue to show you His love.

Love you to the moon and back,
Mommy

———⊗∞⊗———

Did Logan die last night? Every single morning I would wake up, and that would be my first thought. I would lie there as still as humanly possible, with both hands cradling my stomach, as I waited to feel proof of his life within me. My heart would begin to beat faster and louder the longer all remained still. I would feel panic grow in my chest and slowly make its way through my whole body until I was covered from head to toe in fear. I would try to slow my breathing and force some calm into my mind, but it never worked. I could never fully exhale until I felt Logan's familiar bump from within.

I cannot count the number of times I swore he was gone. That process alone aged me *well* beyond my years (I'm totally serious. I was a twenty-seven-year-old suddenly turning gray). I was consumed with the thought that Logan was in pain. It was by far the worst part of it. I felt trapped. I was his mom, and I couldn't keep him safe. The unknown of it all would often send me into panic mode. My mind would go crazy trying to think up all the possible scenarios.

What is going to happen? Is he going to suffer? When is he going to die? What is going to happen during labor? Will he come out alive? Will he come out in pieces?

As horrific as it sounds, that was reality for us. Not many children with OI type 2 made it to delivery because many were never given the chance. There wasn't much of a precedent for us to reference. There was a good chance not only that delivery would kill him but, like the doctor had mentioned earlier, that he wouldn't come out whole. *Potentially gruesome.* How are parents supposed to cope with that?

After doing some research (and because of that early comment from the doctor), we decided we would fight for a C-section when the time came. We knew the doctors wouldn't necessarily agree. I was perfectly healthy, and opting for a surgery that wasn't "medically necessary" was not going to be a popular decision. But we also knew it would be the most gentle way for Logan to come into this world and potentially the *only* chance we would have to see him alive.

—⊛—

We knew we didn't have much time with Logan, so we tried to spend whatever time we did have covering him in love. Logan probably wouldn't be on this earth very long, and as a result, we knew we wouldn't get to experience so many things with him. It was heartbreaking to think of all the landmarks we would miss out on: his first smile, his first steps, his high school graduation, my dance with him on his wedding day. We would have a lifetime of anniversaries and events to mourn.

There may have been many things we wouldn't be able to show him and teach him, but there was one thing we could give him, and that was the unconditional, overwhelming, and selfless love that every child deserves. Our son would not leave this world without experiencing one of the greatest gifts God ever gave us. We made it our goal to give Logan a lifetime's supply of love, regardless of how long we were able to be together. We took him to baseball games and on long scenic drives. We talked to him constantly, read him the Bible, and sang him songs.

7/16/12

My Sweet Boy,

Today we got to spend the entire day with Dad. I think it made you happy, because you were very active. Your father and I took you on a drive around Golden. He showed you where he went to school and took us up on Lookout Mountain. It was so beautiful. I had never been there either, so it was a first for both you and me. There is nothing I love more than being with both of you. Some of the places your dad took us were so beautiful and calm that I actually felt at peace for a bit. We spent the rest of the day at your cousin's first birthday party. Kids were everywhere and it was very loud! I couldn't help but think about how badly I want you to make it to yours.

It's really hard not to let my mind wonder "what if" or "if only." It is in God's hands, and I am doing my best to hang on to hope.

I wish I could explain to you how badly my heart longs for you to stay with me. Everywhere I look, there are babies and pregnant women. Every day I hear about someone else who is expecting. It is so hard seeing all these people with what I desire so badly. It's hard to be happy for them because it only reminds me of what we are in the middle of and the things I may miss out on with you. Please know, I would never trade you for any other child in the world. You are mine and I am yours. God gave you to me, and I promise I will take care of you as long as He allows.

I want you to know how much Jesus loves you. He loves you more than I ever could, which is saying a lot, because you are the light of my life. He died on a cross so we could spend eternity with Him. Because of that wonderful gift, we will also get to spend eternity with you! You are fearfully and wonderfully made, sweet boy, and God knew all about you long before you were in my belly. You are everything to me, and we will make it through this! You were created in God's image, you are covered in our Maker's fingerprints, and He does not make mistakes! I want to repeat that to you, Logan, because you are *not* a mistake.

You are such a joy to your dad and me. We love feeling you move and kick and laugh about your already unique personality. Your dad loves you so much, Logan. He reads you the Bible every night and kisses my belly in the morning before he goes to work. You already look like him, too—my boys are so handsome. I love you. I love you. I love you. I can't say it enough. I am so honored God chose me to be your mom.

Love you to the moon and back,
Mommy

———— ❦ ————

Our families easily jumped on board when it came to our mission to love Logan. Of course he was in my belly, so it was often in unorthodox ways. It brought so much comfort when others would go out of their way to give him attention and remind him (and us) how important he was. It helped me not feel like a crazy person jumping up and down and waving her arms in an effort to get others to acknowledge the life within me. I needed validation and support, and I needed it done in a gentle and graceful way.

One morning, Kelley came over and had rewritten the song, "Jesus Loves Me" for Logan. She walked in the house smiling from ear to ear and got down on her knees, so she was eye-level with my belly. I looked down at her, quite confused as to what was happening when she tenderly started singing,

> Jesus loves you, this I know
> He's going to help your body grow
> Long and strong and pure as snow
> And you'll tell of His glory wherever you go
> Yes, Jesus loves Logan
> Yes, Jesus loves Logan
> Yes, Jesus loves Logan
> He's going to help you grow!

It made me chuckle and sent happy tears rolling down my cheeks. It made me feel seen and understood—like I wasn't having to fight the battle alone. I started singing it to Logan every morning when I showered. I loved that part of our day because he would always start wiggling as I sang and slowly danced back and forth.

Shortly after that day, my mom found a song titled, "Long Way Home," by Steven Curtis Chapman. She shared it with us, and the lyrics—which told of a difficult journey—resonated so much that it became one of several "Logan's Songs." Whenever it would play on the radio, Andy would squeeze my hand, look me in the eyes, and tell me we were going to make it. Sometimes, if we were home, the three of us would enjoy a dance together in the kitchen.

9 — LET GO AND LET GOD

*Father, if you are willing, take this cup from me; yet not my will,
but yours be done.*

—Luke 22:42 (NIV)

Photo by Ken Papapleo

We continued to get closer and closer to our third trimester and the likelihood that Logan could come at any point. Eventually, the day came for us to go to Children's Hospital and have an appointment with a neonatologist. Simply put, we were meeting Logan's doctor so we could discuss our wishes for his care after birth.

I was uneasy about the appointment. I knew it was basically a "this is how he will most likely die" and "how much intervention do you want?" discussion. I still hated being introduced to new doctors. I felt like they viewed me as some sort of an anomaly—some crazy, religious, pregnant woman with no grasp at reality or the deep water she was treading. There was always a tell in their body language—one that screamed to me they disagreed with my choice. At no point did I ever waver or regret my decision, but I just didn't feel like having to explain myself and my beliefs to a stranger—*again.*

Leading up to the appointment, Andy and I had to have a very serious and heart-wrenching conversation. If Logan was born alive and the decision presented itself, would we try to sustain his life with intubation, feeding tubes, or the use of any other intervention? Would we keep fighting for him if given an opportunity?

It was an impossibly hard pill to swallow, but Andy and I knew a time would come where we needed to let go and let God do what He was going to do. It was agonizing, but Logan had a fatal condition. Either God would change that and restore him, or he was going to die. As much as I wanted to continue fighting, I couldn't bear the thought of selfishly keeping Logan here longer than he needed to be. It was torture, but we needed to draw a line in the sand. We needed to *fully* submit to our King and let Logan go, if that was God's will.

Jesus Himself fought this very battle prior to the cross on the Mount of Olives. In Luke 22:42 (NLT), he cried out, "Father, if you are willing, take this cup from me; yet not my will, but yours be done."

Thy will be done. On the surface, it seems like such a simple prayer, but in reality, it is loaded with countless implications. There is nothing easy about fully submitting and surrendering *all* aspects of your life to Christ. I would argue it's a lifelong struggle for most. In some areas of my life, it had been easy, but in others, nearly impossible. I didn't always have a "Jesus, take the wheel" mentality because when it came to Logan, I wanted to drive. I could feel myself in a constant tug of war. One, of course, I had no chance of winning.

Even Jesus begged God to take away the cup of suffering that was before Him. In fact, He prayed with such urgency and anguish that his drops of sweat turned to drops of blood. But in the end, He fully submitted to the will of His father. If that's not leading by example, then I don't know what is.

Not my will but yours. Not my will but yours. I had Jesus's words on repeat in my mind as I walked hand in hand with Andy into the hospital. We were scared and nervous but a united front.

I opened the office doors with my boxing gloves on. I was in no mood to be bullied. I sat in the waiting room running through our defense strategy in my mind. I knew how this was going to play out, but this time I would be prepared. My nerves were visibly subtle to others, but glaringly obvious to me, as I couldn't stop my fingers from fidgeting with the strap on my purse. Then our name was called.

We followed a nurse through a set of very big doors and then, much to our shock, were greeted by a friendly face. Lisa, a nurse who worked at our ultrasound office, was leaning against the wall with a folder (presumably my records) safely tucked underneath her arm. I couldn't have been happier to see her familiar, smiling face. There was no one else in the world I would have rather seen at that very moment. She knew us. She respected our stance. Most of all, I felt like she was our only advocate, and I completely trusted her. I felt a much-needed confidence boost as we entered the boxing ring.

This time around, however, something different and unexpected happened. I judged too soon. I put people I had never met into an awful box that I alone had built. It was unfair and immature. You see, I wasn't walking into a fight; I was walking into a room full of empathy and love.

The neonatologist was kind and compassionate. She didn't question our decision. She even teared up as Andy told her our story and all about our baby boy. The display of emotion and respect for life was refreshing, to say the least. She delicately explained to us what was most likely going to happen after Logan was born—should he be born alive. Because his rib cage and abdomen were so underdeveloped, many of his vital organs would not be able to mature. His lungs were among those organs. So basically, if he lived through delivery, his lungs would not be mature enough to breathe.

I figured that would be the case, but hearing it officially from a doctor knocked the wind out of me. I didn't want Logan to suffer. In the midst of everything else, that had always been my greatest concern. We asked if she could give him something after delivery to make his passing more comfortable. I knew it would only be minutes, but it killed me to think about him struggling to get air. She did her best to assure us that, in her experience, the passing was usually very peaceful. I wish her words could have brought more comfort, but behind the front where I pretended to understand and accept her words, I was actually rolling my eyes. *How in the world can suffocating be peaceful? It's not like he could cry out even if he wanted to.* I felt as though I was going to be sick.

In the end, Andy and I agreed if the situation presented itself and a decision was necessary, we would not intervene. If, by a miracle, Logan came out in better condition than anticipated, we would of course reconsider. But if our situation played out as the doctors predicted, continuing to fight for Logan after delivery would only prolong his suffering.

As hard as I tried to keep fighting for a miracle and show everyone around us we had not lost hope, deep in my heart *I knew.* Deep down in a place I didn't want to acknowledge, I knew we were approaching a point where we would need to finally *let Logan go.*

10 — INTO THE WATER

Therefore go and make disciples of all nations, baptizing them in the name of the Father and of the Son and of the Holy Spirit, and teaching them to obey everything I have commanded you.
—Matthew 28:19 (NIV)

Photo by Ken Papapleo

Rewind to 2010, two years before Andy and I would find out we were pregnant. It was a random Sunday morning, and two of our friends asked us to visit their church. We had been going to the same church for a long time and had no intention of changing, but we thought it would be fun to try something new for a day.

However, after service that morning at Red Rocks Church, we both knew we had found a new home. For the first time in my life, I was excited for Sunday mornings. Church was suddenly a priority and no longer what sometimes felt more like an obligation. I would begin to feel myself mid-week longing to be there, longing to hear what God had to say through the teaching of the pastors, and longing to be a part of a place that was genuinely sold-out for Christ.

It was easy to invest our hearts, our money, and our time there. We plugged in to the community in a way I had never experienced in a church before. We even volunteered every week in the children's ministry before attending service ourselves. That's a testament in and of itself, because spending an hour and a half with a group of fifteen screaming three-year-olds is exhausting. But every Sunday, I would walk out the sanctuary doors feeling refreshed and thinking to myself, *What an awesome day at church.* It was amazing to me that after twenty-five years of growing up in various church settings, for the first time, I knew I was home.

As the next two years passed, I began feeling a stirring in my heart to get baptized again and publicly re-dedicate myself to God. I had been baptized with my siblings when I was little, but now that I was older and understood it more, I felt an urge to do it again.

Our church offered baptisms twice a year. It was always one of my favorite days to attend, as I loved to hear the testimonies and witness life-changing moments. The testimony portion of the service was always so impactful, and although I loved it so much, it was that very thing that kept me from signing up.

Being asked to go through a "mini interview," where I was supposed to share my story, scared me to death. It was incredibly intimidating, and I simply refused to do it. I am shy and introverted, and knowing I would need to go through something so public and personal to get baptized was, unfortunately, a deal breaker for me.

One day, like so many times before, I was crying out for God to restore Logan. But on that day, in pure desperation, I tried to make a deal. Trying to bargain with the Creator of the universe is pretty ridiculous, but I was desperate and willing to try almost anything. I told God if He healed Logan, I would be able to tell *everyone* what He had done for me. I tried to convince Him how much it would impact others to see a genuine miracle firsthand. After all, how could people deny Him after something like that took place? I promised if He fixed Logan's body, I would be a better witness and would even sign up for baptism (even now as I write this, my reasoning seems so childlike and ridiculous that I'm embarrassed to admit it). Instantly, however, I felt convicted. God was gentle but quick to remind me that *regardless* of Logan living or dying, He had *already* done something I should tell everyone about, that something being *Jesus.*

Tears poured down my cheeks uncontrollably, and maybe for the first time in my life my eyes were truly opened to the gift I had been given. *God sacrificed His Son for me.* If He never did another thing for me in this life, I still could not repay Him for the ransom He paid at the cross. It seems so obvious now, but in that moment, the veil that had previously covered my eyes had finally been pulled away. Such a basic truth, and yet, in a way, it had been hidden from me all along.

The insight of that day set me on a journey I never would have imagined. A divine redirection of sorts that would change the trajectory of my life—forever.

There are few times in my life where I can say with certainty I heard the voice of God. I have no doubt that moment was one of those times. His voice was quiet but unmistakable. A few days later I felt Him, once again, make something clear to me.

7/21/12

Logan,

God reminded me today how many times in the past I have prayed for Him to use me to show His love to the world. He then told me that is *exactly* what He is doing with you. I don't know how, Logan, but God is using your wonderful little life to change people. He is using you to show His grace and love to the world. I am so proud of you, son.

Love you to the moon and back,
Mommy

———

I still had *no* idea what exactly it all meant—for God truly does work in mysterious ways—but one thing was finally clear to me. I wanted to get baptized, and I wanted to do it while Logan was with me.

I was terrified to share my story, but I knew it would be a once-in-a-lifetime opportunity. Logan was too important to let my fear win and Satan steal such a beautiful moment between my King, my son, and me. I was still afraid, but full of a newfound courage. I no longer cared if I had to go through something uncomfortable. I knew many people in my situation would want to run from God, but as hard as it was, I wanted to make a stand *for* Him. It was a step of faith for me. It was a declaration that, regardless of my circumstances, He was mine and I was His.

A couple of days later, as I sat in a booth at a sandwich shop, I built up the courage to text a friend from church. She also worked in the children's ministry, and I figured her connections could help get me added to the upcoming baptism. Andy was in line grabbing lunch as I frantically typed out the text. I wanted to get it sent before he came to the table and asked what I was doing. For some reason, I was embarrassed to tell him. I can't even explain why.

I looked at the fully composed text and hesitated to hit Send, until I noticed Andy with our lunch on a tray heading my way. I hit the button without another thought and immediately slammed my phone face down on the table.

When I received a text back later that evening, it wasn't at all what I had hoped to hear. I learned the deadline had already passed to sign up. Due to time constraints, logistics, and the massive amount of people already getting baptized, I couldn't get added on.

I felt my heart sink as I read her text. If someone canceled, I could fill their spot, but there was little guarantee. I would, however, have the opportunity to walk up *during* the service and do an "on the spot" testimony, but I knew I would not have the composure needed for that to work. I was heartbroken and mad at myself and my lack of courage to sign up sooner.

If only I hadn't waited. I ruined my only chance. I had the opportunity to have Logan be a part of something so special. I hate myself. This is something I will spend the rest of my life regretting.

I fell to my knees in the dark basement of my house and cried out to God, *If you want me to do this, then please make it work! I give it to you!* I immediately felt an unanticipated relief wash over me. *My God is bigger than any obstacle. If He wants us to have this, He will make a way.*

THROUGH KELLEY'S EYES

And they were full. Typical. It felt so par for the course those days. Jamie wanted to re-dedicate her life to God and get baptized while Logan was still snuggled up and safe inside her, and the church's list was *full*.

God, why can't you just throw us a freaking bone here?! This had become my standard response to most things during that season of life. It felt beyond unfair to pull the crap card time and time again after we learned of Logan's disorder. I had no oomph left in me to do anything but whine and complain to God about it.

You can't just give her this one thing—this one tiny thing, with all that is going to be taken from her? Honestly, I was so often filled with anger that bitterness was the response that spewed out of me no matter the problem. I was pissed off. Really, I had no one to blame, so I suppose I was angry at anyone who got in my way. That day, it was the church for not squeezing my sister into their baptism service. *And* it was God, because He was about the only one I could constantly yell at. *Done, they suck, and I don't like anyone anymore!*

You want to know one of my most favorite feelings in the whole world? It's that one you get after you completely act like a total jerk toward someone, and then they show up in a big and awesome way. Ahhh, it's so great. It makes you feel *terrible*. But that's exactly what happened. Our church got back in touch with Jamie, and it turned out, they had figured out a way to bend over backward for them.

A couple of days later, I received a call from one of the pastors at Red Rocks Church named JB. I don't know who pulled what strings (well, yes, I suppose I do), but I was getting added to the upcoming baptism. Not only was I getting added, but to make us more comfortable, they offered to come to our house for the interview instead of having us record it at church. They figured it would be much easier to tell my story in the comfort of my own home with Andy by my side. When the interview was finished, they would provide a private baptism and dedication for Logan at a nearby lake. I was so humbled and agreed on the spot. I felt a much-needed surge in my spirit. Even in unthinkable and heartbreaking situations, God's grace still abounds.

After I hung up from the call, I had to share the news with my equally introverted husband that I had sorta, kinda, *somehow* volunteered him for an interview as well. He stared at me with wide eyes and gave me one of those "you're lucky I love you so much" looks.

7/20/12

Dear Logan,

I am amazed at the amount of people fighting for you. All over the world, people are praying for your restoration. God says if we keep knocking on His door, He will answer. There are so many people pounding on heaven's door as we speak. The body of Christ is truly amazing. The way they have come together in support of us is incredible. I feel so blessed to have such wonderful people in my life.

We have hope because nothing is impossible for God. I'm standing in faith today for your divine healing. The Word says if we have faith the size of a mustard seed, we can move mountains. To the world, this may look like an impossible situation, but remember, Logan, we may be *in* this world, but we are not *of* it. God can do anything, and I know He has a plan for you. You have already been a reflection of His love to so many people. Just like He never gives up on us, I, too, promise never to give up on you. Your Dad and I will not quit. We will make our requests to God every day, we will appeal to Him for your restoration, and we will ask in the name of Christ that He would completely heal you.

We are in the middle of a battle, son, but I want you to know how hard so many people are fighting for you. Our battle is not against flesh and blood but against principalities, powers, and the rulers of darkness. Jesus died on the cross to take away our sickness and pain. The price has been paid. We already have victory in Him! Don't be afraid, son. God loves you more than I ever could, and He has a hope and a future and a plan for you. He is with you always and so are we. Take comfort in Him, seek refuge in Him, and trust in Him, because He will never leave you! "I will not forget you! See, I have engraved you on the palms of my hands" (Isaiah 49:16). We have a wonderful Maker, Logan—may His face shine down on you today.

Love you to the moon and back,
Mommy

———

We scheduled the baptism and dedication for the very next week. I had been contracting more than I admitted to anyone, and I could feel time was of the essence.

At an appointment a few days later, a doctor confirmed my suspicions. My body appeared to be gearing up for labor. Of course, they didn't have a crystal ball and had no way of knowing when it could possibly start, but realistically it could happen at any time. As much as I hated to admit it, and as much as I pushed the thought from my mind, I knew there was a chance Logan would not make it much longer.

7/26/12

Dear Heavenly Father,

Your Word says not to be afraid or anxious—please, help me find that place this week. At any time, I could go into labor, or you could take Logan home. I've known that for weeks. But hearing from the doctor yesterday that my body was possibly showing signs of labor was very upsetting. Please, stop the progression of labor inside me! Please don't let my body reject my child! We are not ready. I need more time—please!

I'm appealing to you today to give Logan a long, healthy, and abundant life. Please transform his broken body into a new, strong, and whole body. Please expand his lungs so that he can sing your praises. Heal his arms and hands so that he can raise them up to you, and restore his legs and feet so that he can walk in your footsteps all the days of his life. Please, God, have mercy on him. Please let us make it to his dedication and my baptism. Help us get to a point where we have a fighting chance.

Please give us the right words for our interview. Let your Holy Spirit speak through us and touch the lives of others. May we bring honor to your name, regardless of our circumstances. Please give us clear minds and help us not to be anxious. We ask that you would use us tomorrow to bring glory to your name. Please give us peace and clarity. We are your vessels, and we want our testimony to encourage and impact others in whatever way you have planned. We love you— we trust you—please let our lives be proof of your love.

Thank goodness the week passed and Logan was still safe and sound inside my belly. I was starting to feel more and more anxious about the church's interview coming up. I could feel the oh-so-familiar fears and doubts begin to rise within me. *What am I going to say? How in the world will I be able to maintain composure?*

It's kind of ironic now, looking back, that I tried *so* hard for *so* long to avoid any attention and in the end got way more than I would have originally. In an effort to calm my nerves, I kept reminding myself it was God's will. The door was shut, and He opened it. He already knew exactly what we were going to say, and yet He still wanted us to say it. So the pressure was off. I was going to be honest and open about everything.

The interview wasn't as scary as I imagined. Well, that's not entirely true. It was terrifying—but just initially. Lights, microphones, cameras, and unfamiliar faces filled our living room. I had no idea what to expect, but it was far more intimidating than I ever could have imagined. I could feel heat in my cheeks and hear my heart beating loudly in my chest. I sat snuggled next to Andy on the couch, with my hands tightly gripping my belly. JB sat in front of us and started talking, as if we were at a coffee shop (and not surrounded by cameras). His demeanor and presence were so disarming that my surroundings eventually faded and my nerves settled. For the next hour we simply shared our hearts, our story, and our son with a new person, who somehow felt like an old friend.

Every evening of that week had been full of terrible thunderstorms. I remember thinking we could have a big problem when it came time to jump in a lake. But what an amazingly perfect night it turned out to be. The sky looked like a painting, almost like God had spent the entire day working on a masterpiece of red, yellow, pink, and orange, only to show it off just briefly as the sun disappeared behind the Rocky Mountains. In the strangest way, it felt like a gift. Regardless of the countless Coloradans who could see its beauty as well, I knew He had painted it for *us*. God was truly there. Not that He is ever absent, but in that moment, He was tangible in both His presence and His creation.

Photo by Ken Papaleo

THROUGH KELLEY'S EYES

Our families met at a lake near our house on a beautiful evening where it looked like the sky had been painted with fire. We prayed, we cried, we embraced one another, and felt ever grateful for the moment we shared. It was something beautiful in the midst of all the heartache.

Sometimes we think we know our path more than God. When a roadblock is put on our path, we think it's God's way of messing with us on our journey, instead of realizing that God knows the way. Those roadblocks are an opportunity to sit back and get ready to be amazed by what He has in store for us. A chance to be still and know that God *always* has it sorted.

Photo by Ken Papaleo

7/31/12

Dear Son,

I will cherish today all my life. We went to Standley Lake with those closest to us and dedicated you to God. I am so grateful, because I also got to have you with me as I rededicated myself to our King. Forever I will be able to look back and remember you were with me when I was baptized. It is a memory I will hold on to for the rest of my life. *God is so good.* No matter what we go through, always remember that. I'm so humbled He gave us the opportunity to share our story. I can only hope it will touch lives. You have changed us forever, Logan. God has so much in store for you. Your story will be played at church, and I know your beautiful soul is going to make such an impact. Today was a good day, son. Thank you so much for being a part of it, and thank you for being such an amazing part of me.

Love you to the moon and back,
Mommy

That evening was one of the best and most significant moments of my life. I am so grateful God wove it together so perfectly. I had peace knowing, out of the many things I would possibly never get to do with Logan, his dedication wasn't going to be one of them. Looking back, it's comforting, and yet overwhelming, trying to replay that night in my mind. Logan was there. He was alive. His heart was beating alongside mine. At that moment, my family was *whole.*

As far as we knew, our testimony was going to be played at church during baptism weekend with all the other videos. Although none of it would come to fruition until a month after Logan was born, it turned out God had much bigger plans.

11 — BROKEN TOGETHER

For if they fall, one will lift up his fellow. But woe to him who is alone when he falls and has not another to lift him up!
— Ecclesiastes 4:10 (ESV)

Photo by Jessica Fox

In the middle of the deepest valley of my life, God brought an amazing light in the form of a Colorado-based nonprofit called String of Pearls. Their heart and mission was helping families walk the path of an in-utero fatal diagnosis. I had heard about the group from several different people following Logan's diagnosis, and it turned out to be an immense blessing. It was set up by an incredible woman named Laura Huene. At a routine ultrasound in 2006, Laura and her husband were told their unborn daughter, Pearl, had a rare genetic condition that was almost always fatal.

As I read Pearl's story, I couldn't help but think how similar it was to ours. A fatal diagnosis, the decision to honor life, the uncharted waters of carrying a terminal baby. After experiencing the life and loss of her daughter in a way most people could never relate to and not having substantial outside support, Laura founded String of Pearls.

I couldn't believe there was an organization that perfectly fit our story. We wanted to talk to someone who truly understood, because so few did. I had no one who knew what it was like to carry a dying baby—*until* I met Laura. She was a complete godsend. It takes an amazing person to be called to a ministry that deals with the death of infants and the ultra-sensitive hearts of grieving parents. She offered us support in whatever ways we needed and, most importantly, was a person with whom we didn't have to filter our thoughts. It was so refreshing to finally be able to freely speak my mind and share my heart.

Until I met Laura, I was in a very desolate and isolated place. I was surrounded by people, and yet, on an island all by myself. I was the *only* one carrying Logan. I was the *only* one who would have to deliver him, and I was the *only* one experiencing everything with him firsthand. He had become a part of *me*—a piece of *my* soul that was being torn away. Laura was the first person I met who understood such anguish.

Through her organization, we came to meet another family in our area who had found themselves in the exact same situation as ours. It felt like God connected us, considering how rare of a condition Logan had. Rarer still was finding a local couple who got the exact same diagnosis for the exact same condition and had happened to choose life as well. When Laura told me about the Nichols family, I knew we needed to meet them. She told me they were carrying a little girl named Megan and were just ten weeks ahead of us in their pregnancy.

We met Leslie, Ryan, and their son, Pete, one sunny afternoon at a Starbucks in Denver. I knew who they were the moment they walked through the doors. Leslie looked just like me—pregnant and tired with a halfhearted smile, trying her best to hold it together but silently falling apart. I could recognize the suffering in her eyes, because those very same eyes had been staring at me in the mirror for the last five weeks. From across the room I looked at them like so many people probably looked at us too—on the surface just a seemingly happy family without a care in the world. A young pregnant couple expecting new life with an energetic little boy in tow, off to get some coffee and enjoy a beautiful Sunday afternoon.

In reality, they were a couple in the middle of a crisis. A couple who for months had been in a state of agonizing limbo, wondering if and when they would be burying their daughter.

It made me think about all the other faces sitting around the coffee shop that morning. What stories did these people have? I wonder what they, too, were in the midst of and how many people we pass on a daily basis who are hurting behind their smiles. *Everyone* is fighting a battle. *Everyone* has wounds. Hidden deep beneath a fake smile or calm demeanor, we all are bleeding from something.

Our visit with Leslie and Ryan was just what we needed to give us a surge of strength. It was the oddest feeling to be with strangers yet somehow have a level of comfort and connection to them that normally would take a lifetime to establish. Thanks to the cooperation of little Pete, and due to strategic snack placements, we were able to spend the next couple of hours sharing our stories, our hearts, and our fears.

There were no awkward moments—no uncomfortable pauses. We talked like old friends would and understood each other in a way that literally no one else could. While I was heartbroken they were going through it, too, it was deeply comforting knowing Andy and I were not alone. A bond was forged between our families that day, and I will forever thank God that, even in the darkest places imaginable, His mercies can still be found.

I was anticipating the Nichols family, in a way, paving the road for us. They were the trailblazers in these uncharted waters, and we would follow in their wake, armed with more answers and information when our turn came for Logan's birth. They were set to deliver baby Megan by C-section in two short weeks. I felt more at peace because I would have an idea of what to expect based on her delivery. It was a blessing to possibly have some of my questions answered and, just maybe, have a glimpse of what Logan's birth would look like.

8/7/12

Logan,

We got to meet a very special family last weekend—Leslie, Ryan, Pete, and their sweet little girl, Megan. Megan is special just like you! She is going to be delivered soon, so we are going to keep her uplifted in prayer as much as we can. God is so good to have introduced us to another family in our very unique situation. Ryan and Leslie are wonderful people, and it's amazing the connection we have with them already after only a couple of hours. They understand when no one else can. I can't imagine the range of emotions they must be feeling right now just a week away from meeting their little girl—joy, fear, relief, anxiety. I know we will be there soon enough, but the constant flow of polar opposite emotions has already been a real struggle for me.

I'm so excited to see you and kiss you, but we just don't know what God's plan for your life is. I know how much you have changed my life already, and I can't imagine how God is going to use you to impact others. I don't know, Logan, maybe this has been the purpose of our lives all along—maybe this is what you, Dad, and I were created for.

Love you to the moon and back,
Mommy

I had no idea as I wrote to Logan that fateful morning that a few short hours later, my water would break. I had no idea how close we were to the end.

12 — THE BEGINNING OF THE END

Be strong and courageous. Do not be afraid; do not be discouraged,
for the Lord your God will be with you wherever you go.
— Joshua 1:9 (NIV)

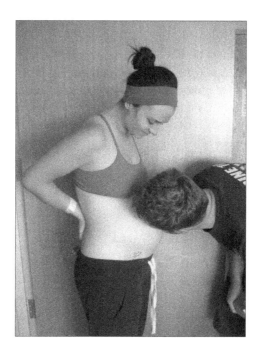

It was August 7, exactly one week after Logan's dedication and my baptism. Nothing about that day felt any different. If anything, I was a tad more hopeful from the connection we had made with the Nichols family just days earlier. I remember spending the early hours of the morning writing to Logan while cuddled in blankets, feeling a bit encouraged, and not wanting to leave the comfort and warmth my bed provided.

But I had a full day of hair ahead, so I shut my journal and dragged myself out of the covers—fully anticipating I would once again enjoy their warm embrace later that evening. As I walked out the door that morning,

I had no idea I would not be returning home for many days—and that Logan would *never* return there again.

———⟨⟩———

It was midmorning, and I was finishing a color application on a client's hair when I felt a big gush. My heart immediately sank into a pit of darkness and fear because I knew my water had just broken. *Please, God, no! Not yet! We're not ready! I'm not ready!*

For a moment, I tried very hard to convince myself I had only peed—definitely the first time in my life I had wished that upon myself. I'd often heard stories of pregnant women mistaking it for their water breaking, and desperately wanted to be one of them. *Please, God, just let that be what this is!* But as I was praying and holding everything as tight as I possibly could—I felt another big gush.

Few times in my life have I experienced such an instant and consuming panic. *Is this it?* I knew it was *way* too early for Logan. He was only twenty-seven weeks old—an age that can be doable for a healthy baby but an absolute death sentence for my little boy. I knew this early the doctors wouldn't give me a C-section like we had hoped. Ultimately, I knew if this *was* the beginning of the end, Logan was going to die.

In that moment, the hope of seeing Logan living on this side of heaven began to slip through my fingers. I ran upstairs shaking uncontrollably and told my boss I had to leave. I didn't know where to go. We still hadn't met our delivery doctor. We hadn't met our delivery team. We hadn't discussed our hope for labor and delivery with *anyone*. We had only discussed care *after* Logan was born. We were not prepared. My mind was in shock. As I stumbled out the door, with my head buried in my purse desperately searching for my keys, a sweet friend and coworker grabbed me by the hand and told me she would drive.

We rushed to my perinatologist's office, which fortunately was just down the street (the same place where we'd found out Logan had OI). They were the only ones I felt safe with, and I had *nowhere* else to go.

My old and kind doctor wasn't there, but thankfully, Lisa was. She continued to be a blessing from God at nearly every turn—always showing up when I needed her most. From what she could see, there was still amniotic fluid, but for the first time, Logan was head down.

Finally, my doctor arrived. He confirmed what Lisa had told us, but also noticed part of the membrane that typically holds everything in could no longer be seen. I hadn't had any more leakage, thank goodness, so they told me to go home, take it easy, and go straight to the hospital if anything else happened.

Finally, Andy arrived and came bursting through the front doors. I could see the panic on his face as he frantically scanned the room for mine. The moment he found me on a small couch in the corner, he rushed to my side. His eyes were wide and desperately seeking answers.

I had started to allow myself to think everything was okay and told him the same. He helped me out of my chair, hooked his arm through mine, and slowly walked me to the car. On the way, I called Kelley to tell her what was going on. I hadn't let anyone know what was happening but decided I should start with her. I was in the middle of explaining the last couple of hours when my water gushed out again. This time, it was unmistakable.

Every ounce of remaining hope vanished in that instant. This was it— we were about to start the journey that would end in good-bye.

Initially, I didn't want to call anyone. I wanted to avoid undue stress, just in case everything turned out okay. My family had been through a lot already. My number popping up on their phones had the power to instantly increase their blood pressure. We were *all* on pins and needles. I wanted so badly to protect them—to shield them from the pain we were causing. Kelley, however, rarely received that courtesy from me— she always had the "privilege" of knowing everything before anyone else.

But now Andy and I were on the way to the hospital. My water was continually leaking, and the clock was ruthlessly ticking. With each passing mile, I was one step closer to good-bye. There was no more avoiding it. The time had come to break the news to the rest of the family.

Throughout my pregnancy, my family had been a constant source of strength for me. They encouraged and supported us at every turn and would effortlessly include Logan when they talked about the future. They had immense faith and never stopped believing in a miracle. Even though I'm sure they didn't fully believe at times, they gave me hope and always spoke life when I felt surrounded by death.

My mom in particular bridged the gap to hope for me in an incredible way. Her heart was crumbling, too, but she never ceased to believe in the power of our Creator. Her faith was immovable and unshakable. She would send me songs, Bible verses, and prayers—basically *anything* to help get me though another day. One day she even sent me a picture of a sunflower on her deck that was severely broken at the root, only to find it days later completely restored. Logan was her *sunflower*, and now I had to call and tell her it was over.

She answered the phone with her usual cheery voice. She was surprised I was calling her in the middle of the day, and she definitely didn't anticipate the grim news she was about to hear. In the silence that followed, I could hear her heart crush. When she found words to speak, I felt the defeat in her voice. She had been a pillar of strength and grace. How I wish I could have protected her from all of this.

The thought of labor is intimidating, to say the least. Knowing what I was about to face was overwhelming, but knowing what *Logan* was about to face was excruciating. I kept hearing the words *potentially gruesome* over and over in my mind. *I'm not ready. Logan is not ready—this is happening too fast. Father God, please have mercy on us.*

I don't remember much of the drive to the hospital after the call with my mom. I don't remember walking through the front doors and finding the labor and delivery unit. I don't remember anything except looking down at a nurse sitting at the front desk and telling her my water had broken. I don't remember what she said. I don't remember how I replied. Suddenly, I was in a little exam room I don't recall walking to. Within minutes, a nurse, whose face I cannot remember, came in and checked to confirm what I already knew to be true—my water *had* broken and labor was imminent.

I was disoriented and numb—dizzy almost. I couldn't focus. The details are now so fragmented. Everything was happening too early and in the wrong way. It had been a painful battle to mentally and emotionally prepare myself for what I *thought* would happen: a scheduled C-section once Logan was full-term, a specialized team of nurses, a doctor who knew about the complications of OI and respected our wishes, and *ultimately* a few moments with our boy.

But we hadn't had an opportunity to meet with the high-risk doctor who would oversee my delivery. We had somehow fallen through the cracks and were left dangerously unprepared. No one in that hospital knew us or our wishes and the reasons *why* we wanted things done a certain way. We hoped to be on the same page as our delivery team and give our reasons for wanting a C-section. And now Andy and I had no advocate. We were in a room with people we didn't know telling us things we didn't want to hear.

"A C-section is simply out of the question. It's too dangerous for you. We probably couldn't even find a surgeon in this hospital that would be willing to do it."

Logan was going to die, so in the doctor's mind, *I* was the only concern. Looking back, I can of course understand where she was coming from (medically speaking, at least), but trying to tell a mother her life is more important than her child's does not bode well under *any* circumstances. *Ever.* It felt like the nightmare I had been stuck in for the last six weeks continued to spiral downward and get more and more horrible with each passing minute.

After some time, the same doctor came back into my room and told me there was another option. For a *brief* second, I felt a tiny shred of hope. *Maybe there is another way.*

The grain of hope dissipated in an instant when her words found their way to my ears. She got down on my level and, in a very hushed voice, as though she didn't want others to hear, offered me a shot that would stop Logan's heart. A more "humane" way to end it, as she so tactfully explained. She was calm, collected, and confident in her opinion. She stood up and brushed her hands back and forth several times—almost as if she had completed a job and was admiring the end result. She had a strange and disturbing smile that sent chills down my spine. *This woman actually believes she is giving me good news.* I wanted to throw up.

Prior to her comment, I didn't feel there was anything that could have been said or done to derail me further. I believed I had already hit the absolute bottom. I couldn't have been more wrong. The pit went further down. After months of fighting for my son's life, I had been offered, in effect, to "put him down."

I could feel my face begin to flush as an immeasurable amount of anger began to swell inside me. I had been *very* clear from the start about our beliefs and wishes when it came to Logan's life. *This is the exact thing I shouldn't have to field right now. If they knew me, she never would have asked.* It's fortunate for the doctor's sake that I was half-naked and unable to get off the hospital bed. What I envisioned doing to her was anything but loving. I hid my face in my hands, shook my head back and forth, and firmly said no several times.

This doctor clearly had been hardened enough over the years that she was left calloused, without tact, and maybe even a bit flippant with her regard to life. After years and years in a life-or-death job, perhaps it's nearly impossible not to become a bit desensitized to death, and there *is* room for grace in that. At that moment, however, the condition of her heart and the many horrible things she had seen to harden it were the *last* things on my mind. As far as I was concerned, there was only one heart in that room where such a needle was welcome, and it was nowhere near my boy. Now, unfortunately, the face of *that* woman, in contrast to the majority of that entire afternoon, I will never forget.

As the day went on, Andy and I were backed further and further into a corner. Checkmate. We had no moves and there was nothing we could do. The doctors had the ability to prolong labor for a while. Although I was contracting constantly, labor hadn't actively started. Since the risk of infection would only continue to increase as time passed, it seemed inducing labor was the safest (and only) option.

Andy and I decided it would be best to wait until morning to make any decisions. I was hoping and praying I would naturally go into labor sometime during the night. Although my body had made the decision for me, it tore me up inside to think of *willingly* taking a medication that would basically force Logan out of the *only place* where he was relatively safe. *I am his mom and it is my responsibility to protect him. I can't do this. Please, God, don't make this decision mine!*

We spent the evening surrounded by family. At one point, Leslie and Ryan Nichols even stopped by. We cried, we prayed, and at times even halfheartedly laughed. It felt like the massive flocking of family that takes place when someone is about to die and everyone has come to say their good-byes. In a way, that is exactly what it was.

As the night got darker and we found ourselves alone in that big room, Andy and I asked the nurse to put the heart monitor on Logan one last time. The staff recommended we not use a monitor as labor progressed, because it would be too stressful to hear Logan's heart beginning to struggle and very possibly stop. The nurse happily obliged. We sat together on that tiny hospital bed for what must have been several hours—crying and listening to the beautiful music that was Logan's beating heart.

Andy and I had prayed so many times for God to take Logan home if he was in pain. In that moment, sitting together, we finally realized that maybe He was doing just that. The decision we had dreaded was made. Come morning, we would induce.

8/7/12

My dear sweet boy,

My water broke today while I was at work. I can't even begin to explain to you the panic going through me right now. All I want to do is protect you, to keep you safe, and to make sure you are not in any pain, but I know it is out of my hands and entirely in God's. Your dad and I are in the hospital right now—waiting. Tomorrow we will talk to more doctors and figure out exactly what we are going to do. Either way you are coming much sooner than we anticipated.

I'm so sorry, son. I feel like I have failed you. I wish my body could have held on longer. I wish we had more time. I wonder if this will be our last night together. Thank you for all the kicks. There is no better feeling in the entire world. You are the best thing that has ever happened to me, and I'm scared of facing life without you. Please know how hard I tried to keep you safe. I would gladly give myself right now if it would spare you. I've begged God to let me take your place countless times. I would take your pain and your sickness, *if only* He would allow. But it appears that's a trade I am not allowed to make. I'm heartbroken, my love. Utterly heartbroken. *I just want you.*

As much as I long to see you alive, if at *any* time Jesus comes for you, please *run to Him!* He has a place for you where there is no pain, no sadness, and no tears. We will meet you there soon enough, and I expect you to be the first one to run into my arms. I love you so much—I know I've said it a thousand times, but I could never say it enough. Even now as it seems we are approaching the end, I am not giving up on you. I will fight for you until you take your last breath—until God decides it's time to bring you home. You are not alone, son. We are here for you, and we will stay by your side *until the end.*

Love you to the moon and back,
Mommy

THROUGH KELLEY'S EYES

My husband, Eric, and I were lucky enough to have work schedules and child care options (aka my mom) that allowed us occasionally to get away in the middle of the week to enjoy a matinee at our neighborhood theater. Not only was it cheaper, but also the theaters were practically empty—except for the ten or so grannies and grandpas that enjoyed the show with us, of course.

I was just about to silence my phone and walk into the theater for two and a half hours of a Batman movie when it unexpectedly rang. It was Jamie. These days, I found myself holding my breath a little every time her face popped up on my caller ID, and the typical greeting she had gotten once upon a time had vanished and was replaced by a blunt, "Is everything okay?" But for some reason, this call had failed to trigger my conditioned alert, and I answered rather nonchalantly. Everything was *not* okay. Jamie thought her water had broken. It had begun.

That's the moment I felt all my hope slip away. Until then, I had made an active choice to believe in a miracle for Logan. Why not, right? People get those from time to time, right? At that point, I remember looking at Eric and saying, "God's not giving us a miracle. Logan's going to die." I had lost all my fight. I was empty.

We left the theater and headed to Jamie's house to grab some stuff they needed for the hospital. It was too soon, and none of us were ready. When we arrived at the labor and delivery waiting room, a herd of waddling pregnant women waiting for their tour of the floor to begin surrounded us. No joke. It was not cool.

Eventually a nurse came out looking for us and led us into a little exam room where they were evaluating Jamie. Blow number one: her water had indeed broken. Blow number two: they weren't going to allow her to get a C-section this early in the game. Blow number three: their only option was to induce labor and pray that it wasn't going to end gruesomely. Done and done. The fight was over. We had been knocked out and were left totally terrified.

They finally moved Jamie and Andy into a bigger, more comfortable room. We sat there as the rest of the family arrived to try to love on them as much as possible. At one point, the Nichols family came to say hello, and I got to meet them for the first time after hearing all about their Megan.

They brought the birth plan they had been working on for Megan, since Jamie and Andy hadn't gotten around to making one for Logan yet. As I sat there reading through it, I held myself together for the most part, but still was in disbelief that this is what it had come down to: the world's most devastatingly sad birth plan.

I thought I had prepared myself for what was going to happen. Time and time again we had been told the end of the story by the world. But as I read through the birth plan, I unexpectedly came upon a section that was just too much. It was instructions on how Logan's body was going to be handled after he passed away. *This is not okay . . . this is not okay . . . this is too much.*

The decision had been made to wait until morning to move forward with Logan's induction in hopes that we all could get some sleep before it began. Sleep—a hysterical notion. A while back, Jamie and Andy had asked me if I would be there for Logan's labor when the time came. An incredible honor. And so, I would return to the hospital bright and early the next morning, with Andy's favorite breakfast sandwiches in hand.

13 — RUN TO JESUS

Yea, though I walk through the valley of the shadow of death, I will fear no evil; for You are with me; Your rod and Your staff, they comfort me . . . Surely goodness and mercy shall follow me all the days of my life; and I will dwell in the house of the Lord forever.
—Psalm 23:4, 6 (NKJV)

Photo by Ken Papaleo

8/8/12

Logan,

It's very early in the morning now. Your dad is asleep next to us. I didn't sleep much—well, not really at all. My mind is racing, and my heart is hurting too badly. I have so many questions—so many concerns about today. I wish I could know how this is going to end. I'm scared for labor, which is unavoidable now, but mostly I'm concerned for you. I am praying God, in His infinite grace, would not allow you to suffer. You are my main concern, and it looks like we will not be meeting at the time or in the manner I was hoping. I am so sorry, Logan.

I know, deep down, it's not my fault, but you are my son—you are inside *me*—and no matter what anyone says, I alone feel responsible for your safety. I wanted you to have all the time you needed, but my body hasn't listened to me. I feel so responsible—I feel like I have let you down. I feel like a failure. I know everyone will tell me differently. I know there is not much I could have done to change or stop what is happening—but I am also the *only* one carrying you. I am the *only* one who is your mother, so really there is hardly anyone who could possibly understand. Sympathy is obvious, but empathy is an entirely different thing. It's one thing to feel bad for someone's situation, but to personally understand the pain is so very different.

You are my baby boy, my first child, and I can't imagine life without you. You have become such a major part of me, and if God takes you, there is going to be a massive hole left in your absence. I will never be the same without you here. A piece of me will be gone the moment you are. But I want you to know, Logan, regardless of all these things, you have made me a better person. You have drawn me closer to God, closer to your dad, and closer to our family. For that I thank you. What a gift you have been. I adore you, my precious little man.

Love you to the moon and back,
Mommy

⎯⎯∞⎯⎯

The first of what would be two of the longest nights of my life was finally over. I wasn't able to sleep, which didn't surprise me. All night I was anxiously waiting for labor to start. I was prepared to begin the induction process come morning, but with all my heart I didn't want it to come to that. I was praying for my contractions to pick up and begin some sort of progression. But there I was, early morning, dark circles—and no labor.

Andy went to get some fresh air, and I was left in our room by myself. I knew he needed a moment to himself, but it left me feeling isolated and incredibly lonely. My phone started ringing with a number I didn't recognize. I *never* answer numbers I don't know. And yet, for some reason, my finger answered before my mind told it not to.

To my surprise, it was our lead pastor's wife, Jill. They were on vacation and somehow got word we were in the hospital and about to deliver. Jill spent the next moments praying with me. She was so kind and had such a comforting spirit. I could feel her compassion from miles away. I was incredibly humbled that someone I had never met, who helped shepherd a church of thousands, would take time out of her family trip to pray for someone she didn't even know. And just for a moment, I felt seen and maybe not so alone. Little did I know at the time that Jill would turn into a pillar of support and friendship in my life for years and years to come.

As I was hanging up the phone, I heard a knock on the door. I figured it was Andy and was curious why he didn't just come in. I opened the door, and to my surprise JB from our church (the pastor who'd baptized me) was standing in the hall. Upon seeing his smiling face, I immediately felt comforted. I knew God truly was with me and cared about even my smallest needs. JB sat and talked with me for a while. Andy and I had gotten very close to him throughout everything, and I was deeply relieved to have him in that room. Andy came back a few minutes later and, by the look on his face, was equally touched by the visit.

Eventually, Kelley poked her head through the door with breakfast in her hands. My appetite was nonexistent, but Andy was happy to have something other than hospital food.

Throughout the morning several doctors were in and out of our room to discuss what the rest of the day would look like. They explained the process of induction, went through details about how things would work, and told me they were in the process of moving me over to a delivery room. I decided to take the opportunity to shower. Who knew how long it would be before I had the chance again. Poor Andy—I made him come too.

I stood in the hot water, holding my belly like I had done so many times before. Slowly rocking back and forth, I quietly sang to Logan with a quivering voice, "Jesus loves you, this I know . . . " My voice fully broke and Andy finished. "He's going to help your body grow, long and strong and pure as snow, and you'll tell of His glory wherever you go." The weight on my shoulders was too much to bear. Like a glass thrown against a wall, I broke. I wept. I couldn't stand. Andy had to hold me up like he had done so many times before.

When I *finally* found the energy to emerge from the bathroom, I was greeted by Michelle, another friend from church. Michelle was actually the recipient of the baptism text I sent all those weeks ago from the sandwich shop. *Wow, three people from one church in the span of a couple of hours.* And just like that, my already great love for Red Rocks Church grew tenfold.

Michelle was sitting next to Kelley and had a little bag in her hand. Inside it was a tiny Bible with Logan's name and a necklace with the letter *L*. I immediately put it on, and every time I looked at it, I was reminded that I needed to be brave for Logan. At different moments throughout the day, I would notice my fist clenched tightly around it, holding on for dear life. In that hospital, it became a semipermanent fixture to the inside of my hand. It might seem silly, but to me it was comforting—like I was going into battle and had just been given a shield.

THROUGH KELLEY'S EYES

With breakfast sandwiches in hand, I arrived at the hospital bright and early the next morning. Walking into the room to see the pastor who'd baptized and dedicated Jamie and Logan was unexpected and welcomed. Then to hear that the head pastor's wife, Jill, had gone out of her way to call and encourage Jamie meant the world to me.

At that time, I was employed at the church and worked in the tiny-person Sunday school department. My boss, Michelle, knew Jamie and Andy from the countless Sundays we had all spent pretending we knew how to teach Sunday school lessons to a herd of three-year-olds. Part of our job was to plan and host the child dedications for the church. Every baby who was dedicated received a tiny little Bible with their name engraved on the front.

Well, the next visitor of the morning was Michelle. She had brought a tiny Bible with "Logan Andrew Stewart" engraved on the front, along with a beautiful necklace that had an *L* and his birthstone dangling from it. That necklace actually hung around Jamie's neck from that moment on—for *years*.

I remember sobbing with Michelle in that small hospital room as the two of us sat listening to my baby sister sobbing in that small hospital shower. The things we will always remember.

We were finally moved to a delivery room where the long process of induction would begin. I stared at the ceiling and studied its imperfections as doctors administered a medication that would start my labor. I wanted to get up and run away. I wanted to be *anywhere* but there. I had fought *so hard* to keep Logan in me, and now I was letting doctors give me something that would force him out. *How could it have come to this?*

From that point on, my awareness of time faded. It was a continual process of pills and procedures that seemed to have no end. It felt as though every step was a struggle. Procedures that were "normally" simple turned out to be difficult. Measures that were "normally" effective turned out to be unproductive.

Hour after hour passed. Eventually, in the middle of the night, I had to get an epidural in order to have a procedure done to help manually progress my labor. After a short amount of time passed, it was evident my epidural didn't fully work. My left side continued to gain feeling while my right side stayed numb. They continued to give me more medication through the IV hoping it would migrate, but eventually one side was fully responsive, while the other was completely immobile. It seemed as though *nothing* was going in our favor.

Hours crept by. With the curtains drawn, I didn't even know if it was day or night. I was *desperate* for sleep, but the pain was overwhelming. Panic washed over me in waves. Finally, I asked Kelley to take my journal and read it out loud. I needed a distraction and I wanted Logan to hear the love I had for him *one last time*. She and Andy squeezed on to the tiny hospital bed with me, and read my journal from cover to cover.

Soon after, the contractions moved to my back and down my leg as they continued to intensify to a breathtaking level. I became furious with God. I looked at Kelley, and I could see on her face she, too, couldn't take much more. I saw her eyes begin to fill, as she clenched her jaw and left the room. She made up some excuse—I knew it was in an attempt to regain her composure. I knew we all had the same thoughts running rampant through our minds.

Why God? You are going to take Logan at the end of this! We are going to watch him die! Or he could come out in pieces! Can't you at least let the epidural work? Can't something go smoothly?

Andy began to panic as my arms and hands started shaking uncontrollably. The nurses assured him it was normal, but I felt like the situation was spinning out of control. My support team had *understandably* reached their limit. To make matters worse, it seemed like there was no end in sight.

After more hours than I can recall, we were *finally* told it was time to call our family and have them head to the hospital. Logan was coming soon.

THROUGH KELLEY'S EYES

It's unbelievable how incredibly crappy and frustrating Jamie's delivery was. *Everything* was difficult. Nothing seemed to work like you would hope, and I couldn't even begin to understand where God was in all of this. It was so lonely—just the three of us thrown into a situation that was *far* beyond us. It was painful. It was terrifying. It was exhausting. I can't begin to tell you how many times I had to step out of that delivery room and sit on the floor in the hall and cry, just to release the incredible amount of anxiety and frustration I was feeling. In the midst of it all, Jamie's *only* concern was for Logan. Was he in pain? Was he scared? Did he know we were there and how much we loved him?

Throughout her pregnancy, Jamie had written letters to Logan in a journal that our brother, Jordan, gave her. I knew she had been using it, but I had never read any of them. After twenty-four hours of labor, Jamie decided she wanted her letters to Logan to be read out loud to him *one last time*. But neither she nor Andy thought they could do it, so she asked me.

As we all sat squished together on an extremely uncomfortable hospital bed, I started to read an amazing love story about two parents and their sweet son. I was utterly blown away by the words coming out of my mouth and the incredible steadfast faith they had—a faith I felt I had lost along the way. *That's* where God was in all of this. It was humbling and something I will always cherish. It was the calm before the storm.

Shortly thereafter, Jamie was finally far enough along that they could begin to administer Pitocin to try to move things along more quickly. I remember calling my mom and telling her they should probably head down to the hospital soon, since they lived so far away. It was literally only *moments* after I hung up the phone that Jamie suddenly started yelling that she needed to push. I remember running out to the hall calling for help and was followed back into the room by a flood of people.

It was insane how many people were in that room. The doctor checked Jamie. She was spot on. It was time to push. I felt like I was going to vomit.

So much had led up to this moment and so much uncertainty along with it. Too many doctors had said horrifying things, and I didn't know if we were about to witness the miracle of life or the gruesome death they had predicted. I was terrified.

They had me and Andy hold Jamie's legs. Sweet Andy kept trying to count out contractions for Jamie, because she said it helped, but the poor guy had no idea what he was counting. It felt like pure chaos, with all eyes glued on Jamie. And then it happened. And everything became still and silent . . .

Everything happened so fast. One moment I was *supposedly* two hours away from delivery, and a few minutes later I was yelling at Andy and Kelley that I needed to push. I could feel Logan coming out. I knew there wasn't much time. Andy told me not to push yet, and Kelley ran to get help. People were suddenly *everywhere*, frantically trying to get set up in time. My doctor came running through the door with a nurse on her heels who was simultaneously tying her gown and handing her gloves. I had gone from "getting closer" to "fully dilated" in a matter of minutes.

My instincts were telling me to push, but my heart was screaming no. I knew pushing meant good-bye, and yet I also knew if Logan was still alive, all the pushing could crush him. We hadn't checked on his heart in quite a while, but if he was still with me, I needed to get him out as fast as possible. The contractions were intense and coming back-to-back. I could hardly catch my breath.

The scene was frenzied. I yelled at Andy to count for me. I felt like I had no idea what I was doing, and by the look on Andy's face he was equally clueless. I needed some direction, and for me, someone telling me how long to push seemed to help. My sweet husband began counting, although I'm pretty sure, in the chaos, I heard him start at seven.

After just a few minutes of pushing, I could feel that Logan was close. It was time. I couldn't stop thinking about what all the pressure was doing to his little body, and I was determined to get him out on the next push. Another contraction was fast approaching. I pushed with everything I had, and out he came.

Instantly, a chaotic scene turned completely quiet. Everything was suddenly still. Even if Logan was alive, I knew I wouldn't hear his cry. But oh nged for the beautiful noise. Time seemed to stand still as I sat up to get my first look at him. *Did he make it?* I didn't know what I was about to see. All I kept hearing in my mind was *potentially gruesome... potentially gruesome... potentially gruesome.* And yet, when I saw him for the first time, when my eyes *finally* found what they had been so desperately searching for, all that was before me was my perfect little boy.

He was alive. And he was absolutely beautiful. He was wiggling his shoulders, and I could see his chest moving ever so slightly. They immediately handed him to me, and I was finally face-to-face with *my Logan*—the boy who had been a part of me for nearly seven months, the boy I had spent countless hours talking to and praying over, the precious little life I had fought so hard to protect. The one thing in the world I loved most, and the one thing that held the biggest piece of my heart, was finally in my arms. *Hello, my sweet boy.*

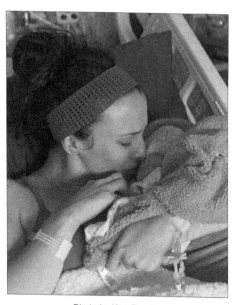

Photo by Ken Papaleo

He looked like Andy: same gorgeous full lips, same dimpled chin. Yes, his body was broken, but through my eyes he was the most beautiful thing ever to grace this planet. I stared at his beautiful little face with wonder. I kissed his warm cheek, nuzzled his tiny nose with mine, and told him how much I loved him. *Please, God, don't let him suffer. Please, God, don't let him be afraid.*

The love I felt for the child before me was *indescribable*. It was as if in one moment I was able to understand (to a small extent) the love Christ has for us. I would have given *anything* to take his pain away—to cast his illness to the deepest, darkest depths of this planet. I knew the overwhelming love I felt for Logan paled in comparison to God's affection for us, for He loves us with a fierceness we cannot comprehend. But in that very moment, as I held my son in my arms, I saw God more clearly than I ever had before.

I passed Logan over to meet his father. I had been holding him for the past twenty-seven weeks; it was time for Andy to have a turn. Andy sat there with a tiny two-pound bundle in his arms, tears streaming down his face, and said, "Hey buddy," to his son for the first time. Logan looked so small in Andy's big frame. He opened the blanket and traced his hands across Logan's little body, almost as if checking to see if everything was in place. Ten fingers and ten toes—they were all there.

Logan had come so quickly that no one in our family had made it to the hospital yet—besides Kelley, of course, who hadn't left our side in over twenty-four hours. It's a lot to ask a person to be present for something so heart-wrenching, and Kelley did it gracefully. She had given us a priceless gift. There was so little I could do to say thank you in return, but Logan's heart was still slowly beating, and there was one gift we *could* give her. It was an opportunity only *she*, of all our family, would ever have: holding Logan while life still filled his body.

Kelley placed Logan close to her face and gently rocked him back and forth. Tears rolled down her cheeks as she sang her rendition of "Jesus Loves You" into his perfect little ear. Babies can recognize voices and sounds they repeatedly hear in the womb, and if there was one thing in this world Logan would have been familiar with, it was that song. It was such a tender moment, and I know his aunt's sweet voice brought him comfort in the last minutes of his life.

It felt as though we hadn't even finished saying hello before it was already time to say good-bye. Logan was in my arms once again. It didn't matter how tightly I held on, because I knew God was calling him home. I finally let go. *Please, God, take him.* It was *by far* the hardest prayer that has ever left my lips. I passed him to his dad one last time. "Run to Jesus, Logan," Andy whispered in his tiny ear. Then . . . he was gone.

A nurse quietly walked to Andy to check what we already knew to be true. A bruise emerged on Logan's chest where her stethoscope was placed. "Time of death . . . 12:37."

There was a strange sense of peace as Andy and I looked into each other's red, swollen eyes. It may have been short-lived, but there was an unexplainable calmness that could have only come from God. As much as we didn't want Logan to go, it was a relief to know he was no longer suffering. *It was over.* The unknown was now known. All the questions had been answered. Logan was safe and in the arms of Jesus, and one day we would meet him there. We were given 54 minutes to pour out a lifetime of love on our sweet boy. Even though it felt like an impossibly short amount of time, we knew it could not compare to the eternity we will get to share with him one day.

I sat there with Andy by my side and stared at the body of my little boy. *Did that really just happen?* It just didn't seem possible. *Logan is dead.* I kept repeating it in my mind, but I couldn't comprehend what it meant.

Photo by Ken Papaleo

THROUGH KELLEY'S EYES

Logan had come into this world and wiggled. He was alive! He was our perfect boy. Here was God again, in this perfect moment.

There are really no words to describe how it felt watching Jamie and Andy meet their sweet boy for the first time—saying hello, knowing that good-bye was right around the corner. They asked a couple of times if I wanted to hold Logan, and while I honestly couldn't wait to hold him, I kept passing up the opportunity. I wanted them to get as much time with him as they could, knowing it was quickly running out. Finally, they insisted, and finally, I happily agreed.

I sat in a rocking chair with my sweet boy, not knowing how to give him all the love I had for him in the few minutes we were going to have together. I decided to sing him our song, even though I know I have the worst voice ever. So we rocked and sang and snuggled, and that's our story for now. Moments later I watched Logan peacefully pass in his daddy's arms. As weird as it sounds, I felt a strange sense of release. No more confusion, no more fear—just a sense of clarity and peace.

I sat on the hospital bed with my sweet boy cradled in a bundle of blankets on my lap. I hunched over so my face was just inches from his, trying to take in every piece of him. I traced my fingers over his perfect little features. My tears dropped on his belly. The world around us felt frozen in time. The two of us had been a team for seven months. We were one and the same—and now we were not.

My mind began to wonder if I gave Logan all he needed in his short life here. *Was there an area I lacked? Could I have done more for him? Been a better mom somehow?* I tried so hard to be everything he needed and everything he deserved, but I knew I had probably fallen short in some ways. I wanted to give him everything, yet in that moment, as I looked down on his little two-pound frame, I realized he had given way more to me than I ever could have given to him.

He made me a mother. He taught me a love I never understood. He gave me insight into a God who *willingly* sacrificed *His* son for our freedom—a God who gave His son as ransom, knowing fully that His gift wouldn't be accepted by all. If only we could fully understand the depth of love that is capable of such a choice.

Once again, like so many pieces of this story, the next moments are black, fuzzy, and distorted in my mind. I just can't remember, and it frustrates me deeply. I know at some point Logan was put in a onesie and wrapped in the monkey blanket Andy had picked. I know Laura, from String of Pearls, arrived and made some footprint ornaments and molds. I know at some point we were told our families had made it to the hospital and were in the waiting room. I know I asked Kelley to go talk with them. But I have no idea on the timing or order of any of it. I know I was *really* anxious about the scene our families would be walking into, and my heart broke knowing what they all were feeling in anticipation of what they were about to see.

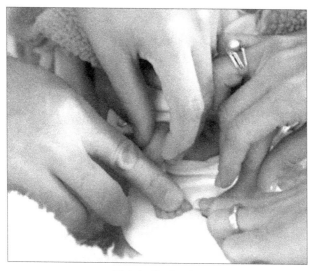

Photo by Ken Papaleo

THROUGH KELLEY'S EYES

The nursing staff let us know that some of our family had arrived and were in the waiting room. I hadn't spoken to anyone since that last call to my mom. No one knew that Logan had arrived, and no one knew that he had already passed. The staff still had some work to do on Jamie before more family could come into the delivery room. So Jamie and Andy asked if I would go out and speak to them. I literally have no clue what I said to anyone. I only remember walking into the waiting room, seeing everyone, and bawling uncontrollably. It was probably a good forty-five minutes before Jamie and Andy were all set to have the rest of the family meet Logan. The hospital was kind enough to let us all sit in a little conference room down the hall while we waited, instead of that stupid lobby I had grown to hate so much.

Finally the time arrived, and the family got to lay their eyes on our little man. One by one, they got a chance to hold him. My husband, brother, and the crew of our little ones arrived a bit later, all excited to meet their new little cousin. We had tried to explain the situation to them when we found out Logan was sick, but we quickly learned they didn't get it. This became apparent when they started talking about bringing him home so they could play with him. How was I supposed to explain something to them that I could hardly absorb myself?

It was agonizing to introduce Logan to our family for the first—and *last*—time. One by one I watched grandparents, aunts, and uncles take Logan into their embrace and cry. With each and every set of arms it was like a fresh lash had been laid on my back. I was tied to a whipping post, and all I could do was watch the scene unfold before me. Logan wasn't just a loss to Andy and me but to the entire family. For Andy's parents, Logan was their very first grandchild.

My dad, who was a professional photographer, brought his camera and took a hundred pictures. My sweet grandma, who had Alzheimer's, rocked him back and forth for quite some time. She looked to be in heaven and had a big smile on her face. I don't think she understood what had happened, and no one had the heart to try to explain it to her. My brother sat by my side and commented on Logan's cute nose. My oldest niece and nephew knew that "Logan was with Jesus," although I'm not convinced they understood what exactly that meant. They were so sweet, commenting on how cute he was, giggling at his small toes and wanting to hold his hand. They asked when we could bring him home, and just like that, another lash dug into the flesh of my back.

Photo by Ken Papaleo

Eventually the Nichols family was able to make it to the hospital as well. I hadn't asked any other friends to come, but there was a different connection with them, and we told them they were welcome to meet Logan if they wished. I can't imagine what was going through their minds as they stared down at Logan's little body. Baby Megan was being delivered in just five short days. Was this a glimpse of their future as well?

Looking around, I was sitting in the middle of a scene that just couldn't be real. It was so far from the original picture of what I thought that moment would look like: laughter, tears of joy, and the unmistakable cries of new life.

A hospital employee who handled logistics when a death occurred came in and introduced herself. We were nearing the end of regular hospital hours, and she basically told us it was time to take Logan's body. I don't understand why, but she very casually told me I could keep him overnight, or he needed to go with her. I guess she had been a bit desensitized to her job as well.

The thought of my son's tiny body being placed in a fridge all alone in a massive hospital made me sick to my stomach. I just couldn't do it. I couldn't let her take him. I can't even try to explain it, but I didn't want him to be alone and cold. He was gone. I knew that. But I was not ready to say good-bye, and I still felt the need to protect him somehow. We

105

decided he would stay the night in our room and made arrangements that the mortuary would pick him up the next morning.

THROUGH KELLEY'S EYES

That day I saw a lot of hellos and *too many* good-byes. Then the time arrived for me to say mine. And just like that, I found myself driving away from the hospital, as if nothing had changed in the world, but knowing too well the planet had shifted and I would *never* be the same again.

14 — THE SORROW MAY LAST THROUGH THE NIGHT

Jesus wept.

—John 11:35 (NIV)

Photo by Jessica Fox

I remember sleeping better than I had anticipated that night. I hadn't slept in two days, and my body and heart had never experienced such an extreme level of trauma or exhaustion. My mind fought the sleep, but my body ultimately won the battle. I woke up early in the morning. The room was so quiet, so still. The sun was just starting to come up and send its warm rays through the sheer curtains covering the window. Andy was asleep on the little couch next to me.

For a brief moment I forgot where I was and what had just happened. I looked up and saw the tiny outline of my son's body in the hospital sleeper by my bed. It hit me again like a ton of bricks. *I'm in the hospital and Logan is dead. My baby is dead.* The phrase began to swirl through my mind relentlessly—bouncing off every part of my being and wreaking irreparable and catastrophic havoc wherever it touched. The concept was foreign and felt like a lie. Regardless of how many times I repeated it, it wouldn't absorb.

I felt the overwhelming urge to start screaming at the top of my lungs, but I didn't want to wake Andy—not yet. He looked so peaceful, and I wanted to delay the reality I knew he would be waking to.

I picked Logan up and sobbed silently. The tears were pouring down my face and soaking the monkey blanket he was wrapped in. I had never felt such relentless pain, such sorrow, such agony. Never had my soul been torn to pieces. *It goes against nature to watch your child die. It is supposed to be the other way around: Logan should lay me to rest!* I buried my face in his blanket to smother the noises coming from within me.

My head started to throb, and with each sob I attempted to contain, the pain and pressure only increased. My soul was screaming, but my body couldn't keep pace. I had to resort to taking big, slow breaths in an attempt to subdue the onslaught of emotions. Thank goodness I somehow stayed quiet enough not to wake Andy.

Once again, the room was still and calm. It was just me and Logan. I was marveling at his face, his tiny nose, his beautiful lips, trying to soak it all in—trying to do *all* I could so I would remember that moment forever. Even though Jesus had already taken him home, I knew it was going to be the last time I had both of my boys with me—the last time on this side of heaven my family would be whole.

As hard as I tried to ignore it, I couldn't drown out the noise of the clock relentlessly ticking away in the background. I knew in a couple of hours I would have to leave him behind. I knew another moment was soon approaching where I would have to pass my son over, close the door behind me, walk out of the hospital, and head home without him in the backseat of our car. With Logan still in my arms, I picked up my journal, and finished a good-bye letter I had started the night before.

8/9/12

Dear Logan,

Today you met Jesus. You came into this world at 11:43 a.m. and left at 12:37 p.m. For 54 minutes God gave us the gift of your heartbeat, your warmth, and your amazing life. You were more beautiful than I could have imagined—*perfectly* crafted from our Maker's hands.

Today was the best day of my life, but also the worst. I finally got to kiss you and hold you, but I also had to tell you good-bye. I have peace knowing you are no longer in any pain—your body has been restored, and you are with your Maker. You are the greatest gift we have ever been given. Your life was brief but beautiful. I want you to know how much I am going to miss you. My heart will never be whole again because *you* made up so much of it.

I feel so empty without you here, but I know you are in better hands now. I know you are happy and safe. It's just so hard, because everything in me longs to be with you. I'm holding you in my arms at this very moment. I know your soul is no longer here and this is just your body, but I am so afraid to say good-bye one last time. I can see you and touch you and kiss you—all these things will be a memory a short time from now—one I hope I can hold on to forever.

How do I say good-bye? Where do we go from here? How do we carry on without you? I guess these are things we will slowly and painfully figure out. I want you to know that because of you, heaven is going to be more crowded. God created your life as proof of His love, and I know lives will be changed because of it. In your twenty-seven weeks, you have accomplished more and made more of an impact than I have in my twenty-seven years.

As your mother, I want you here with me, but I know God had a different plan. And even though I can't fully see it, I know eternally the lives that will be saved are worth the pain and sorrow I am feeling now. It's just so hard not to be selfish—not to want you to myself.

Your dad and I love you so much, son, and we are so proud of you. You will always be our greatest accomplishment, but now it is time to say good-bye. We will miss you more than words can express. We love you, and we will see you soon. Godspeed, little man.

Love you to the moon and back,
Mommy

———⊗———

The time for our discharge had arrived. I didn't think I would be able to pass Logan's body off to a stranger. Luckily, Andy's parents had volunteered to stay with him until the mortuary could pick him up. At least my last memory would be of him wrapped up in his grandparents' loving arms. I kissed his tiny nose one last time and forced myself to walk toward the door. My feet felt like lead—every step near impossible. Before the door shut, I looked back at him one last time. *Goodbye, Logan.*

———⊗———

Like so much of my story, many of the details of Logan's time here are blurry in my mind. Waking up that morning was like waking up from a surgery where something was amputated. I was still under the effects of lingering anesthesia, and everything was fuzzy and dreamlike. I could tell something was gone, but I didn't fully understand what. I could tell it hurt, but I couldn't fully understand how bad. The pain was intense but still being tempered by the anesthesia. I knew the shock would soon wear off, and I would have no protection from the full impact and gravity of what had just happened.

I wish I could go back and replay my time with Logan, because I do have such a hard time remembering. I long to be there again and see him full of life, remember the smell of his soft skin, and feel the warmth of his body against mine. It is difficult to comprehend, but in a single instant we experienced both the best and the worst this life has to offer. I myself am still not sure how the two can coexist in the same moment. All I know is that they can and they did.

I am eternally grateful God gave us the opportunity to see Logan alive. He was here. We got to meet him, tell him we love him, try to give him a lifetime's supply of kisses, and ultimately hand him into the arms of Jesus. As absurd as it may seem to some to be grateful, I still am. I understand it could have gone very differently. Logan could have died during delivery. It could have been "gruesome." I may never have had the few cherished memories I hold. Yes, I'm heartbroken, but I'm also appreciative. Yes, we had to feel him grow cold in our arms, but more importantly, we got the blessing of first feeling his warmth.

We drove home in a fog. Andy and I sat in *complete* silence. I'm not sure we spoke a single word the entire way. My mind was fuzzy. I remember watching people drive by in their cars next to me—mad that they were self-consumed and unaware of what was going on around them. I was angry my world had shattered, yet everywhere I looked, life was continuing *uninterrupted*.

Nothing had changed. *Nothing.* It was a beautiful day. People were outside eating lunch, laughing, walking their dogs, and all I wanted to do in return was scream at the top of my lungs. I resented their happiness and most of all their *seemingly* blissful ignorance to the realities and fragility of life.

Truth was, I wanted it back. I was envious. I wanted to be as unaware as they all seemed to be. I wanted to be back in the sheltered world I used to live in, yet I knew I would never return to that place again. I was being pushed down by the claustrophobic and relentless weight of knowing life would *never* be the same.

Just blocks from our house, we somehow ended up blocking part of an intersection while waiting at a red light. I'm not even sure what happened. Andy was as disoriented as I was and probably shouldn't have been driving in the first place. Although we knew we were stopped somewhere we shouldn't be, neither of us could figure out something as simple as backing the car up.

Car after car drove around us, laying on the horn, yelling obscenities, and giving us not-so-polite gestures. In return? We sat there frozen. Not showing an ounce of emotion or consciousness to our surroundings. Our eyes were glazed over, as we both were somewhere else. Everyone passing us was full of anger yet obviously unaware of what had led us to that place. If only we'd had a glowing sign on our roof that read "Please be kind—our baby just died."

Walking in the house was an eerie feeling. Everything was just as I had left it three days earlier—dishes in the sink, my pajamas crumbled on the bathroom floor, Logan's room sitting nearly empty and untouched next to ours, my blankets still pulled back on my bed from where I had crawled out of them just days before. *What do we do now?* Andy and I crawled into our bed, pulled those very same blankets over our heads, and didn't emerge for several days.

Time seemed inconsequential. Minutes, hours, and days passed. All the while I felt unaware. *What day is it? How long have we been lying here? Actually, I don't care how long I have been here. I am never going to leave.*

I felt immobile—emotionally, mentally, and physically paralyzed. The days following any delivery are uncomfortable, to say the least, but for most the discomfort is dulled by the joy and responsibilities a new baby brings. I had *no* distractions from what my body was going through. The physical pain could not compare to the emotional, but it was a constant reminder of what I had lost.

My body didn't know there was no baby. My milk came in, and I had no choice but to suppress it. I was so engorged and in so much pain, I couldn't move my upper body for several days. Andy became my arms. He had to help me on and off the couch, in and out of bed, and with anything that was above chest level. There was nothing I could do except wait it out, as the volume of milk only continued to increase. I knew any type of release would only prolong the process, although inevitably the milk had nowhere to go and started to leak out. It was torture knowing it was supposed to be feeding Logan. On several occasions, I would break down and scream at my body at the top of my lungs, "There is no baby to feed! Please stop!"

I hated my body. I hated *anything* that reminded me of what I did not have. At the same time, in the strangest way, I was afraid of my body going back to normal, removing all proof that Logan ever existed. With every ounce of energy that remained in me, I just wanted my boy back.

15 — SOMEONE ELSE'S MIRACLE

But Jesus looked at them and said to them, "With men this is impossible, but with God all things are possible."
—Matthew 19:26 (NKJV)

Photo by Jessica Fox

Five days after Logan died, it was time for baby Megan to be delivered. It was the first thing important enough to motivate Andy and me to get out of bed. I think I may have even showered and brushed my teeth — seemingly simple activities for most, until you find yourself trapped under a blanket of sorrow that steals any and all energy.

We in no way felt ready to leave the house, but we wanted to be there for Leslie and Ryan. Regardless of what we had just lost, we knew we needed to be a source of strength for them, just as they had been for us.

No one knew what to expect. I'm sure, for the Nichols family it was quite unnerving just days earlier seeing how our delivery played out.

Is Megan going to die too? She certainly had a much better chance. After all, she was thirty-seven weeks and would be delivered via C-section. We never voiced it, but I think all of us quietly assumed Megan would be meeting Logan very soon.

———⊗⊗⊗———

I sat staring at my phone, anxiously waiting for *any* news from Laura, who was waiting at the hospital. When the text finally came that Megan had successfully made it through the C-section and was screaming, I experienced something I never could have anticipated. There is no way to explain it without sounding completely terrible, but again I want you to *walk with me* in this, so here goes . . .

I had fallen in love with the Nichols family and considered Megan partially my own. I was *ecstatic* she was alive. Lungs capable of screaming were a great sign, and yet, I was angry. Not because Megan was alive but because Logan was not.

Why would God choose to save only one? How come I never got to hear the beautiful sound of my baby's cry? Why would God answer their prayers and not ours? Where was our miracle? I couldn't believe the thoughts running uncontrolled through my mind. *What is wrong with me? Megan is alive! Stop this, Jamie!*

Within moments, I received a *second* text from Laura. "What you are feeling is normal. I am so sorry this is not your story." I fell to my knees and cried on our office floor. *How in the world did she know? I guess I'm not completely terrible after all.* I wiped the smeared mascara off my cheeks, regained my composure, and went upstairs to tell Andy it was time to leave for the hospital.

———⊗⊗⊗———

The *last* place in the world parents who just lost a baby should go is the labor and delivery unit of a hospital. In fact, I would say *any* place would have been a better choice for our first outing.

We walked in with a brave facade and good intentions but found out rather quickly it was a bad idea. A *very* bad idea. I knew it would be hard.

I didn't fully comprehend *how* hard until I had to watch wheelchair after wheelchair pass by with new happy moms holding new pink babies.

I thought I was going to be sick. Every fiber in me was fighting to run out of that hospital and never look back. I could feel the ever-so-familiar urge of a scream rising within me. Thank goodness Laura was there. She cracked a joke only people in our shoes would understand, and the momentary laughter reset my system and gave me strength to stand my ground—for a few more minutes, at least.

Finally, Leslie came out of her C-section. We only got to see her for a moment, as they wheeled her by us in the hallway, but our eyes met and it was enough. Leslie and Ryan had tons of family visiting from out of town, so Andy and I decided it would be best to go home and come back the following day. It was already such an overwhelming situation for them, and we didn't want to be in the way. Hand in hand, we walked (and by walked, I mean practically *ran*) out of the hospital.

The next day we found ourselves, once again and much too soon, right back at the hospital to meet Megan. I apparently was a glutton for punishment. They were exactly where we expected to find them: the NICU. Leslie looked drained of every ounce of life within her. Her eyes were red and yet sparkled, as they were filled to the brim with fresh tears ready to spill. Ryan looked tired, too, but he greeted us with a halfhearted smile. He was trying hard to be the strong and optimistic one. After knowing him for only a short time, I had already picked up that he was a "glass half full" kind of guy and always did his best to focus on the positive in their situation. I'm not entirely convinced he really felt that way, but he certainly put on a good front.

At that point there was no estimation on how long Megan would live. She was breathing on her own, which was absolutely amazing, but being fed through a tube. Like Logan, she had fractures throughout her tiny body. She looked so incredibly fragile—like a baby made of glass. Her body was very similar to Logan's, but bigger and less broken. It was hard not to let my mind wonder what could have been *if only* Logan had made it full-term and had been delivered via C-section too. It was eerie as I stared at Megan lying there fighting for her life against the very disease that just days earlier took my son. I stared at her tiny broken body and began to boil with anger toward the cruel disease that had broken it in the first place.

I would have given anything to have had a similar outcome with Logan, but I could see the fear and torment on poor Leslie's face. Megan was finally here and alive, but there were still so many questions that could not be answered. I did not envy Leslie in that regard. The doctors knew little of what to expect. It was touch and go for a while, but as we would all come to know over the next years of her life, little Megan was *and still is* a fighter. A miracle for sure—just someone else's.

—❦—

On the way home from the hospital, my heart was shredded beyond recognition. I was happy for the Nichols family, although the road ahead of them was uncharted and scary, but I also felt that, unlike them, God had forgotten us. Question after question ran through my mind. *Why, God? Why?* I didn't want to see Logan in pain, but I would have given *anything* to have had more time with him—time to take him in, hear his cry, and memorize the features of his face; time to let his grandparents see his body full of life, instead of the empty shell where life used to exist. What I would have given for his sweet eyes to lock with mine, or to have had a few pictures of him that illuminated life rather than exuded death.

The myriad of thoughts running recklessly through my mind were interrupted by the ringing of my phone. I looked down to see it was JB from Red Rocks Church.

He was calling to ask if Andy and I would be willing to do another interview with the church—a follow-up of sorts. He informed us the pastoral staff felt God wanted to use our story for more than a video clip during baptism Sunday. If it was okay with us, they wanted to create an entire sermon surrounding our sweet Logan and his story. The timing was almost uncanny, as the next series they were entering was titled "Before I Die."

Really? An entire sermon? An entire Sunday about my boy? I was shocked. Never could I have imagined what God had planned, starting with the first text I sent the church just weeks ago regarding my baptism. I never would have believed the road God was leading us down. All along, His hand had been picking up the pieces of our lives and building something beautiful from the rubble.

Without hesitation, we agreed on the spot. I was a bit shocked at my newfound boldness. The *old* Jamie would have surely shied away from any more attention. But I was no longer that person. I was Logan's mom, and *she* was being transformed into something new.

16 — UNTIL WE MEET AGAIN

God is our refuge and strength, an ever-present help in trouble.
Therefore we will not fear, though the earth give way and the
mountains fall into the heart of the sea.
—Psalm 46:1–2 (NIV)

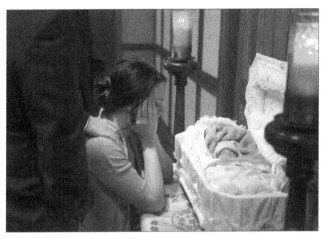

Photo by Ken Papaleo

It was a beautiful and sunny morning when we laid Logan to rest. He had been gone only a week, and I found myself *once again* having to face something that made me physically ill. No one should ever have to bury their child, and the thought of it literally made me sick to my stomach. I knew I would be putting the thing I loved most in this world into the ground. With him, I would also bury my heart.

Driving to the cemetery felt surreal. *I'm going to bury my son today. I have to watch as they lower him into the earth and cover him with dirt.* I was anxious and didn't know if I should look at him again. I was scared about what I would possibly see. What changes had taken place in the span of a week? Would he still look like Logan? Would I recognize him? On the flip side, if I passed up an opportunity to see him again, would I regret it the rest of my life?

The anxiety on Andy's face was clear as day and rivaled my own, and I could feel his nerves peak as we got closer to the cemetery. It was *his* job to carry Logan's tiny casket to the plot, and it was an impossibly heavy responsibility. It would be one of the hardest moments of his life. He knew it, and I knew it. I was secretly happy it was his job and not mine.

We pulled into the funeral home, and I could feel my pulse instantly quicken. A warm sensation began to crawl up my neck, turning my cheeks a bright shade of pink. I prayed my face was not as red as it felt. My heart started beating so loudly it drowned out all the other noises around me. My hands were shaking, and noticeably clammy, as we slowly walked through the parking lot. I felt off balance and had to steady myself on Andy's arm.

As soon as we walked inside, we were greeted by the director of the funeral home, who somehow knew exactly who we were without us having to say a word. I guess our outward expressions must have been yelling, "We are burying our baby today," as loudly as those words were on repeat in my mind. The woman gave us a halfhearted smile and led us into a private viewing room.

I decided to have Andy look at Logan and then tell me if I should. That was the plan at least. But when we got into that little room, and I saw the tiny white casket where the body of my son was, I couldn't keep myself away. I *ran* to his side, fell to my knees, and sobbed uncontrollably. He still looked beautiful, cozily wrapped in the second monkey blanket we (Andy) had picked out just weeks earlier—the one I had prayed *countless* times we wouldn't have to use for such a purpose. The matching blanket he was wrapped in at the hospital had found a permanent place in our bed.

Time ticked away, but I felt frozen in it, like I was still in a horrible dream that was stuck on pause. An endless supply of tears streamed down my face. My body shook with each fragmented breath. I have no idea how long we actually knelt by his side, just staring at his sweet face. I couldn't take my eyes off him, regardless of how hard I tried. It could have been five minutes, it could have been thirty. I guess I'll never know.

Before we invited the rest of our family in, we read our good-bye letters to him one last time. We then put a stuffed animal, our letters, and a picture of us by his side. Our families quietly filtered in and one by one said their good-byes. The room was full of whispers, almost as if a baby was sleeping. Oh, how I wished that had been the case.

I'm not sure why everyone always has that response at funerals, myself included. Are we afraid to talk, or do we just think whispering is more respectful? I genuinely have no idea, but it provided an eerie background nonetheless.

We were eventually told it was time to close the casket. Panic set in yet again. *Please don't make me shut it! I can't stand the thought of never seeing him again!* I kissed his little nose one last time. I looked around the room hoping I could buy a few more minutes. *Everyone* was looking at me. *Everyone* was ready. I was not—but time was out. I forced myself to close the top. We were escorted outside where a funeral car was waiting with an open door. Behind us, Logan and his casket followed in the loving embrace of his grandfathers.

Andy and I wound through a never-ending maze of roads and head-stones with Logan's casket resting on our laps. We took advantage of our last few moments together and opened the lid of his casket to look at him one last time. His sweet face looked so perfect. So peaceful. *How could he have been so broken—so sick? How could all I have ever wanted be so close, yet so incredibly far away?*

As the car came to a stop, I could feel Andy suddenly tense. He looked at me with big, glistening eyes. The moment he had been dreading was here. It was no shock to me, but he handled it with poise. He alone carried Logan to the graveside, as the rest of us somberly followed in his wake.

Photo by Ken Papaleo

The service was short but beautiful—a brief message from JB, a dove release, and "Amazing Grace" being played by bagpipes as Logan was lowered into the ground. We covered his casket in sunflowers, as they had become one of the many things that reminded us of him.

I didn't realize it was possible to be jealous of a piece of earth, but in a strange way I was—for it would be holding my son when I so desperately wanted to. I knelt by the deep hole and took in my surroundings. The scene was so unfamiliar: a place I did not know but a place that would not be foreign for long. Pretty soon I would effortlessly navigate the winding roads leading to Logan, know each and every headstone near his, and lose track of the number of times I had sat in that very same spot.

Photo by Ken Papaleo

There was a heaviness to my feet as we walked back to the car. I could hear the beeping of a truck preparing to dump the contents of its bed on top of Logan's casket. I didn't know where it came from, but I picked up my pace. I didn't want to hear the sound of massive amounts of earth falling down on my boy, and I certainly didn't want to *see* it happen. I was desperately hoping to be long gone by then. I picked up my pace even more, but before I was able to get to the car, I heard the unnerving noise of dirt collapsing down behind me.

It stopped me in my tracks. It sent sickening chills down my spine and left a grimace on my already puffy face. It sounded *unavoidably* final. I would be lying if I said I didn't briefly scan my surroundings for a shovel.

THROUGH KELLEY'S EYES

It's weird that after all the things I had been through during Logan's short life—Jamie's pregnancy, his diagnosis, her labor, and his passing—one of the darkest, most depressing realizations I experienced was that the world kept turning, even though Logan was no longer in it.

The first time I came to this rather upsetting conclusion, I was making preparations for Logan's burial. I took over the task of preparing the flower arrangements for the service, which, if you know me, is hysterical—but nonetheless, I was determined to pull it off. Sunflowers. All Jamie wanted was big glass vases of sunflowers.

I thought I would spruce them up a bit by adding coppery brown, red, and gold ribbons. I figured I'd cruise into Hobby Lobby real quick, grab myself some ribbons, and be on my way to Costco to pick up the flowers. Immediately upon entering the store, I remembered Hobby Lobby had an issue with pre-holiday preparation. I kid you not, it looked like Christmas had vomited all over the store, and there I was, on my way to pick out dumb ribbons for my nephew's funeral. I never thought the sight of stockings and ornaments could prove to be physically painful, but they destroyed me on that August day.

I made a beeline for the ribbon section, plopped down in the middle of lace and burlap, and cried. *Christmas.* The world around me was planning for Christmas, and I . . . was planning a baby's funeral. The world kept turning, and I *hated* it for that.

Photo by Ken Papaleo

121

And then I found myself in a green cemetery, staring at a deep hole in the ground. Right next to that hole were sunflowers decorated with coppery brown, red, and gold ribbons. I thought I was going to be sick.

The very next day, we had Logan's Celebration of Life service at our church. We kept his burial private but still wanted to share and honor his life with our extended family and friends. It was important for us not to hide him *or* our story. Losses like ours felt very taboo, and in our minds the only way to provoke change and break the stigma was to bring it out into the light.

I couldn't find anything to wear that morning. I emptied my closet trying to find *something* that fit my awkward, post-baby body. But no such thing existed. I felt terrible and I looked terrible. The mirror in front of me only validated those feelings. I ended up on the floor, crumpled in a ball and crying with a pile of dresses underneath me.

Andy tried to help, but I was in no mood to be consoled, and it ended in an argument. As much as I hated what the mirror was reflecting back at me, the frustration had little to do with my appearance. *Nothing* was okay. Logan was dead—and to top it off, I had nothing to wear to his service. It wasn't the biggest of my issues, but at the moment it felt *insurmountable*. I finally pulled the wrinkled long black dress I had worn for Logan's burial out of the dirty clothes basket. It still smelled like dirt and grass from kneeling by his grave the day before, but I threw it on regardless.

Once we arrived at the church, we were taken to a second-floor room to wait while our guests filtered in. I stood at the window that looked down at the parking lot below and watched cars gradually fill the spaces. I had always been the person *showing* support, not the person *receiving* it. I wished desperately I was one of those people below, who just had to endure a sad morning and then could return to a normal life. But I wasn't, because it was *my* boy who had died.

We were incredibly humbled with the amount of people who came to pay their respects to Logan and share their condolences with us. Andy and I stayed up late the night before and talked extensively about how we were going to navigate his eulogy. We ended up deciding to read the good-bye letters we wrote in the hospital on the day he died. I wasn't sure how I was going to have the composure to get through it, but I knew I needed to do it.

I walked up to the stage, feeling every pair of eyes on me. *Am I going to cry? Will they be able to understand what I say through the tears? Will I have to walk away before I'm finished? Why in the world did we invite all these people? Maybe this was a bad idea.* But when I got to the microphone, something shifted, and there she was again: Logan's mom. And *she* was bolder and braver than I had ever known myself to be.

As I stood on the stage, I looked out at a sea of eyes staring back at me—some as red and puffy as mine, some heavily laden with sympathy, and some avoiding contact and *noticeably* uncomfortable in such a delicate setting. I had never given a eulogy, let alone one for my own child.

I can do this. One line at a time. Breathe, Jamie, just breathe. "Today you met Jesus—" It was the hardest line to get out. I felt as though my voice was going to fail me, but surprisingly, it never did. I had read that letter so many times it had become a part of me. It was my last moment with Logan. He was in my arms as I wrote those very words. The tears that now fell on the paper I was holding were then falling on my son as I tried to say good-bye. I was sharing not just a letter but one of the most intimate and private moments of my life. *They have to know. I need them to understand.*

My dad and I had spent countless hours in the days leading up to Logan's service creating a slideshow of his story. We knew it would be really hard for everyone to watch, but we also felt it was the only way to help people understand what we had been through and truly honor him. Words could never do his life justice; they would have fallen short every time. But what we could not do with words we *could* show with pictures.

As the slideshow was being played, I kept my eyes down and glued to the "L" necklace Michelle had given me at the hospital. I hadn't taken it off since that day. I heard the familiar music of the slideshow surround me but refused to take my focus away from my fingers nervously fidgeting with the little bead. I knew if I looked up, I would not be able to contain my emotions. My effort was in vain as the pictures played seamlessly in my mind.

For the remainder of the service, I felt like I was the mistaken epicenter of what had to have been someone else's story. I watched as loved ones got on stage and spoke about the life and death of a little boy. I looked around and saw many familiar faces with glistening eyes. There were some faces I didn't recognize or couldn't place, which made it feel even more like someone else's story. All the while, I sat stoic and unmoved—one hand still sealed to my necklace and the other in a seemingly permanent death grip with Andy's. *Surely it's not my son they're talking about? Surely this all isn't for us?*

We finished the service outside, where we released balloons in his honor. I kissed our balloon and asked God to please let it somehow find Logan's tiny hands. I knew it was childish. More than likely, it would find its way tangled in a tree somewhere, but I asked regardless. *Maybe, just maybe, this balloon will make it to him—maybe, in a few minutes, he will be holding what I am holding now.* The thought sounded peaceful and warmed my heart for a brief moment. If only there had been a *real* way to send him our love.

I clung tightly to Andy's arm, and together we stared at the sky until Logan's balloons disappeared from sight. When my eyes finally came back to ground level, all I saw were faces. We were surrounded by them. Faces were everywhere of people who had come to support us—faces I now can't remember.

THROUGH KELLEY'S EYES

An incredible amount of family and friends showed up to Logan's service. A very special group of those individuals had practically taken over *all* the planning for us, and I was so grateful. We just told them what we wanted and, *poof,* done.

As sad as the service was, it wasn't until after it ended that I felt an overwhelming wave of depression. I remember sitting in my car watching the interactions of a few young families outside the church where we held the service. The adults were just casually chatting with each other happily while their kiddos ran laps around their legs giggling and screaming. It was at that moment that it hit me: "They get to be done now." As sad as these last couple of hours were for them, they now get to load up their families into their cars, head home, and continue on with life.

I knew at that moment we would never get to "be done," and I would never choose to "be done." I would grieve the loss of my nephew for the rest of my days. Before this moment I thought the hardest stuff was behind us. I remember thinking we just had to make it through this last service, and then we'd be okay. In reality, the trauma behind us—the stuff that felt almost unreal, because it was too messed up to have possibly happened— would never fully go away. And the hardest stuff was life moving forward, life that knew loss, fear, loneliness, and depression like it never had before.

Needless to say, I spent the rest of the day sprawled out on my living room floor and unable to peel myself up off the hardwood, while my kiddos ran laps around me giggling and screaming. This is the challenge anyone who knows great grief must face: not *moving on* from the ones we have lost but choosing to *move forward*—choosing to honor their lives in a way that would make them smile. Sometimes, though, we just need to lay on the floor for a bit.

The couple of days leading up to Logan's service were so full of preparations that my pain was partially and momentarily numbed. Well, that's actually ridiculous—but it *did* dull it to an extent. I was utterly devastated, but Andy and I were so busy trying to figure out what needed to be done and working through the various ins and outs of planning a service, that I wasn't able to dwell too long on the reality of what had just happened.

It was *after* the funeral, when it felt as though I had already reached the lowest low of my life, that I got a new and very unwelcome sinking feeling. As Andy and I drove home, my only thought was, *Now what? How do I live in a world that is crumbling around me? Now what do I do with my shaken faith? My broken life? My child—in the ground. My marriage— vulnerable. My work—unimportant. My life—broken. Now what, God!?*

The anesthetic of distractions had vanished. All that remained was a raw, searing pain that had boiled its way to the surface. *Am I just expected to start living again? Go back to work? Pretend like I care about hair? Pretend like I care about anything? Am I just supposed to put a smile on my face and act like I'm okay?*

I felt alone. Even with Andy right there by my side, I felt alone. Everyone had gone home. The sadness of their morning could now be forgotten as they carried on with their normal routines. They were all off to have lunch and enjoy the rest of their Sunday. And here we were, driving home from our son's funeral and heading back to a life we no longer knew. The world kept spinning for everyone—but us. Our world had lost its color *and* its rotation. *Our world* was black and white and shattered into a thousand pieces.

17 — A MATTER OF
THE HEART

The Lord is near to all who call on Him, to all who call on Him in truth.

—Psalm 145:18 (NLV)

Photo by Jessica Fox

THROUGH KELLEY'S EYES

Here's a PSA for everyone: you can't distract someone from the fact that their baby just died, just in case you are wondering. I know, it's a shocking epiphany, but there it is.

A few days after Logan's service, Andy had to leave Jamie alone for the first time. His brother was getting married, and with Andy being the best man and the wedding being only weeks away, he had a lot of responsibilities. So Jamie and I decided the best course of action for the day was to redecorate her guest bedroom, as they would soon be hosting family from out of town for the same wedding. We had gray paint, wall decor, and, God forbid, a brand-new IKEA bed frame. I know what you are thinking—even on their best day, the jolliest person around is going to plunge into a deep, dark place trying to assemble *anything* from IKEA. They have really good prices, but what were we thinking?

Needless to say, Operation We Are Just Not Going to Think About It had commenced. Soon enough, the fumes of wet paint had filled the house. While the paint dried, we moved on to assembling the IKEA bed frame, and surprisingly, it was pretty easy. Not what you were expecting, huh? The whole redecoration went off without a hitch, and by the end of the day, we had ourselves a lovely and welcoming guest bedroom.

So what's the point of my story? The point is this: even on days like that, when *nothing* went particularly wrong, *everything* was still completely *wrong*. Sitting in the victory of a perfectly executed bedroom remodel, we cried because we knew it didn't help. We didn't feel accomplished or proud—just empty.

Our hope that the pain would lessen as time passed was pure crap. It almost felt like, as time passed, we became more and more aware of what we had all lost. We'd lost a lifetime with Logan, smelling his little baby head, watching him fall asleep and drool on our chests, and enjoying the funny expressions he'd make while dreaming. And that was just the beginning.

No first holidays, or teeth, or steps. No first days of school, or dates, or driving lessons. Nothing. And there was nothing we could do to lessen or distract ourselves from it; we just had to sit *in* it. Not even Operation We Are Just Not Going to Think About It would work. Turns out you can't distract someone from their grief.

It had only been ten days since we had lost Logan, and I found myself alone for the first time. Andy's brother was getting married soon, and he had a lot of best man stuff coming up. I didn't want him to go. I understood he needed to, but I wasn't ready to be without him—not even close. But that morning, the door inevitably shut behind him, and my tears were left alone in an empty, quiet, and painfully still house.

Kelley was coming over to help me renovate the guest room. Nothing like some paint fumes to distract a grieving heart, but in our naïveté, we had high hopes it would help. But she hadn't arrived yet and before I knew it, I was driving to Logan's grave. I couldn't stay in the house by myself for one more second, and I had nowhere else to go. After getting lost in the cemetery and trying my best to navigate through my tear-filled and blurry vision, I finally found the little white angel that marked the spot where he was buried.

Proof of his recent burial was evident in the fresh dirt piled much higher than the grass surrounding it. The flowers that days earlier were beautiful, bright, and alive had succumbed to the heat of the sun and lay on top of the dirt, lifeless and brittle. It was as if that one spot in the cemetery was screaming out to the world that our loss was recent and my wound was fresh. *A bunch of dead sunflowers—what a perfect addition to the day.*

I lay down by his grave in the bright morning sun and traced my fingers through the soft dirt. Not caring about the dirt on my clothes or those around me, I openly cried until my tears ran out. I had my journal with me and, in a completely raw way, poured my heart out to God.

8/19/12

Dear God,

How am I supposed to keep living with this pain? How do You expect me to go on without my child? The ache is too intense—it does not relent. I cannot breathe with this weight on my chest. Where are you? Why do I not feel your comfort? Your word says you draw close to the brokenhearted. I am in a thousand pieces—where are you? I know you are good. I know your plan for Logan was great and that he changed lives. I know your ways are not like ours, and I believe you picked us to be his parents for a reason—but why?

We are not strong. We are not brave. We are not courageous. We are not any of these things people seem to think. I am dead inside—there is nothing left in me. Everything I was has been buried here with my son. I can't sleep. I can't eat. I can't even find the energy to pray. You still are and always will be my foundation. My core beliefs in you will never change. I know the truth, and nothing will ever take that away, but you let my baby die when you could have saved him. Now his body lays beneath me in the cold ground. Why did you give him to me in the first place? Did I have to watch my son die just to fulfill the purpose you had for his life?

Are we just a Sunday church service to you? Is the cost of my forever broken heart worth being an inspiration for a day? And now, when I need you the most, when I am in complete agony—I can't feel you! Don't be silent now! Haven't I given enough to deserve at least a little of your peace? Stop dragging me through this valley. Please, Father, pick me up and carry me! I need you to show up. I need you to give me something, anything. I know when we are weak you are strong, but I can't feel your strength! I can't feel you.

Please don't let this break me, Father. I don't want to be bitter. I want to be a reflection of you and your love. I want to come through this a better person, a better wife, a better friend, and hopefully, someday, a better mother. Please tell Logan how much I love him. Give him the hugs and kisses I am unable to. Tell him how much we miss him. Tell him I cannot wait for the day you call me home.

———— ❧ ————

"Raw" may have been a bit of an understatement. Not sure what word to use, but those words *far* exceeded raw. After reading that letter, some will question my faith, my heart, my motives—maybe even if I have the *right* to classify myself as a believer. "You can't talk to God like that!" Am I right? Well, that's great and all, but I did. Some will question if I have the right to offer guidance to others when it comes to life, loss, and faith. Some may assume I am defenseless against such accusations, as if my only play is to wave the white flag, recede, and accept my faults for what they are.

However, if you're one of those accusers, in the most polite voice I can muster, I want to tell you something. I *need* to tell you something. It's not that I feel as though *I* need protecting; it's that the person you are reading this book *for* probably does. You may feel justified in your opinions about how we *should* and *should not* talk to God. You may have a lifetime of Bible knowledge in your head and verses to back up your opinions. However, you have a lot to learn about Jesus if you think the honest cry of a mourning heart is enough to push Him away.

I had probably never been more honest with God in my entire life. That morning at Logan's grave was possibly the very moment I *finally* let my walls fall and *finally* allowed the posture of my heart in relation to my King's heart to be 100 percent unapologetically *real*.

I shared it for *you*—the person who would feel relief from the honesty of my words. I shared it for the person who has felt the same way—the person who found themselves in a graveyard when they were expecting to be in a nursery. I shared it for the person who has a tiny box on their night-stand that is now the keeper of their life's greatest love. I shared it for the family member or friend who feels helpless watching someone they love try to live without a piece of their heart.

I would be lying if I said I didn't initially consider editing parts of that letter to save face. But I know too well what is at stake, and I realize my readers' hearts are more important than my image. It is okay to be mad at God. It is okay to feel abandoned. I refuse to hide the messy parts of faith in order to look like I handled things better and never felt anger toward God. That would be a lie. I wanted to show you where my heart was, just in case your heart is there too.

If that is where you find yourself today, I wish more than anything I could squeeze your hand and give your tears some much needed company. I wish I could give you a hug and pray with you. I can't give you the hug, sweet friend, but I would absolutely love to pray with you.

Heavenly Father,

In these moments, it's hard to find the right words. It's hard to know how to pray and exactly what to pray for. All I can ask is for your healing hands to fully surround the person reading this right now. Let them feel you—truly feel you. Quicken them to hear your voice and notice your delicate fingerprints on the broken pieces of their lives. There is no one who can begin to mend their heart besides the one who first created it.

Remind them of your extravagant love, a love that can fully handle the honest cries of an aching heart. Shield them from those who would tell them otherwise and continue to remind them, "There is no condemnation for those who are in Christ Jesus" (Romans 8:1).

Your forgiveness trumps it all. Amidst the questions and amidst the heartache, remind them how much they are cherished and the sacrifice you made at the cross, just so the two of you would never be separated. "I am with you always, even to the end of the age" (Matthew 28:20). Show them you are present regardless of their circumstances, and continue to embed into their hearts the truth that there is nowhere they could go where you cannot follow and no sin too great that you cannot forgive.

I thank you for Jesus. I thank you that because of your sacrifice we have the promise of redemption and of a day where tears will be no more. Your word says you count our tears and keep track of them in a bottle. Today I pray we all can find great hope in anticipation of such a day where that bottle is obsolete.

Some may argue it's wrong to question God. I would argue the condition of one's heart is *far* more important than the occasional words that may come out of our mouths during turbulent times. Do we need to be careful with our words? Of course. However, there is a *big* difference between questioning *why* God allowed a certain event to happen and questioning His goodness or sovereignty. An honest cry from a worn heart is starkly different from bitterness and rebellion seeping from a hardened one. The *posture* of our heart is what God sees, and even though I am in no way proud of some of the things I said, I know He still calls me beloved.

Through Logan's death, I never turned away from God. My faith was still intact, but our relationship needed time to mend. I still trusted His heart, but I questioned His hand. He still was who He had always been to me, but I would be lying to say a piece of me didn't feel betrayed. A crack had emerged in my foundation. It was small—but there nonetheless. It never matured or threatened to crumble my faith, but I did trip on it from time to time. Sitting alone in the graveyard that day, I was engulfed in sorrow. I was mad. I was hurt. I felt abandoned.

In the weeks that followed Logan's death, and especially in that moment, I wanted God to show up in a very tangible way. I wanted a big, booming voice to knock me over. I have since learned that many times the words of our Creator are still and small. Looking back, I can *now* see that God's tears, as I lay on the ground that day, were mixing with mine. My sorrow was not lost on Him, and He had never left my side.

8/22/12

Dear Logan,

You will have been gone for two weeks tomorrow. It feels like it has been ten years. This journey and your death have completely drained me of all I am. I miss you so much. The idea that I have to live this life *without you* is hard to grasp. I will never be the same again. How could I after losing a vital part of my being?

What I would give to have you back in my arms again. I know our entire family is hurting. But I feel so alone in all of this. You were with *me* for seven months. *I* had to deliver you, and *I* am the one living with a body that will not stop reminding me what I lost. I miss you moving in my belly. I miss singing to you in the shower and reading to you in the morning. I miss talking to you throughout the day. Everywhere I look, I see you. Everywhere I go, I see what I lost. My body still thinks I have a baby to feed. I want to scream to it that you are gone and to stop torturing me!

I hate the bitterness that rises in me when I see babies and pregnant women. I don't feel like myself. I hate who I am right now. I feel like I have been robbed of my joy. This all feels like a horrible dream. I watched you die, I had to bury you, we had a funeral—can this really be my life? How can you actually be gone? I just want to be where you are. I know God is by my side. He has just been so quiet. Regardless, if it wasn't for Him, I wouldn't be here now. I feel like He is dragging me through life as I kick and scream in protest. But at least He is still there. I get mad when I see happy people. I'm mad that life just keeps going for everyone else—I want to scream at the top of my lungs, "My baby is dead! Does anyone see me?!"

I know I just need time. I know I will be forever changed, because you are no longer with me, and I know I will eventually learn how to live without you, but I want you to know, sweet boy, that I will *never* forget you. I am so thankful you were so strong, that you were such a fighter. Thank you for staying alive long enough for your daddy and me to see you, to hold you, and to kiss you. I hope in that short time you felt our love.

In all of this darkness, I can still see that God is good. I am so glad, if you are not able to be with me, that you are with Him. You are in the one set of arms capable of loving you more than mine. He is a good Father, Logan. I love you so much, son, and I will see you soon.

Love you to the moon and back,
Mommy

⸺⸻⸺

I would have moments where I was at peace with God and moments where I wasn't. I tried really hard to fight against my anger toward him, especially in those first months. I tried to push it down and hide it away. I didn't want Satan to have any victory in our story, and sometimes it felt as though lashing out at God or admitting my anger toward Him was putting a point on the enemy's side of the scoreboard.

But here's the problem with that logic: I was trying to hide a piece of myself from my Creator, and it was a futile effort at best. An *honest* relationship built on trust is a *strong* relationship. God created me and *all* my emotions. He certainly can handle each and every one of them. All He desired was a relationship with me—the good, the bad, *and* the ugly. All of it. I learned I could not carry the weight of my anger and needed to allow my King to carry it for me. If I didn't face those feelings head-on and with God by my side, they would have gotten bigger and uglier and increasingly harder to carry with each passing year.

If that is where you find yourself today, let it out. Don't listen to voices that tell you to do otherwise. God is with you in *all* of it, and He is *for* you. So be unfiltered. Be raw. Be honest. Just be *in* Him.

18 — BEFORE I DIE

And be sure of this: I am with you always, even to the end of the age.
—Matthew 28:20 (NLT)

Nearly a month had passed. I wasn't sure how it was possible. It felt like just yesterday—but also a lifetime ago. Sometimes it didn't feel real at all.

I was sitting on my couch, in what had become a very familiar cloud of sadness, when my phone rang. It was our church. They had called to tell me Logan's story was going to be featured the upcoming weekend, and by default our second interview would have to take place in the next few days. At the news, a mixture of fear, excitement, purpose, and sorrow washed over me.

It had been hard to talk about our story the first time around, and now that Logan had died, it would be even harder. I was anxious because I wanted to be completely honest with what we had been through, and I didn't know how it might come across to others. Andy and I firmly believed we needed to be as sincere as possible and not sugarcoat anything—regardless of how it could make us look. In the midst of all those insecurities, I still felt a peace in my spirit I couldn't explain.

Logan's church service was exactly one month from the day we lost him. Some would say that's a coincidence, but I don't believe in coincidence. I believe in divine appointments and a Creator who is meticulous and intentional in everything He plans. It felt like a sliver of grace from Him—a gift to help carry me through the first of many "firsts" and anniversaries.

Walking through the sanctuary doors that morning felt different from the hundreds of times I had done it prior. I tried to look calm and collected on the surface, but on the inside my heartbeat was bouncing frantically throughout every part of my body. My hands felt as though I had had a few too many cups of coffee—and by a few, I mean like ten. I could feel their tremor and decided it was best to hide them in the pockets of my jacket.

I was grateful to find a seat and have a moment to close my eyes and focus on slowing the pace of my breath. I hooked my arm with Andy's and cuddled in as tightly as I possibly could. *Calm down, Jamie. Just. Calm. Down.*

Then church started, as if it were any other Sunday morning. We prayed, we sang, our pastor got on stage and, like so many times before, began his message. He talked about trusting God through unthinkable circumstances and wanting to share a story about a family who did just that.

I suddenly realized he was talking about Andy and me. I rolled my eyes at myself and the ridiculous amount of shock I felt in hearing my name, even though I *knew* it was coming. Familiar faces filled the screens in front of us, and I became aware that I had no recollection of what I had actually said in our interview.

I could feel eyes on us as the people nearby realized the faces up front matched the faces sitting next to them. I could hear sniffles, and when I was brave enough to look around, I could see hundreds of tear-filled eyes.

How can any of this be real? The story in front of me is awful and heartbreaking. I have never seen so many people openly cry here. Ugh, that poor fam—oh wait . . . that's my family. That's my story. I am the one whose son died. These tears . . . are for us.

And just like that, it was over. People started funneling out of the sanctuary into the bright morning sun. I kept my head down, because any type of eye contact surely meant recognition. I wore a hat to church that day *and* made sure to put my sunglasses on the instant we walked outside, but my attempts to "Clark Kent" myself didn't work as well as

I planned. Turns out, even with my accessories, I was still very recognizable. Apparently, my ever-evolving and new identity as Logan's mom was indeed a bolder make and model—but still a *shy* one.

Andy and I were impossible to miss. People surrounded us. They were kind and loving. They hugged us and wiped tears from their eyes as they explained how moved they were. They thanked us for our bravery in sharing Logan with the world and said that his life would forever change theirs.

That morning will always be one of the most significant and humbling moments of my life. We felt loved and validated. It was incredible to know thousands heard our story and knew Logan's name. It felt like our loss had suddenly been gifted a purpose, yet as we drove home, my heart was *still* conflicted. My heart was *still* broken.

9/9/12

Dear Logan,

You have been gone for exactly one month. Today after church (which was about you, by the way) Dad and I visited the cemetery. They finally put grass on your plot, but it's still void of a stone that marks your name. We walked around for a while trying to find a headstone we liked the look of. I haven't been able to pick one, but I never imagined I would "shop" in a cemetery. Even now I can't seem to wrap my head around it all. I just need to accept you are gone and begin the long process of healing. I need to be thankful for the blessings God gave us with you during the seven months we spent together—the fact you were born *alive* and the way God is using your life to change people.

Today, on the one-month anniversary of your birth, our church did a sermon about *you*. What Satan meant for evil God remolded into good. He is using you to impact people, and He is doing it in a way we can actually see. I know that is a blessing many grieving people don't get to experience firsthand. We may not see exactly how you are impacting people and changing lives, but I know without a doubt that you *are*.

I can feel in my core there is so much more coming our way and more work to be done, and it confuses me. I don't understand what it all means. I don't know what God is asking of me as we move forward, but I can feel He is asking me to do *something*. I can only hope it becomes clear in time.

It was so weird seeing your Dad and me on the big screen at church and hearing our pastor quote things we said. It was weird having people approach us after the service and tell us we are an inspiration. I don't feel like an inspiring person—not even close.

People acted like we were so special, but there really isn't anything very special about me. I'm broken but still believe God's Word—that's it. It's hard to see what is special about that. But this is God's deal, and all I can do is hope and pray that in our brokenness we can still be the example He deserves. But right now, in *this* moment, my soul is in anguish, and from where I'm sitting, the cost of one inspirational church service feels like a lifetime of agony for me.

I know God will forgive me for such thoughts, and I pray He won't let this break me. He still is my everything—He still is my hope. Miss you so much, buddy.

Love you to the moon and back,
Mommy

Logan's service gave us a sense of purpose. And yet when the day came to an end, our brokenness remained the same. Beauty *can* grow from ashes, and while I was grateful to see a tiny green seedling emerging from the rubble of my life, it didn't make those ashes disappear. Those ashes still covered everything for miles and miles.

Several months prior to that Sunday, Andy said if God was going to let Logan die, then he wanted to be shown *why*. He wanted God to reveal to him what "good" could come from the death of his son.

"And we know that in all things God works for the good of those who love him, who have been called according to his purpose" (Romans 8:28 NIV). In the Christian realm, we hear this verse *all the time*, and we commonly use it in an effort to comfort others in the middle of struggles (I have *much* more on this topic later). But nowhere in the Bible, that I'm aware of at least, does it say God owes us an explanation as to *how* or *why*. But Andy didn't care.

I *gently* tried to tell him he couldn't expect God to show him clearly why Logan died—he just needed to trust something good would come from our situation, because that is what God's Word promises. I tried to explain how many tragedies take place every day without that question being answered—that many times we will never know or understand the *why* on this side of heaven.

Ultimately, God honored Andy's prayer, even though He certainly didn't have to. It wouldn't (and didn't) make our loss any easier, but there was comfort in being able to see the ripple effect of good beginning to expand from the epicenter of Logan's far-too-short life.

Thousands of people heard Logan's story that Sunday. I had no idea then, but that sermon was just the beginning of what Logan's little life would accomplish on this earth. It was a catalyst in my heart for ministry and loving on broken hearts. A spark ignited that morning, and it opened my eyes to see there was another unknown road ahead that God was going to ask us to walk.

I could continually feel Him whisper, "This is just the beginning." But it wouldn't be until two years later that the picture God had been painting and the work He had been doing, unannounced to me, would finally start to become visible. Did He have more planned than I could have ever imagined? Oh my goodness, yes.

I may never know on this side of heaven the full extent of Logan's impact, but I trust and choose to believe there is someone, somewhere who needs to hear his story. I choose to believe that maybe God allowed all of this to happen to my family because it would help at least one person. For all I know, all of this could have been for *you*.

19 — AN UNEXPECTED FILTER

My command is this: Love each other as I have loved you. Greater love has no one than this: to lay down one's life for one's friends.
— John 15:12–13 (NIV)

Photo by Jessica Fox

A tiny poisonous seed—much like that of a lone cancer cell, small and inconspicuous at first but with malicious intent and unlimited growth potential. A tiny poisonous seed had been planted in the fertile soil of my heart, and it was growing like cancer.

Pieces of me were changing, my life was unrecognizable, and Satan didn't hesitate to seize the moment and fertilize his deception. Unknowingly, I was feeding a monster, and what was once just a small seed was rapidly becoming a full-grown thistle.

In a muted but persistent voice, the weed spoke lies to my exposed and vulnerable mind. It told me I was a burden to everyone around me. It told me I was tainted—that people didn't *actually* want to be around me but felt obligated to keep my company. I was nothing more than a charity case, a way for someone to check their good deed box for the day. I was the girl with the dead son. I was tarnished, no longer valuable, and ultimately, *unlovable*.

And so, the thistle's barbed roots grew deeper and deeper, mercilessly wrapping their way around my heart. Any attempt to untangle them or remove them simply made me bleed more. I would try to tell myself it was all in my head, that I was hypersensitive, paranoid, and spending way too much time trying to dissect the thoughts of others. But regardless of how hard I fought, the world around me would only confirm my fears.

Eventually I saw two groups: the people who were no longer in my life and those who still were but only out of obligation. There was no middle ground, and so the thistle grew. It tactfully highlighted the people who had abandoned me, the people who avoided me, and told me I was nothing but a hindrance to those I believed still loved me. Choking it out was nearly impossible. I didn't recognize its presence in my life, and that made my heart an easy place for it to thrive.

What I was actually experiencing at the time was a filter—an unexpected (and at the time *unwanted*) sorting of our friend circle. Andy and I were enduring a series of secondary losses that were no fault of our own, but simply the collateral of Logan's death. I never could have imagined the countless levels of loss we would endure on top of losing Logan. I had never even heard the term *secondary loss* and didn't realize the way it tiptoed in on the heels of our *primary loss*. I was naive to think Logan would be the *only* thing taken from me.

It was no coincidence that the timing of that filter's arrival in my life would coincide perfectly with the growth of that thistle. Unfortunately, Satan is more clever than we would like to admit.

11/20/12

Dear Logan,

Your due date has come and gone, and now my thoughts have gone from "I would have been this far" to "You would have been this old." I've realized I will be mourning your loss for the rest of my life. Each day, month, and year that passes, we will be missing some milestone we would have shared. This is something that will always follow me—a shadow that goes everywhere with me, a shadow that constantly reminds me what I am missing. I want so badly to give you a bath, push you on a swing, and give you your first haircut. How naive many parents are to take such simple things for granted.

Thanksgiving is soon. At the beginning of this year, I had this day planned very differently in my mind. I played it over so many times in my head. Even then, it almost seemed too good to be true—I guess this time around, it was. I know I still have so much to be thankful for, but I'm haunted by the memories of watching you die. I'm haunted by the memory of waking up the day after you passed with your lifeless body at my side. I'm torn by the image of your father carrying your tiny casket and strangers putting your body in such a dark, cold place. *No* parent should have to put their child in the ground.

I am so tired. I feel like I have aged a hundred years. I can feel your death changing me, like I'm a shell of who I used to be. How long can a person continue in this manner before they finally disappear into nothing? I miss you so much that sometimes I pray for God to bring me home too. I'm needed here, but it feels like half of me is already dead, so sometimes I wonder what's the difference. It's not that I want to die; it's just that right now I don't care to live.

People treat us differently now. Just more collateral from your death, I suppose, but hurtful nonetheless. I just want to hide in the house away from *everyone*. Friends are disappearing. Calls and texts are slowing. Our circle is getting much smaller. When I walk into a room, conversation always seems to halt. Those who are "brave" enough to be in my company carry heavy eyes, a head tilt, a half-smile—a sense of duty in their time with me. I must have the plague. I better start acting okay so at least *this* part of my life can turn back to normal.

You seem so far away, but I know with each passing day I am one step closer to seeing your beautiful face. I hope God will tell you about us. I hope right now you are sitting on Jesus's lap and He is bragging about how much your parents love you. We will have so much to catch up on, my dear, sweet boy. It's a good thing we will have all of eternity to do so.

Love you to the moon and back,
Mommy

Grief makes people uncomfortable. It was one of the first lessons I was forced to learn in the wake of loss. There were many things I anticipated I would face after Logan's death, and although it seems obvious now, I was in no way prepared for those around me to be noticeably rattled in my presence. I guess I assumed bereaved individuals didn't notice the uncomfortable nature of those in their presence. I couldn't have been more wrong.

Before Logan *I* was the one who would see a grieving friend, feel my heart begin to quicken, and inevitably fumble my words. *I* was the one who maybe, sorta, kinda avoided eye contact whenever possible or maybe, sorta, kinda didn't go out of my way to make sure my path crossed theirs on a regular basis. The feeling must be universal, because once I found myself on the bereaved side of things, it was painfully obvious Andy and I made people uncomfortable. It hurt to see some of our friends avoiding us. When we did see familiar faces, I got tired of the awkward silence, the fake smile, or even worse, the complete avoidance that anything had happened.

If you're taking notes, jot this one down: we notice. The majority of you are not great actors (neither was I), and it is easy to tell if you would rather be anywhere but where you are. Your inability to step momentarily into our pain simply gives us *more* pain.

In a situation like ours, it was only natural to expect a rush of support, and for those closest to us to walk through the muck and the mire with us. For the most part, that is exactly what we got. In fact, it would be an absolute injustice if I did not acknowledge the massive amount of support we received. God was gracious in bringing us an amazing group of loving people—family, friends, coworkers, our church, and even complete strangers. At times it was overwhelming, but also incredibly humbling.

However, when we first received Logan's diagnosis, the last thing on my mind was how the process of saying good-bye to our son would lead to the process of saying good-bye to certain relationships. While friends had come and gone in my life, I had never lost a friendship solely due to circumstances in my life, ones that were also entirely out of my control. "Fair-weather friends" had never applied to my story, but I guess to be fair, my weather prior to Logan had been mostly sunny.

I didn't realize the new and uncharted season would not only be the darkest and hardest because of our loss but also refine the list of those who would (and would not) continue to do life with us. Andy and I quickly learned that sometimes the people you trust and rely on the most are the ones who shy away, and the people you never expected are the ones who come running to your aid.

Logan's death stole motivation from every pocket of our lives. We had been drained of every ounce of energy—like we were nothing more than severely cracked water bottles. Water couldn't come in nearly fast enough to keep up with what was being lost, leaving us feeling empty and exhausted. I never knew grief could present itself as fatigue, yet with more depths and layers than I would care to count. Everyday tasks like getting out of bed, doing laundry, going to work, and making dinner felt almost impossible. So naturally, maintaining relationships within our social circle was not a high priority. We stopped reaching out, not because we didn't care but because we didn't have the bandwidth to.

During that time, the family and friends who pursued *us* were the ones we cherished the most. We were greatly blessed to have people in our lives who kept in touch on a daily and weekly basis. They brought us food, even if we didn't want to eat, sat with us even when there was not much to say, brought us to the movies even when we were reluctant to go, and did almost *anything* to get us out of the house in which we'd begun to hide.

Andy and I were not the most fun people to be around. I knew that, and can't say I would have called us on an open Friday night. And yet, some friends *did*. We knew a metaphorical rain cloud hovered over our heads, and we felt no one in their right mind would *choose* to spend time with us. That, of course, wasn't the case for all, but here's the hard truth: some of our *best* friends completely dropped us after Logan died. We were *already* hypersensitive to being a burden. We were *already* hearing the thistle's poisonous melody playing in our minds. So when our dear friends left, it only confirmed the thought we had already been fighting: our story *had* made us unlovable.

As painful as it was at the time, it turns out that filter was a blessing, for it let the surface-level relationships in our life slip away, and held tight to the friendships worth saving. At first, I hated it and the way it pushed itself into my life without asking permission. I hated how friends seemed to be dropping like flies—how people I had known my entire life *still* hadn't reached out. But in time, I came to respect it and eventually even *love* it.

Were it not for the filter, we would have missed out on the most incredible friends this life has to offer. God had them waiting, not quite out of sight, but not front and center either. I'm not going to name-drop them (because I promised I wouldn't), but I know when they read this, they will know. I did, however, find a bit of a loophole and placed one of their faces at the beginning of this chapter with mine (sorry, my beautiful friend, but I'm not sorry).

They could have invested their time in other people and more mutually beneficial friendships, but they didn't. They made it a point *not* to distance themselves from us. In fact, they did the opposite: they *pursued* us. They leaned into the uncomfortable when others looked away.

No matter what we did or how we acted, they just kept coming around. Andy and I were convinced we would inevitably scare them away, and yet every week they continued to call, text, or stop by. They had never lost a baby, but they talked about Logan freely and let us vent in whatever ways we needed. They weren't judgmental of the occasional harsh or off-color things that would come out of our mouths. Instead, they would just shrug it off and laugh along with us.

They were supportive of where we were in the grieving process and never tried to force the "hurry up and grieve" mentality of our culture. They were some of the *only* friends we felt normal and safe around. They didn't treat us differently. They continually made all the plans to get together, knowing full well we wouldn't take the initiative. Even through all our imperfections, they loved us. Want to know the best part about them? Beyond a shadow of a doubt, I knew they loved Logan too.

To those dear friends of ours—thank you. Those two words fall impossibly short, but it's all I have to offer. We are forever humbled by the love and kindness you have shown us. You have become a part of our family, and Andy and I are honored to do life with you. You were evidence of God and His love, even in our darkest hour. We will forever thank that unexpected filter for catching you, and will forever thank *you* for ever so carefully severing our thistle's roots.

I have now sat on both sides of tragedy. Live long enough, and most will be able to say the same (lucky us). I have seen those close to me suffer, and I have experienced the pain firsthand. It has been eye-opening to have the ability *now* to take a step back and look at tragedy through *both* lenses.

When someone I love is hurting, there is an innate pull in my core to help. Some people are built to be caretakers, and I have always considered myself a part of that group. With all my heart, I want to take away the pain. Even before I lost Logan, I knew, unfortunately, it was impossible. Typically, it left me feeling helpless, like I was good for a hug and a warm meal but nothing after. That "nothing after" is the problem.

Following a death, and after the initial flood of support, families (or individuals) are eventually forgotten. It's not intentional; it's just a byproduct of the never-ending chaos of life. And typically, unless someone has personally experienced a loss of similar magnitude, they are often-times ill equipped to handle the ultrasensitive nature of grief. Unless it has touched you personally, it's impossible to understand how the death of a loved one is a *lifelong* pain—one that requires *lifelong* support.

It's too easy in our human nature to go back to our normal routines, lose track of time, and eventually forget the bereaved altogether. The result? Isolation of a group of people who need to *not* be isolated. Making matters worse is the blatant uneasy demeanor many people exhibit in the aftermath. Some can't handle it and some simply don't want to, but the cost, once again, is the same: isolation of the bereaved.

Those friends of ours I talked about moments ago knew how to love and support us *only* because tragedy had already touched their lives. The price of our lifeline was the death of my dear friend's mother. That's *really* hard for me to accept sometimes. Sitting in darkness was familiar to *her*. Pain was familiar to *her*. Isolation was familiar to *her*. So, when she saw us sitting in that familiar place, she grabbed her husband's hand, and together, they bravely held ours. They willingly crawled into the darkness with us. In turn, we were blessed with the most incredible friends this life has to offer—at a devastatingly high cost. That is immensely tragic, yet somehow, profoundly beautiful.

Keeping the company of someone who has just lost a loved one carries an undeniable strain. Our minds can't help but search for words capable of healing, oftentimes forgetting that no such words exist. When I saw people for the first time after Logan died, I could feel their hearts tense. I could see their minds hard at work trying to find the right words. But there were no *right words*. I just needed them to acknowledge my loss, say my child's name, and allow me space to say it too.

There were so many times I just wanted to yell to those around me, "It's okay to talk about Logan! He is not a taboo subject. He is my son! Stop making excuses for why you haven't stopped by or called. Be someone for me to pray with, confide in, and cry with. I am still me! Don't abandon me now when I need you most!" I desperately wanted one thing, and that was the people I loved to love me back. It was that simple. Friendship is a back-and-forth dance. Each one with a unique rhythm and melody. So many of the people around me acted as if our music had stopped playing, when in fact our song had just changed.

I understand our situation made those around us tense. As a whole, our culture has done a terrible job allowing people time and space to openly lament a loved one's passing. Add to that the death of a baby, and you can see where we run into issues. There is nothing in this life more fragile than grieving parents. *But* at a time when I felt as though things could not get worse, in a way they did because of people's erratic behavior.

When I was pregnant with Logan, sometimes I was treated like I was carrying a corpse in my belly, not a living and beautiful baby boy. People were distant and removed. They were *clearly* troubled with my situation. But guess what? *So was I.*

Some parents were standoffish toward me with their children. Both my pregnant friends and friends with new babies kept their distance. It seemed like they were afraid to be around me. More likely, they thought it would hurt to see them or their little ones, knowing I was going to lose mine. But I didn't see a difference. To be completely honest, pregnant bellies and tiny babies *did* sting—a lot. People's inclination to keep their distance wasn't entirely wrong, because in all honesty, I didn't really want to see them. But do you know what hurt even more? Being blatantly avoided by those individuals who had previously played a role in my life simply because my kid was going to die. A much better response would have been for those individuals to acknowledge the tension and follow my lead. With both tact and delicacy, they could have shared their fears and ultimately given *me* the choice.

For example, let's say a friend was having a birthday party and wanted us to join, but knew a brand-new baby would be there. Rather than choosing by default not to include us or choosing to include us without acknowledging the obvious triggers, they could say, "We are having a party and would love you guys to join. But you need to know a newborn will be there. We understand if that is too much for your hearts right now, but we would love to spend some time with you." Now *that* is a good friend.

Here's another example: "As you know my baby shower is coming up. I just sent out the invites and wanted to let you know it was on the way so you can be prepared to receive it. You know how much I want you to be there, but I understand it would be very triggering for you." *That* is a good friend.

Do you want to know the cherry on top and the biggest kicker in all of this? For those friends *not* to be offended if (and most likely when) my answer was no. Now *that* is a great friend.

Being intentionally left out or completely looked over wasn't even the worst of it. I repeatedly had friends hide their pregnancies from me. I found out on social media one of my oldest and best friends from child-hood was pregnant, and not just newly pregnant but over halfway there— oh, and she had just found out it was a girl. *Wow, really? Facebook? You didn't think that was information I should have learned directly from you?*

When I confronted her about it, she said she just didn't know how to tell me, and so she didn't. It cut one of the most fragile parts of my heart. I was being ostracized simply because my kid was dead. Of course, she knew I would inevitably see that post. And you know what? It would have been really nice if it hadn't blindsided me while I was carelessly scrolling through my newsfeed waiting for my burrito at Wahoo's Fish Tacos (in front of fifteen other people). If she only had the courage and compas-sion just to tell me herself, it would have protected me from being the girl crying in the take-out line. Now I can add that to the list of places I can no longer go, thank you very much. Was her intention to cause additional pain? Of course not. She loves me, and to this day she is a dear and cher-ished friend of mine. But did she hurt me with her actions? Absolutely.

The way the pregnant community treated me felt very reminiscent of high school—the whispers, the secrets, the awkward pause in a conversa-tion that would happen just as I entered a room. And no, staring at the ceiling is not going to conceal the awkwardness of those moments. *Do they think I am a monster? Just because I am in the middle of my own grief doesn't make me unable to share in their joy—well, a tiny bit, at least. I mean,*

I really don't want to hear you're pregnant, but you are. So just suck it up and tell me. Told you I would be honest in these pages.

And so, I'll say it again: hearing pregnancy announcements stung. And believe me, when you don't want to see or hear them, they are *everywhere*. But it hurts tenfold to learn someone you love has chosen to avoid you and *purposefully* hide their news. I already felt isolated, and those times made me feel like I was the *only* person in the world. Our situation may not have been fixable, but the reactions and behaviors of others were.

A word of advice: if you are hiding or delaying telling that one friend about your pregnancy because of their loss, you are probably doing more damage than good. Find an appropriate time and privately tell her or him. And if you notice they flinch—that maybe for a second, you see pain behind their smile—that's okay. Love them anyway.

20 — SMALL TALK

Let your conversation be always full of grace, seasoned with salt, so that you may know how to answer everyone.

—Colossians 4:6 (NIV)

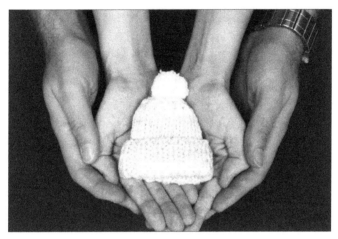

Photo by Ken Papaleo

The bipolar nature of my grieving mind was confusing and complicated, for as much as I truly wanted to talk about Logan in some situations, in others, I truly didn't.

Please don't ask. Please don't ask. These words resided in the forefront of my mind anytime I found myself in a public setting. Whether I was meeting someone new, grocery shopping, or having an unfamiliar client in my chair at work, I always struggled with how I should navigate a certain question that would inevitably come up.

"Do you have any children?" There was a part of me that wanted to lie. I wanted an easy out, and bringing up my child who had died was anything but. However, I felt like I was dishonoring Logan if I didn't acknowledge him. I felt like he deserved to be mentioned, even if it caused me, or the other person, some momentary discomfort.

It just seemed much easier to smile and say no, rather than share the most intimate and painful part of my life—with a complete stranger.

However, the times I chose that route, it almost always ended in regret. It made me feel like I was ashamed of him, and that was most certainly not the case.

But was I oversharing if I casually mentioned my child had died to the woman checking me out at the grocery store? Did she understand the repercussions of such a seemingly harmless question when she asked? Did she have any idea where innocent small talk could lead? No, probably not.

On the other hand, should I have been dishonest about Logan's life only to spare *her* an uncomfortable moment? It has taken a lot of living to get this answer, but again—no, probably not. It might be a bit of a shock, but turns out it was not my job to protect the asker of such questions. An uncomfortable moment for them was leaps and bounds better than what had become an uncomfortable *life* for me.

On the flip side, I can't tell you how many times I mentioned Logan to a stranger and then ended up needing to console *them*. There is a look I have become very familiar with that happens the moment you tell someone your baby died: mouth open, eyes wide, and usually some sort of awkward pause as they try to absorb what they just heard and think through how they will respond. One of three things usually follows.

One, they apologize and change the topic as quickly as possible. Two, they apologize and start crying. Three, they pry and want more details. There were times I didn't mention Logan *solely* because I didn't have the energy to field the many responses I might get. It turned into a game of roulette that I wasn't always willing to play.

It may seem trivial to those of you who can't relate, but early on, the stress of being asked about children led to serious anxiety attacks that I still struggle with today (stay tuned, I have a whole chapter on that later). The inevitable pockets of small talk that used to flow so easily had suddenly turned into an almost guaranteed conversation I didn't want to have. I would trip on my words *every single time.*

It was interesting how Andy and I differed in this area. I stumbled and searched for words. I was so easily rattled by the question that you could almost physically see the tug-of-war happening in my mind as I struggled to find the right response. Andy, on the other hand, rarely mentioned Logan to strangers or new acquaintances. It made him uncomfortable, and he was more reserved with those he did not know.

I knew Andy and I had the same struggle, even though his manifested mostly on the inside. I knew it tore him up as much as it destroyed me; it just wasn't obvious to the outside world. I, on the other hand, could see his whole body tense whenever the question arose. I could see his anxiety skyrocket. Our eyes would inevitably meet, and it was almost as if in that moment we carried an entire conversation without a single word being spoken. He would look at me, seeking approval for however he'd handled it, and regardless of what my heart was feeling, I would return his glance with a nod and a smile.

However, in the complex mind of a woman, even though I typically wasn't angry when he didn't acknowledge Logan, I could feel the ache in my heart increase. Sometimes it increased so much, it felt a lot like anger. Sometimes, I guess, maybe it was. But then I would realize the source— and my heart would soften. How can such a simple question continue to cause such chaos in our already overwhelmed hearts? I was frustrated because I should have been able just to smile and say, "Yes, I have a baby boy at home."

I made sure to tell Andy often that there was no right or wrong way to handle the question, and whatever he felt like doing or saying was okay. Kinda funny, because I hadn't even made peace with my own responses or offered that level of grace to myself, but I hoped he could do so.

One Saturday morning, Andy and I decided to go grab a cup of coffee. The day was open, and it seemed like a nice way to spend some time together and kick off a calm weekend. While waiting in a line that wrapped around the small shop, an innocent conversation between Andy and another customer found its way to the topic of children. I knew the question was close. It was only a matter of time.

I was not in a "chatting with strangers" mood and made sure to face the counter with Andy to my back. To my surprise, when the dreaded question arose, Andy sweetly mentioned his little boy. My heart swelled with pride. Perhaps something was beginning to shift in his healing process. I knew how hard this was for him and what a big step it was for his heart.

My big, proud smile was interrupted, however, as curiosity got the best of the old woman. She began to prod. I heard Andy's once-confident voice crack and his words become flustered.

I turned around. Andy's eyes screamed for help. But I was in too much shock. I began glancing back and forth between Andy and the face of the rude lady, completely baffled at how brazen she was. I kept my eyes on Andy's and watched his demeanor change as he became increasingly upset with the situation.

Finally, she crossed the line. "How did he die?" Andy, now with a very red face, responded by saying Logan had a fatal bone condition. Unsatisfied, she countered, "No, how *exactly* did he die?"

"He suffocated!" Andy snapped back, drawing the attention of other customers in line. We locked eyes, knowing what the other was thinking, grabbed our coffees, and walked out the door.

Unfortunately, sometimes being honest can open the door to more pain. Needless to say, after the coffee shop event, Andy often deferred to his previous go-to when asked about kids.

THROUGH KELLEY'S EYES

Life is messy. God created us to experience life alongside a precious few people, while spending fleeting moments with most others. Because we were created to be social beings, it is inevitable that at some point in our lives we are going to step right smack dab in the middle of someone else's pain. There is so much hurt in the world that there really is no way around it. Be it a divorce, the loss of a loved one, a job that didn't pan out, or a friendship that went sour. *Everyone* has wounds.

It's never fun when you're the person who unexpectedly walks all over someone's else's pain by asking them that one question they are secretly begging the universe not to ask. "Are you married?" "What do you do for a living?" "Are you still friends with so and so?" And for my sister and Andy the nasty one was, "Do you have any children?"

I don't know how many times I had to stand and watch Andy and Jamie squirm trying to figure out how to answer that one. They didn't want to dishonor the memory of their boy, but they also didn't want to tell a stranger their baby just died and have to watch them wipe the look of horror off their face. The world is full of loaded questions, loaded *and* damaging if you happen to ask the wrong person, the wrong question, at the wrong time.

So what's a person to do? And the million-dollar answer is—I literally have no idea. Honestly, none really. I have a few questions I'm more careful to ask strangers because of the path my family has been on, but I know there are other questions I wouldn't think twice about.

So, we can either hide in our houses and never speak a word to each other again, or we can venture out into the world very certain we will inevitably put our foot in our mouth. The key here is not spending energy trying to avoid each other's pain but praying God would prepare us for when He chooses to throw us into it.

For me, that started by praying every day that God would help me to see the people around me like He does. I mean really *see them*, not just fly past them on my way to the produce section. And second, if I *did* happen to step into someone else's pain, I asked God to help me carry myself in a way that doesn't add to their wound.

When the time comes that I ask that one person that one wrong question, I hope I stop what I'm doing and engage. I pray I don't look away awkwardly and start fumbling in my purse or stick my nose in my phone. I hope I take the time to hear their story, *if* they want to share it. I hope I don't feel the need to pretend I can relate to their pain, but instead voice that I hurt for what they have endured. I hope that when the encounter is over, they leave knowing they were not just a blip in my day, easily forgotten, but feel seen as another human with a story that deserves compassion.

My reaction to the cringe-worthy question "Do you have kids?" has evolved over the past ten years. I have seasons where I *always* mention Logan and some where I don't. I have learned ways to respond that are honest without being *completely* translucent.

If you have living kids, you can always respond with how many you have "at home." Technically, it's correct; it just doesn't dive into the details of how many of your children are "in heaven." If you don't have living kids, but a child of yours has died, simply say, "I don't have kids at home, just yet." It's a bit of a stretch, but it works. If you have multiple children and are wanting to acknowledge all of them, you can easily say, "I have an eight-year-old, a six-year-old, *and* a son who would have been ten." If your only child has passed, you can easily say, "I have a son who would have been two." Typically, that response is not followed with more questions. Either way, just know there is no right or wrong answer here.

I have learned over the years to give myself grace when I decide to bring up Logan's name and grace when I decide *not* to. It doesn't lessen or reflect poorly on my love for him. It doesn't mean I am ashamed of his life or dishonoring his memory. It simply means sometimes my heart is willing to share and sometimes it is not—and that's okay.

21 — REMEMBER ME

Come to me, all you who are weary and burdened, and I will give you rest.

—Matthew 11:28 (NIV)

Photo by Jessica Fox

As the days, weeks, and months progressed, life continued all around me. My world was stalled, but it felt as if there was an expectation that it shouldn't be. We had gotten to a point where everyone seemed to be "over it" and sometimes hinted that I should be too. To them Logan was a problem to overcome. There was a timeline and a deadline, it seemed, and I had exceeded *both*. A massive disconnect existed between *their expectations* and *my realization* that I would never "move on" from Logan's loss. Best-case scenario, it would simply integrate within my life.

But if I couldn't learn to separate my social life from my grief, would the number of people who wanted to stay in my world only *continue* to deplete? If people knew how broken I still was, would I face additional losses?

I eventually found myself in a place where I would no longer say Logan's name. In specific settings, he became off-limits, and I intentionally had to stop myself from bringing him up. There was nothing worse than mentioning him and, in response, seeing people tense and change the subject. I didn't want to be the one who *always* cried, and I felt if I continued to show my true colors to the world, then at some point the world would stop looking my way. I didn't want my grief to push those I loved away—especially the ones who had actually held on.

And so, I began a season of pretending. I picked up the pieces of my very broken heart and put them where no one could see them. Down in the deep recesses of my being, they sat in a corner, covered in a blanket of dust and shame. I made my inner circle—the people I still trusted with Logan—incredibly small. The world around me became malignant and unsafe. And yet, day after day after day, I faced it with a smile and acted as if all order had been restored in my life.

But I saw Logan *everywhere* and in *everything*. It was so hard for my mind to catch each and every thought of him that wanted to escape my lips. I wanted to talk about him freely, like a mother ought to talk about her son. I longed to hear his name come from a mouth other than mine. I wanted to know someone else's heart was hurting. I wanted . . . to be remembered.

The irony in all of this, as I look back with more wisdom, is that those around me likely felt *they* were the ones who couldn't say his name. I learned people were actually afraid to bring him up in fear of renewing pain. In many (but not all) situations, it wasn't a lack of *love,* but rather, a lack of *understanding*.

On the rare occasion someone else *was* brave enough to mention Logan on their own, I wasn't angry or upset. I was relieved. It was a gift when someone would *willingly* crawl down into the pit I was in and sit with me. One of my biggest fears was that Logan would be forgotten, that I would be the only one left to say his name—that I would be the only one left to remember.

The truth was, I cried *every single day*. When someone was courageous enough to talk about my loss, yes, sometimes I would break down. But I was going to cry regardless, and from time to time, it was just nice for my tears to have a friend. Logan's name being mentioned didn't remind me he died. It reminded me he *lived*.

Logan has been on my mind every minute of every hour of every day since the moment I said good-bye to him. That may sound a bit extreme to some of you. The only way to explain it is comparing it to what I would assume it would be like to lose an arm or a leg. Sure, the wound would eventually "heal" (well, to an extent at least), but that limb would always be noticeably absent, regardless of the passage of time. I assume a part of that person's consciousness (even if it was deeply hidden) would *always* be aware, in some way, of what should be there but no longer is.

Logan was a piece of me—a piece I no longer have. A part of my heart is *gone*. It's not just broken. It's not just cracked. It's not simply wounded and needing time to rest. A part of my heart has been amputated. And that part will not return to me on this side. I will never "get over" his passing or forget his absence. Just as a person learns how to live without a limb, as time passes, I will simply learn how to live without Logan.

———

People continued to become more erratic, foreign, and unpredictable as time continued. And I didn't have the bandwidth or patience to navigate *any* of it. As a result, I got very good, very quickly, at "faking happy." It was easier and more comfortable for those around me to believe I was fine. And as far as the world could see, I was.

I can't count the number of times I would hear, "Oh my gosh, I'm so happy to see you looking so well!" I would smile, nod, and say thank you. Simultaneously, my mind would be in a deep argument with their "observation," desperately wanting to explain just how "not well" I was doing. My jaw would eventually start to ache, and I would realize I had been clenching my teeth for far too long.

It was simply easier for the world to believe I had moved on and had turned back into the same Jamie they knew before Logan. The truth was, I wasn't. Not even close. I may have looked alive and well, but I was really a walking, talking, empty shell. I was smiling on the outside but screaming on the inside. Never in my life had I been a good liar, but I suddenly could have won an Academy Award for my performance.

I did bring up Logan occasionally, and only to a select few, and most of the time I was able to do it with a stoic face. I eventually found it easier to avoid the drama and the tears, even if I was with someone I trusted. I was protective of my tears. They sometimes felt like the only tangible proof Logan existed, and I saved them for private moments, like my car ride home from work, hiding in the shower with my music blaring, or sitting by Logan's grave with my journal open.

> I may look strong to you,
> But inside I am falling apart—
>
> You may see a smile,
> But underneath it I am broken—
>
> I may look brave and courageous,
> But really I am afraid—
>
> I may seem calm and quiet,
> But I'm actually screaming in pain—
>
> I may look alive,
> But I have never felt so dead—
>
> I may seem like myself again,
> But I will never be the same—
>
> I'm not just another face in a crowd,
> I'm a mother—without her child.

These words poured out of my heart as I sat by Logan's grave one chilly morning. I would have moments of overwhelming sorrow. They made me feel claustrophobic. It was like I was being smothered by a blanket of grief that weighed a thousand pounds, and no matter how frantically I tried to find the edge of it, I couldn't. I couldn't catch my breath. I would twist and pull and try to escape in every direction, but I was never able to find my way out from underneath its consuming weight.

At those times, I would hide at Logan's grave. Being where his body was eventually helped me find my breath again. I knew he wasn't there, but it was all I had. In order to be as close to him as physically possible, I would drape my body on the barren ground where he was buried. I couldn't stand the thought of his body being cold and alone. It was all I could do to give him my warmth.

The thought of him being cold was *always* upsetting to me. Maybe it was some motherly instinct that remained deep within me, unwilling to accept that Logan was gone and refusing to believe he no longer needed me to protect him.

One evening, I found myself driving with Andy past the cemetery in the middle of an unseasonably early snowstorm. As we reached the point where I could see the cemetery across the freeway, I was suddenly hit with overwhelming pain. Without any warning, I started crying—well, that's a bit of an understatement. Andy was quite confused, because prior to that moment I seemed totally fine. I was almost embarrassed to admit it, but the sudden and unexpected trigger of emotion was because Logan's body . . . was covered in snow.

The rest of that evening, as I sat cuddled in blankets on the couch and trying to stay warm, my mind was miles away in that graveyard. I could hear neighborhood kids playing outside in the snow. I could hear their giggles and laughter, and the next day I knew I would see their footprints all over the street.

But my son was not playing in the snow. My son was buried *underneath it.* I knew his soul was in a better place, but his body was there, and it was *alone.* It was dark. It was quiet. It was cold. There were no tiny footprints scattered in the snow and no laughter filling the air.

I couldn't use the heat of my body to warm his. I would never have the opportunity to wrap him in a blanket, sit him by the fire, and place a cup of hot chocolate in his hands. I was his mother, and yet I could not mother him. I couldn't keep him warm, and it only reminded me that I couldn't keep him safe.

I wondered how many more triggers were in front of me and when they would rear their ugly heads. One thing I knew for sure was that every year, as the seasons shifted and the first snow fell from the sky, I would be hit with a wave of sorrow. I knew I would always think of my firstborn, alone in that place, wrapped in the earth when he should have been wrapped in my arms.

How is it possible to be triggered by beautiful, white, and glistening snow? I just couldn't process it. The sight used to bring happiness and joy. Now it only brought emptiness and a longing that couldn't be satisfied

A couple of days later, Kelley decided to share a strange experience she had with me. She told me I would probably think she was crazy but needed to get it out. I laughed out loud thinking of that snowy night and said, "Try me."

Turns out, she was driving home in the snowstorm (in the car right behind me, in fact), and as she passed the cemetery, she was suddenly flooded by a wave of emotion, because it was snowing on Logan's grave.

I'm pretty sure my mouth hit the floor. We had the same breakdown, on the very same drive, at the exact same time. Sometimes, as the ones who experience loss firsthand, it's easy to overlook or forget that, even though we may not see it, others are grieving too. In a strange way, it comforted me knowing that Kelley had the same response. The way it soothed my heart cannot be explained. It was like she had unknowingly stepped beside me under the giant slab of concrete I was struggling to carry above my head.

Suddenly, her face was wet with tears next to mine, and she reached her arms high in the air beside me, helping hold the weight. There is *immense* power in being remembered. There is an even *greater* power in empathy. I never questioned her love for Logan. I knew it was grand. But in that moment, I knew she truly loved him with a fierceness that matched mine, and for an instant I didn't feel alone.

Plus, crazy loves company. I felt like I was losing my mind that night in the snow. And if I was losing my grip on reality, at least Kelley was too.

THROUGH KELLEY'S EYES

Grief isn't always rational, but that doesn't mean the feelings it invokes are any less real. After Logan passed away, I found myself in tears quite often—sometimes for reasons that would make sense to most people and other times for reasons I wouldn't bother sharing with *anyone*.

One such bout of grief occurred one snowy evening while driving past the cemetery where Logan was buried. This wasn't an abnormal occurrence, considering the cemetery was next to the main highway in town. Logically, I knew that even though Logan's body was laid to rest in that cemetery, he didn't actually live there. I knew he was whole, healthy, and at peace in heaven.

Illogically, though, the thought of his little body out there alone in the cold, covered in snow, was more than I could bear. The tears started to flow, and there was nothing I could do to talk myself out of it, even though it made no sense at all. What started as a slow trickle down my face quickly became a full-body sob, which, as a side note, is not the best safety choice when it comes to operating a vehicle. But sometimes that's how grief goes.

Most of the time, I chose to keep a lot of my grief to myself. I didn't want to burden anyone else with it, because I'm a pretty private person. I wasn't interested in other people's opinions on how well or how poorly they thought I was handling my emotions. For reasons unknown to me, this time around, I chose to share my irrational grief episode with Jamie.

It turned out, she'd had the exact same experience. It turned out, we both found ourselves in the grip of cold, snowy, crazy grief, which led me to believe maybe there is no such thing as irrational or rational grief. Maybe, at the end of the day, grief is just . . . grief.

It's painful and crappy and often lonely, unless we choose to go out on a limb and share our grief with others or, even crazier, if we choose to enter into someone else's grief. The truth is, we all will grieve at some point, so why not work to make those seasons of life as normal and accepted as the joyful ones?

22 — IT IS WELL WITH MY SOUL

But those who hope in the Lord will renew their strength. They will soar on wings like eagles; they will run and not grow weary, they will walk and not be faint.

—Isaiah 40:31 (NIV)

Photo by Ken Papaleo

*D**ear God,*

Months have come and gone, and not one of those days has been absent of tears and suffering. I don't know how much longer I can carry on like this. I know joy and happiness are two very different things—joy comes from you alone and should not be dependent on

162

our circumstances. However, I am still waiting for you to help me figure out how to restore mine. I feel so empty right now, I could just crumble into pieces. No matter how hard I press my face into Logan's blanket, I can no longer smell his sweet scent. Sometimes I feel as if I almost smother myself searching so desperately in that blanket for evidence that he really was there—for something *to hold onto,* anything *to hold onto.*

I know my life will be redeemed someday, but what if that redemption isn't received until I get to heaven? I'm struggling, because if I get pregnant again, a part of me feels like I am owed a healthy baby. I know that is completely absurd—you don't owe me anything. But if something bad happens again, I know I will be fighting the feeling that you betrayed me. I'm terrified to try again. It's not a perfect world—and at the end of the day, I could very well have two headstones side by side. Many people lose more than one, I very easily could be one of them.

Regardless of what my future holds, I want you to know I love you with all my heart. I don't doubt you are good. I just don't understand the way you move sometimes. I know expecting it all to work out next time around is potentially setting myself up for a lot more pain. But I also don't want to wait an entire pregnancy for something terrible to happen, and I know you don't want that for me either. Please, God, bless us with a healthy *baby. Please let me keep the next one.*

Andy asked me the other day what I needed. I told him, "I need a miracle." Thank you for reminding me today that I already had one. Thank you so much for the life of my son—he was so beautiful, wasn't he?

I would be lying if I sat here and pretended like getting pregnant again wasn't on my mind soon after losing Logan. However, even thinking about it made me feel guilty. The idea also terrified me in a way I can't begin to articulate, yet it also often consumed my thoughts. It seemed counterintuitive to have such an overwhelming pull in my heart after what I had just endured. It seemed absolutely crazy to open myself up to that pain once again, but for some reason it was one of the only things besides Logan that occupied my mind.

I think a part of me knew there was a level of healing that could not take place until I became a mother to a child I would be able to keep. I wanted to not just "technically" be a mom but a mom who *actually* had a baby in her arms. God had placed a longing in my heart, and as the months passed after Logan's death, my eagerness only grew. I was desperate for a little hope, a little light in the darkness, and the chance of a new little life.

It had nothing to do with trying to replace Logan. The only people who think a new child can take the place of one who was lost have never lost a child. I was so close to bringing a baby home and then, in an instant, so far away. It was nearly impossible not to calculate how long it would take to have another child. Best-case scenario, it was still an eternity away.

To say I was afraid would be an understatement. I was consumed by fear. I knew it had reached a dangerously unhealthy level, and I knew it was not what God wanted for me, but I wasn't sure how to control it. A part of me believed that surely God would not allow me to endure such pain again, and another part of me knew that wasn't how He worked. There is no promise we will never have to bury more than one child, and there is no pain quota we can meet and then live life free of tragedy.

12/1/12

Sweet Boy,

I can't remember what my life felt like before tragedy touched it. Your daddy and I talk about it often. Did we laugh more, worry less, and live carefree? Were we filled with joy and expectant of all the good things on the horizon? What were our worries when all seemed so *calm*? For the life of me, I just can't remember.

If I could go back and relive a moment, it would be when I was pregnant with you and had no idea what was coming our way. We were deep in discussion over the perfect name and the cutest room decor. We were excited about the future, ready to be parents, and anticipating only good things. I could feel you move, was less nauseous (well, kinda), and had finally started to settle and anticipate your arrival. I was happy, innocent, a tad naive, but *full of life*. My world had not yet been pierced, and my life had not yet been broken.

In those moments, I had no idea my innocence would soon disappear. I didn't know it was possible to forget what a peaceful life felt like. When I think back to that version of myself, I see a Jamie I no longer know—but a Jamie I greatly miss. It would be such a gift to feel what she felt one more time. It would be such a gift to go into another pregnancy expecting to go home with a baby in the end. I feel like I have been robbed of the joy I deserve to feel should God give us another child. I'm broken and terrified to try again—and yet it's the only other thing I think of beside you.

I feel crazy to be willing to open myself up to that pain again. And then in the same breath, I feel angry. I shouldn't have to be thinking of another pregnancy right now. I should be watching a movie with you asleep on my chest. This isn't fair. *None of this is fair.*

Love you to the moon and back,
Mommy

There were several headstones in the graveyard that belonged to the same families. I would stare at the names and dates and think about the poor parents who buried their babies just a year or two apart. Sometimes I would look at the open plot sitting next to Logan's and wonder if, one day, it would belong to us as well. *What if God lets this happen again?*

Can I survive burying another child? Would I want to turn from Him if I lost baby number two?

I was so afraid, not only of the pain, but of the impact on my relationship with God if my next child *also* died. It was such a fight to stay in His Word and by His side after Logan. Did my faith have a breaking point? Was I only following Christ because I thought I would have more "favor" and live a less painful life? That is never promised in the Bible. In fact, it seems more the opposite. Even at times of weakness, in my core, I knew God was good and would remain my Savior come what may.

The day we found out Logan's sickness was not genetic, but rather a sporadic mutation, is a morning I will never forget. It was the moment we found out we *could* try to conceive again.

I was at my salon when an unfamiliar number appeared on my phone. As I said before, I very rarely answer numbers I don't know, but once again, this was a time I decided to pick up. As soon as I heard who was on the other end of the line and the knowledge she possessed, I could instantly feel my heartbeat pounding throughout my entire body. *This is it. This is the moment I will find out if I will ever be pregnant again.*

Why, in a time like that, does it always feel like it takes *forever* to get to the point? I just wanted to hear, "You can try again!" And thank you, sweet Jesus, that is precisely what she said—eventually.

My cheeks were instantly wet with tears, but for the first time in months, they were happy tears. Well, maybe they were terrified, hopeful, totally panicked, *and* happy tears. Thinking of going through another pregnancy was scary, but to think I might not even be able to try was heartbreaking.

Some of you reading this have a different story. Maybe what you heard was more along the lines of, "This could happen again." If that is you, *I am so sorry.* Heartbreak upon heartbreak. Yes, you can adopt, and that is probably what everyone is telling you. No, they have no idea how upsetting their comments are.

Before our genetic testing, Andy and I decided we would adopt if we were at risk for a repeat. That being said, you need to know it is okay (and even necessary) to mourn this loss. After all, that is exactly what it is: another loss. Before we heard our results, I remember fearing, *I will never be pregnant again. I will never get to feel life within me again. I will never have the moment I was supposed to have when a beautiful, screaming pink baby was placed on my chest. I will never know what our biological children would have grown up to look like.* I will say it again—that is absolutely something to mourn. Don't let anyone tell you differently.

I wish I could give you firsthand advice and words of wisdom, but I just can't. It's not my story and not my place. Just know, I am praying for you. As I type, I am asking God to give you clarity and direction. May you feel His presence wherever you go, and may you feel His peace in whatever way you choose to move forward.

Terrifying. I had asked around, and the consensus seemed to be that *terrifying* was the predominant feeling among bereaved moms concerning pregnancy after loss. Some waited years, and it was terrifying. Some, just months, and guess what? It was terrifying. I knew it would be a long and turbulent road, and I knew I wouldn't always handle it well. I was angry the joy many get to experience during pregnancy would be forever robbed from me, but at the same time, I knew I was blessed to be given another opportunity at least to *try.*

And that's exactly what we did. In early 2013, Andy and I learned God had given us another precious baby. Grieving a life *and* growing a life is no easy task. It's nothing short of a roller coaster of emotions that all seemed to coexist simultaneously. There were ups. There were downs. There were moments of panic and moments of peace. There were two weeks when, once again, we had to face markers on an ultrasound and the reality that something could be wrong. And there was the moment I fell on my knees and thanked my King when we found out all was well.

When anxiety and fear would begin to take root, I would recognize the source, rebuke it, and pray for the child within me. *It is well with my soul. It is well with my soul. It is well with my soul.* I repeated those words every day, all day, until I eventually began to believe it. That hymn, penned by Horatio Spafford in the late 1800s, truly became an anchor for me as we walked the long and scary journey of our second pregnancy.

When peace, like a river, attendeth my way,
When sorrows like sea billows roll;
Whatever my lot, Thou hast taught me to say,
It is well, it is well, with my soul.

I had always loved the famous hymn, or any song inspired by it, but it wasn't until I found out the story surrounding its origins that I realized how powerful of a testament it was.

Horatio Spafford, in my opinion, is a modern-day version of Job. For those of you unfamiliar with the book of Job in the Bible, it is about a man who lost everything—and I mean *everything*. And yet his faith in God remained.

But much like Job, Spafford lost practically everything he loved. The Great Chicago Fire of 1871 took his wealth, pneumonia took the life of his four-year-old son, and a ship collision over the Atlantic took his remaining four daughters. His wife survived the accident and sent him the now famous telegram that read, "Saved alone . . ."

Spafford traveled to meet his wife, and as his ship passed the place where his daughters died, he wrote the now famous hymn, "It Is Well with My Soul." That story puts a new light and depth of meaning behind such seemingly simple words. Spafford lost it all, and still, in the midst of his grief, he was able to proclaim, "It is well with my soul!" I didn't want Spafford's story, but I so admired his faith.

Through God's grace alone, I was able to get through another pregnancy. It was messy and it was beautiful. And at the end of it all? A little bit of redemption was placed in our arms.

9/17/13

My dearest Logan,

Exactly a year, a month, a week, and a day after we had you, your little brother, Sullivan, was born. He came into this world on a very rainy day, and oh my goodness, does he look like you! The joy that fills my heart is immeasurable—but at the same moment it's matched with an eerie sorrow, because this is what I so desperately wanted to experience with *you*. Every moment I have with Sullivan just makes every experience I missed with you all the more real. What I would have given to have these moments with you as well.

In no way does Sullivan replace you, nor was that ever our intent in having another child. Your little hands will always hold my heart. Now there are just two more little hands to help carry the weight. I could have never imagined the magnitude with which my heart was able to love until I had you boys. Because of you, I am a better mother. It's true—you gave me so much in your time here, and for that I cannot thank you enough.

I know the journey ahead of me is going to be difficult in its own right, but now I have a different perspective on the gift I have been given. I will give Sullivan my all, I will never take him for granted, and I promise I will try my best to be all your little brother deserves. I promise I will tell him all about you and our journey together. I will tell him how loving you was one of the greatest honors of my life. We are a family, Logan—and we always will be—even if we are not all together on this side of heaven.

Our next hello will not end in good-bye. With all my soul, how I long for that day. Just thinking about it now brings tears to my eyes—the moment I get my arms around you, I am never letting go. I will never stop wishing you were here, but I know you are in the one and only place, and with the one and only person who can possibly offer more love to you than I am capable of giving. I am so grateful it is in those arms that you rest tonight. Good night, sweet boy.

Love you to the moon and back,
Mommy

———— ❧ ————

This is a redemptive piece of my story. After all the tears, pain, and all sorts of ugly, Andy and I began a new journey with Sullivan Logan Stewart. Two short years after Sullivan arrived, another pair of hands wrapped themselves tenderly around my heart with the arrival of our third child, Emersyn Grace Stewart.

Without a doubt, those two have been beacons of light in our lives. Sullivan and Emersyn are proof of God's mercy and grace and have been a soothing balm to my very broken and bruised heart. I thank God *every day* for redeeming a piece of our story and bringing so much love and joy into our home once again. They are affirmation of the gracious God we serve—a God of hope, a God of new beginnings, and a God of redemption.

There is nothing else in this world that could compare to the love I have for *all* of my children. After I lost Logan, I wasn't sure if I would ever be capable of loving in such a capacity again, but it's as if the door to my heart that slammed shut after Logan died was blown wide open once more.

God gave me two more *priceless* gifts, and I promise all the days of my life to give them every ounce of love that is within me. I will not take them for granted—not for even a second. As Sullivan and Emersyn grow, I will continue to tell them all about their big brother. One day I will be able to fully explain to them how brave their brother was, and how our family will all be together again someday—and this time forever. My family may be broken, *for now*, but it's still beautiful.

For those of you who have lost one or many little lives and have yet to have a living child, I have an idea what is running through your head. I remember how many people came out of the woodwork saying things like, "I lost my first, too, but now I have three healthy kids." Almost every time someone shared their story of loss, it was followed by, "But *now* I have (fill in the blank)."

It was encouraging to hear it was possible for life to continue and be happy again after loss, but it never provided me much comfort. *Just because God gave you more children doesn't mean He will give me more. That is your story—not necessarily mine. What if I am never able to have another baby? What if they all die?*

Sometimes it's so hard to look back at some of my journal entries and read the thoughts I had, but it is exactly what I was thinking. When others shared their stories of having healthy babies after loss, I would smile and pretend like their words were comforting.

I believe with all my heart that God does not place dreams and desires on our hearts just to dangle them in front of us, always right out of arm's reach. That would be cruel, and our God is anything but. I don't believe He would do such a thing *knowing* we would never be able to get our hands around what we desperately longed to have. I am obviously not God, and I certainly do not know His plan for each and every one of you, but I do know this: He redeemed parts of my story, and He will redeem parts of yours too. It just doesn't always look the way we had originally planned or fit in the timeline or box we tried to design for it. God designed you, and *He* is the one who placed the desire to be a parent on your heart. He did that for a very specific reason, and it's not to torture and tease you throughout life.

Andy and I used to say to each other, "We will be parents again, one way or another." So my prayer for you today is this, that *one way or another*, God would grant your heart's desire and that *one way or another*, you would know the pure joy of not just being a parent by title but also raising a child. Until that day comes, may you feel the overwhelming presence of our Father, and may He give you the grace you need to keep pressing forward.

23 — LETTERS TO HEAVEN: A WALK THROUGH THE YEARS

To every thing there is a season, and a time to every purpose under the heaven: A time to be born, and a time to die; a time to plant, and a time to pluck up what is planted; a time to kill, and a time to heal; a time to break down, and a time to build up; a time to weep, and a time to laugh; a time to mourn, and a time to dance.

—Ecclesiastes 3:1–4 (NKJV)

Rewind with me for a moment to the time *before* Sullivan was born, and Logan's first birthday was heading our way full-steam. I was *very* pregnant. I was exhausted. I was hopeful. I was heartbroken. The world loves to label our losses as old once we get to the one-year mark. By that time, we've been able to process, to cope, to accept, and ultimately to *mend*.

I hope your eye roll was as large as mine as you read that. It's simply not true—not even close. As we neared Logan's birthday, I was *not* healed. I was *not* at peace with Logan's death. Things had *not* returned to normal, and I was *anything* but okay. I couldn't figure out how time had moved so fast, yet somehow, so incredibly slow. I couldn't process how Logan had already been gone 365 days. So yes, you could say my wound was still very fresh—*even* after a year.

To the world, I had passed the allotted time to grieve. I was also pregnant again, so in others' eyes, my "replacement baby" was on the way, and life was good. What is there to be upset about, right?

Again, my eyes are rolling. The notion that twelve quick (or excruciatingly slow) months equate to healing, and the assumption that one child can simply be swapped out for one another, is completely absurd. But again, so is the way our society handles loss. To our culture, I had crossed back to the real world after a *brief* visit on Grief Island, and all was well. But that was far from the truth.

In reality, I was trapped in the juxtaposition of carrying one child in my memory while carrying another in my womb. I was grieving the loss of a son while anticipating the arrival of another. I was a mess, but it had almost been a year and my time of support had, by the world's terms, *expired*.

As we began to near Logan's first birthday, I started to have a lot of anxiety about what the day would look like. The day he was born and the day we lost him were one and the same, so it was both a day of celebration *and* a day of great sadness. Trying to navigate a birthday absent of a birthday boy would be no easy task. The anticipation was brutal. The day itself? It felt off balance, foreign, and heavy. Do we *celebrate* because he lived or *mourn* because he died?

8/9/13

My dearest Logan,

Happy birthday, sweet son. One year has come and gone since you left us, and I can't believe it has already been that long. It feels like a lifetime ago, but somehow, in the same moment, it feels like *only yesterday*. My heart has been so heavy in the weeks and days leading up to today. I'm just not sure how to handle it. How am

I supposed to feel? *Joy*, because I was able to have you, if even for just a moment? *Sorrow*, because, even after a year, my heart aches for you with an intensity I cannot explain? Or maybe even *anger*, as I'm reminded, once again, that instead of having a lifetime of memories with you, I will have a lifetime of days to mourn. I just don't know, Logan.

The only thing I'm sure of is how desperately I miss you. I often wonder who you would have been. What would you have liked and disliked? I don't know the things about you that a mother is supposed to know about her child, and to be honest, it makes me angry. It breaks my heart that I wasn't given the opportunity to know the ins and outs of who you would have been. I'm supposed to know you more than anyone, yet I don't know you at all.

I wish my biggest concern as your birthday approached was trying to decide what present to get or what kind of cake to make. Instead, I'm left trying to figure out how I am supposed to spend a birthday for my child who is no longer here.

Your dad and I went up to Evergreen and sat by the lake as we watched the clock go from 11:43 to 12:37. I felt my pulse begin to quicken and my anxiety rise as the minutes continued to pass and we got closer to the time we lost you. I knew a year ago, at that very moment, we were getting ready to say good-bye. I closed my eyes and relived it all. It was like losing you all over again, except this time I had the foresight of knowing all that would take place in your absence—all the pain, all the sorrow, all the tears. I think I have cried my weight in tears this last year. Actually, I think I have cried much more than that.

We sent you letters on balloons. I know it's kind of childish, but I'm choosing to believe you actually got them. It comforted me to think that maybe, just maybe, the letter I was holding would somehow find its way into your sweet little hands—that *maybe* you weren't that far away after all.

I'm so sorry I didn't write to you for a while. No matter how many times I tried, I just couldn't. I wanted to, I just didn't know how to verbalize what I wanted to say, and I felt so drained that I couldn't find the energy even to try. I was so torn as to how I *should* feel, still very much in the middle of mourning your loss, but at the same time trying to embrace the hope of new life with your little brother growing in my belly. My heart was being torn in two different directions.

I don't want people to think Sullivan is merely a replacement, because he isn't—I could never replace you. Such ways of thinking are unfair to you *both*. I feel like I am obligated to be happy because I am pregnant again, but I'm not fully happy. I am hopeful to be a mother again, but in my mind, having a child *live* feels impossible. And then there is a part of me that feels guilty—like it's a betrayal to you to be happy in anticipation of another baby. I don't know, Logan. I just don't know.

As more time passes, it is becoming more and more obvious that I truly buried a piece of myself with you. I am beginning to accept that there is a part of me that will *always* be missing. I hope, as every year passes, I will find an easier way to navigate your birthday. I know it's an ignorant thought. I think I just need to stop having expectations of how I should or shouldn't feel on the day. Maybe I just need to be okay with being sad. Maybe I need to stop fighting the grief and accept it as a reminder of what I had. It is honestly one of the only things I have left that ties me to you. Maybe I just need to accept that it is okay to hurt no matter how much time has passed.

I hope you are dancing with the angels today, my love. I just can't imagine all the things you have seen and experienced in this last year. What a wonderful day it will be when you finally get to show it all to me. Happy birthday, Logan.

Love you to the moon and back,
Mommy

Years have passed, and Logan's birthday has continued to come and go. Seasons continue to change, and time continues to tick away. Each year on Logan's birthday, I allow myself to sit and remember. No matter how much time passes, in an instant I can be right back where I was many years ago. In my experience, the passage of time has been abstract since the day I lost Logan. Sometimes it even feels like it never happened at all. Then I see evidence of him scattered around my home, and I cannot question his existence.

Many times, throughout the years, my grief visits unexpectedly without warning me of its arrival. However, every time Logan's birthday approaches, I know it is headed at me full steam.

8/9/15

My Sweet Boy,

Every year I hear the same question. August arrives, and it's time to think about your birthday—again. Somehow another year of life absent of you has passed, and all that remains is the question, "What do you want to do for Logan's birthday?"

What do I want to do for your birthday? Now there is a loaded question. I think this year, I would like to answer it differently than I have in the past . . .

I *want* to run into your room, jump on your bed, and yell, "Wake up, Birthday Boy!!"

I *want* to give you kisses and tickles until you open your sweet little eyes and your room fills up with laughter . . .

I *want* to dance and parade our way down the hall to the kitchen where Dad is making his famous Mickey Mouse banana pancakes. Yours, of course, will have chocolate chips and whipped cream today. After all, only the best for my birthday boy . . .

I *want* to sit next to you as you eat, run my fingers through your crazy hair that seems to be a trademark of my children in the morning, and admire God's handiwork . . .

I *want* to bring out the biggest birthday present you have ever seen and watch pure joy consume your face as you squeal in anticipation about what could possibly be hidden inside . . .

I *want* to watch you tear into your package with the zeal and aggression only a little boy could muster and take a picture just at the moment where your eyes finally meet what they were so desperately looking for . . .

I *want* to hide my laughter as your little brother chases you around the house trying to get his little hands on your new possession, as you scream and cry in protest . . .

I *want* to spend the entire day by your side being able to hug you, kiss you, and pick you up and toss you in the air whenever I feel like it . . .

I *want* to look into your big blue eyes, cradle your face in my hands, and tell you how much I love you and how you are my heart's delight . . .

I *want* you to be so tired after such a long and fun day that you fall asleep in your bed before we can even finish our prayers, and I want to stare at your beautiful sleeping face with awe and wonder and thank my King endlessly for you.

But instead . . .

I will go to your resting place, drape my body over where I once buried yours, and cry my weight in tears, because those things will never be, and that is not our story.

I will send you a balloon with a letter saying how I miss you so, and with a childlike faith, I will believe it somehow ended up in your little hands.

And through it all, I will choose to believe that God is good—even though so much around me today screams the opposite. I will choose to thank my King for you, even though I had to say good-bye too soon. Until we meet again, sweet boy.

Love you to the moon and back,
Mommy

8/9/17

My dear, sweet Logan,

I just told Sullivan that today is your birthday. He instantly squealed, clapped his hands, and jumped up and down in anticipation of your big day. He said we should have chocolate cake with chocolate sprinkles—and probably some chocolate cupcakes too. He then casually asked how we were going to go up to heaven to get you.

Moments like this catch my breath. His innocence is so beautiful and refreshing, yet it also cuts deeper than almost anything I have experienced since you've been gone. I told him we couldn't go get you, and the look on his face said it all: "How are we supposed to celebrate Logan's birthday if he's not here?" I ask myself that very question every year.

Sometimes the life I lead feels like a facade. I keep putting one foot in front of the other, make myself continue, consume my time with family, kids, work, and all the while keep forcing down the ever constant—but deeply hidden—need to yell your name. My life is good, but often I live in a perpetual state of denial when it comes to you. This is my normal now, and for the most part, I have learned how to embrace it—well, more so how to tolerate it. I talk about you when given the chance, and most of the time, I am able to do so with a straight face. A select few have the ability occasionally to break through what has become a very thick shell and bring me back to you. In those moments, I allow myself to remember. I sit in the tears, the pain, the ugliness of grief, and *I remember*.

I still laugh, I still smile, but deep beneath it all, *I still hurt*. You're gone. My sweet boy is gone. You should be turning five, and according to your brother, I should be baking a *ridiculous* amount of chocolate treats. *Instead*, I will pick out flowers for your grave. I will take way too long choosing the right ones, fuss over the color scheme, and then meticulously arrange them at your grave because . . . *it's all I can do.* There is nothing else. You are not here, and I cannot "go up to heaven and get you." If only God would let me borrow you back for a day.

And yet, even in your absence, you gave us a great gift this year. Ironically, you are the one doing the giving on your fifth birthday . . .

On the day you were born, we were able to hold you for 54 minutes before Jesus took you home. What is the value of a single minute? Some could argue not much. After all, so many come and go throughout a day, a year, and, ultimately, a lifetime. I would argue that mere minutes create moments, and moments make our memories. Sometimes—like in the story of your life—a memory is all we have to hold on to. The number 54 has since carried a very special meaning in our family. Just a number to some, but to us, it represents *you.*

Your dad figured out recently that 54 in Roman numerals is written out "LIV." You may not understand the significance of this, son, but Roman numerals don't make words often—let alone appropriate ones. Some would say that's a crazy coincidence, but I don't believe in coincidence. I believe God's hand is always moving for a purpose, and I believe He loves us so much that five years ago, He chose the length of your life—down to the minute—so that today, we could be reminded of that great love. Had your life been a moment shorter or a moment longer, we would not have such a beautiful and poignant reminder that you did indeed "LIV." I need that reminder today as we try to navigate *yet another birthday* without our birthday boy.

I then realized, for the first time in five years, that we actually could get you something for your birthday. Forever "LIV" will mark my skin the same way your life has marked my heart. Now, every time I look at my wrist, I will see you. I will carry a piece of you with me wherever we go, I will honor your life proudly for all to see, and for you, my sweet boy, I will "LIV" this life to the fullest until the day I, too, am called home.

Thank you for reminding us to keep pressing forward, even when we cannot see where God is taking us. Thank you for reminding us we can trust His direction and trust His character, even when we don't understand His ways. And lastly, thank you for reminding us that even if God leaves *mountains immovable*, we can still know for certain that He is good.

Happy birthday, my love. I am sorry I cannot be with you today.

Love you to the moon and back,
Mommy

Photo by Chesney Midcap

8/9/18

My beautiful son,

Every year, as your birthday approaches, I am at a loss for words. Yet when I finally find myself facing the day of your birth and death, the words pour out endlessly, almost as if they have been held silent by a dam, just waiting for that one time a year when I allow myself to open the floodgates. I only write to you once a year. I used to write to you every day, and then gradually it became a few times a month, and then a few times a year, and now—August 9th.

I also used to hate Thursdays, because you died on a Thursday. And then, eventually, I stopped counting the weekdays and just hated the ninth of every month. Now, six years from your death, I no longer count weeks, and I no longer count months. I only keep track of one day a year. Just so happens that day is today. Ironically, it also happens to be a Thursday—a bit of an extra punch in the gut to put on my tab for the day. In a way, we have come full circle, yet I still don't have a party to host or a cake to make. I don't have a birthday boy to spoil. I don't know what else to do, so I do the only thing I can to honor you: I write.

Your birthday seems to be the one time I find the energy to do something I truly love but at the same time find incredibly draining. If I'm honest, it's like having a one-sided conversation. Like spending too much time picking out the perfect gift, wrapping it beautifully, waiting anxiously for the big day to arrive, and then putting it on a shelf to *forever* collect dust. I pour my heart and soul into your letters and try my best to believe they somehow actually end up in your little hands. *But do they?*

The child within me wants to jump up and down and scream, "Yes! Have some faith! Of course they do!" The practical adult in me looks down at that very child and rolls her eyes. Here's the thing, Logan: the Bible says in heaven there is no sadness, no tears, no heartache. My letters, in contrast, are *always* sad. How could they not be? You are not here. My life is blessed. My heart is full. But there is still this intense ache and this hole in the shape of you. I guess I just don't think it's realistic for you to read my letters, because they would in turn make you sad.

I know God can do anything and of course has the ability to filter you from the pain and still let you get glimpses of me, but do you see the bigger problem? Something so sad has *no place* somewhere free of sorrow. Even if God would show them to you, I almost wouldn't want Him to. I don't ever want you to feel what I do. I never want you to know this pain. So today, on your sixth birthday, I am doing things a bit differently.

In the Bible, God tells us to have "childlike faith," and in that spirit, today I am also resorting to "childlike reasoning." After this, I may be the one now getting the eye rolls, but it's for you, son, so I simply don't care. This year, I celebrate you. This year, I am doing my best through the tears to make this a joyful day and a letter full of just one thing: love. This year, I will send you something different, something that maybe, being void of my pain, might make it past those pearly gates and into your beautiful hands.

So, God, this is in your hands now. Would you please make sure it gets to my son?

Dear Logan,

Happy birthday, baby boy! All I want to tell you today is how much I love you and how proud I am that you are mine. There is a story I told you long ago, that I now tell your brother and sister often. Today, for your birthday, I want to tell it to you again . . .

One day, God was creating a heart. He took extra time and special care with this heart, and when He was finished, He said to Himself, "Wow! This is one of the most beautiful hearts I have ever made! It is full of so much compassion and love! It looks a lot like mine. Now, who in the world should I give this heart to?" So He searched and He searched and He searched, and then He finally said, "Of course! Logan Andrew Stewart! He is exactly who I made this incredible heart for!" He then put that beautiful creation into you and breathed his life into it. *Ba-bum! Ba-bum! Ba-bum!* And that, my boy, is the day your heart started beating. God gave you a heart overflowing with compassion for others, Logan, and He is going to use it to change the world. So now, take that precious gift, let His light shine out of it, and go change the world!

And guess what, Logan? God did exactly that. Through your heart, He is changing the world. You, sweet boy, are making a difference in ways you would never imagine, and I couldn't be prouder. I cannot wait to tell you all that has happened because of you. I can't wait for you to run into my arms so I can hold your face in my hands and tell you just how delighted I am that you are mine.

I love you, buddy. Now go have the best birthday ever and take a very special birthday walk with the Creator of your heart. I can only imagine time in heaven is different from time here, so, at the end of that walk, turn around, and maybe I will be there.

I love you to the moon and back,

Mommy

Thank you, God, for giving me not just one but three *of your most beautiful creations. Why you chose me for such incredible gifts I do not know. I don't deserve them, but I am forever grateful. What I do know is this: my Logan the Compassionate, my Sullivan the Loving, and my Emersyn the Brave, will change this world, and I have a front row seat to watch it happen. Today, above all else, I choose to focus on that.*

For as long as I have breath, I will write to Logan on his birthday. It is one thing that ties us together, and one of the *only* ways I feel I can still be a mother to him. I long for the day when I will no longer need to write to Logan, because I will be where he is. There is just so much distance to travel between where I am and where he waits.

PART II:

IN THE WAITING

W hen you have a child in heaven, a piece of your heart is there too. Forever changed and incomplete, a part of you walks through this life desperately waiting for the next. A silent but ever-present battle ensues. We sit on the fence of this life and eternity, not sure which side to fight for—not sure where we belong. In this season of waiting, there is much to learn. In the waiting, joy and sorrow can coexist. In the waiting, beauty can be found among the ashes. In the waiting, faith can grow. In the waiting, God is still good. *Logan, my sweet boy, this is the space between here and you.*

The following chapters hold the moments I've experienced and the lessons I've learned on the road of infant loss. I wish I could say my journey mirrored only health and wisdom, but that wouldn't be entirely true. In reality, some things were carried well and some things weren't carried well at all—but we did learn a thing or two along the way. I hope and pray the road we walked (both the good moments and the bad) can serve as a baseline to those of you who have found yourself on a similar path. No one would choose for their feet to find this unthinkable road, but we are here nonetheless—so let's go for a walk.

24 — WALK WITH ME

Carry each other's burdens, and in this way you will fulfill the law of Christ.

—Galatians 6:2 (NIV)

Photo by Jessica Fox

The summer after Sullivan was born, we signed up for a 5K that supported the infant loss community. For the walk, each team was encouraged to make a shirt with their baby's name on it—an idea I absolutely loved. I knew I wanted a big 54 on the back to honor the minutes we were able to be with Logan, but other than that, I had no idea what to do. I reached out to my sister-in-law, Emily, who is a talented graphic designer, and asked if she could help with the design.

To my delight, when she sent over a mock-up, right above Logan's name were the words "Walk with me." *Walk with me.* I said it over and over in my head several times, and each time a bigger and bigger smile emerged on my face. I had no idea how or where she came up with the three simple but immensely powerful words, but it did something to my heart.

That is exactly what parents on this journey need, I thought. *We need people to walk with us. Not drag us. Not make our pace match theirs. Not be on our heels with a stopwatch, yelling that we go faster, but to walk with us. Hmm . . . I really, really love that.*

And from that day on, the phrase stuck with me. I filed it in the part of my mind where we store things we know we will need to remember *someday* for *something.*

Let's rewind all the way back to Logan's sermon at Red Rocks Church and the pull on our hearts that God was going to use us to build something new. For years after Logan died, I felt God tenderly pushing me in a direction I didn't understand, but I believed each and every day the picture of His new calling on my life would eventually become clear. *If you lead, God, I will follow. You are doing . . . something . . . and despite the cost, despite what you ask of me, I will follow You.*

I'm sure on the surface it sounds inspirational and beautiful—like Andy and I took a giant, blind leap of faith over a canyon's edge while holding the remnants of our broken hearts in our outstretched hands. Just at the moment where gravity *should* win, our feet landed on the invisible path God placed there to catch us. This path would take us over the obstacles, the dangers, and the trials below. It would safely guide us to the other side, where all our questions would be answered and all our needs for the mission would be fulfilled.

Well, as poetic as it sounds, that is exactly how it *didn't* happen. The process was slow, complicated, and full of more challenges than I ever could have imagined. In order to build new things in me, old things had to be torn down. God had to remold my heart, and the process was painful—*incredibly* painful. He pushed me and my family to our limits and asked us to do things I would have before thought impossible.

I often questioned God on why He didn't just give me certain talents, strengths, and abilities from the start, since He knew I would one day need them. It seemed *if only* He had built me differently, the process would have been much easier in the end—for me at least. But I knew there was purpose in the process and that He had built me exactly the way He intended.

The level of sacrifice along the way was steeper than I care to admit. I learned opposition didn't mean God wasn't *for* us, but that someone else was *against* us. I learned my pain was actually a weapon—that what Satan meant to destroy my family would one day, and through God's grace, hold other families together.

And so, in 2015, with Andy and Kelley by my side, and after enough blood, sweat, and tears to last us *several* lifetimes, a nonprofit was born. A name had sat in the recesses of my mind for two years and I *finally* understood why. *Walk With Me*—a place where loving hands could meet broken hearts.

We now willingly immerse ourselves in the infant loss world, where our heart, as you can guess, is helping families through the unthinkable. *Walk With Me* was born out of heartache—out of lessons learned from stumbling around in the dark and learning how *not* to walk the road of grief. It was born out of the love I had for a little boy for which I had no outlet. It was driven by the anger of losing my son and hoping my marriage wasn't next. It was born out of loneliness—out of the desire to be affirmed in my grief and simply understood, but knowing so few truly had the ability to understand. It was born out of frustration that our culture is so afraid of grief and often chooses to look away from those in the midst of it. *Walk With Me* is the physical manifestation of my broken heart's desperate cries in those early years. It's what Andy and I longed for but didn't have enough of.

Our organization now has the honor of walking into the most delicate and tragic parts of life, where we get to meet children *few* will ever see. We get to hear stories *few* will ever know and have the privilege of being trusted in the sacred spaces into which *few* are invited. The weight and responsibility of what we have been gifted is beautiful, heartbreaking, and not lost on us.

We offer support and education at local hospitals, donate keepsake kits, and have a mission to educate our community and change the way our society looks at grief. We provide families with counseling, support groups, community events, and financial assistance for things no parent should ever have to pay for—like the cremation or burial of their child. Most importantly, though, we provide the supportive community that every bereaved parent deserves *and* needs, but rarely finds. We are a safe place. Together, we remember, honor, and celebrate babies. Together, we fight for hope.

What started as a legacy for Logan has turned into the legacy of hundreds of children. God's hand designed it from the beginning. It is beauty and heartache wrapped so seamlessly and intricately that the two cannot be separated. In so many ways, *Walk With Me **is*** my baby. It's all I have left of Logan. As much as I *still* wish my story with him had been different, I am grateful to have a place where I can see his beautiful fingerprints. Logan is the heartbeat of *Walk With Me*, and I am immensely proud to call him mine.

Losing Logan changed the trajectory of my life. I lost my world the day he died, and now, in a plan only God could have designed, infant loss *is* my world. My story, as broken as it may be, is now my strength. I can still feel God telling me there is more, and if I'm being honest, I still struggle to know what He means. For now, I know He wants me to share, and as long as I have a voice, I will do just that.

8/9/19

Sweet Boy,

Another year has come and gone. My world has circled the sun seven times now since you first left. I have woken up 2,556 times without the ability to say good morning and kiss your sweet face. I have gone to bed 2,556 times without the ability to tuck you in and say our prayers together. I have missed reading you books, making you snacks, kissing your ouchies, watching you cruise around playgrounds and tickling your tummy until laughter-filled tears rolled down your cheeks—more times than I could possibly count. Now take that unknown number and multiply it by a million. That's the amount of times I have missed cradling your head in my hands, looking into your big blue eyes, and saying, "I love you." You are not in the world I'm in, and I'm never going to be okay with it.

I feel like I am having to fight to celebrate your birthday this year. I can't even fully explain why. We have done our usual routine. The grief and hope dance is similar as in years past, but something just feels *different*. I feel like the further I get away from you, the harder I have to convince this world that you and this day are important.

Why does what is so obvious to me (seemingly) feel so foreign and excessive to others?

People assume time equals healing. Many people believe the process of mending a broken heart is linear. Almost as if we carry our grief in a bag hurled over one shoulder, and with every step we take, a grain of our sadness falls through the bottom. Almost as if with enough steps and enough time, our grief will eventually "disappear." Unfortunately, that just isn't true.

Grief changes and evolves, but it never fully leaves. The only consistent part of grief is its inconsistency. It's not a wound that heals and leaves a scar. It's a wound that scabs over and then is repeatedly torn wide open again and again with no warning. Time doesn't equal healing in the way most assume—time just changes how much (or how little) my wound bleeds. Time is simply a Band-Aid on top of a chronic wound.

This year I feel like the world is looking down at me with a megaphone saying, "Your time is up, Jamie. Your 'almost son' had his moment. Stop fighting. We are tired of listening. Raise the white flag and move on."

Well, the world picked a fight with the wrong family. The world around us hasn't paid close enough attention and has overlooked the army we are building. We are training this army to teach those whose feet have freshly touched the unfortunate gravel of this road, that they never need to succumb to the pressure of "moving on." We are going to teach them that grief is *normal* and has no timeline. We are going to teach them the healthy way to walk this path. And slowly, one family at a time, this army will grow. We will set an example and one day the world will be the one to raise its white flag.

Lately, I've had pockets of tension when it comes to the dreams I have for *Walk With Me* and its future. If we stay small, I know we are still making a difference. It makes me feel bad when I dream big about all *Walk With Me* could become. Greedy almost—like I should be happy and content with where we are and all we have accomplished. Maybe I am worried my intentions are not pure?

Maybe I am letting pride take the wheel? I can't explain it, but something has changed in the last month.

I'm not sure how, but a fire is growing, and it is not fueled by status or pride or power. Rather, by compassion and love and empathy. I realized all this time I have not been dreaming too big. I have been dreaming *too small*. This is so much bigger than all of us, Logan, and it is not *because* of us but *in spite* of us. We are *so* flawed and cannot take any credit. God is just that good. All I know is that you, sweet boy, have started a movement. I can almost see you and Jesus looking down at us with big grins, shaking your heads back and forth and saying, "They have no idea what's coming . . . "

In all of this, the hardest pill for me to swallow is still the fact that I don't know the inner workings of you. I am your mother, and I should know you better than anyone, and yet, I'm left to wonder who you would have been. What would you have loved? What would you have been scared of? Would you have been into sports, music, or art? Maybe all three? What would my CliffsNotes response have been when someone asked about my oldest child?

Your little brother has a *huge* heart. He is a feeler and has big responses with everything he does. He analyzes all he sees and is very cautious of his surroundings. His mind is very calculated, and he wants to know how everything works. Self-preservation is at the top of his list. He is gentle and kind (with the exception of his interactions with your little sister, because he beats her up quite a bit). CliffsNotes explanation—*Sullivan is my sensitive and compassionate kid.*

Your little sister, on the other hand, couldn't be more different. She is a tomboy in a princess dress. She loves all things girly on the surface, but is as rough and tough as most little boys on the inside. Her spicy attitude assures me she is going to be strong and independent. She is a leader, will try almost anything without hesitation, and is as resilient as they come. CliffsNotes explanation—*Emersyn is my brave and courageous kid.*

So where does that put you, Logan? It drives me crazy that I do not know.

Last year, we decided your favorite food was Italian and that would be the cuisine we eat every year on your birthday. This year, we decided your favorite color was yellow—like a sunflower, of course. Your cousins agreed that you didn't really like traditional cake but preferred the ice cream variety instead. As a result, your grandparents bought you one this year. Looks like our tradition is growing. Your aunt Kelley said you definitely loved ducks and Macho Man Randy Savage. That one makes me laugh and certainly would have made for an interesting combo of bedroom decor. But hey, kids are weird, so it sounds good to me.

We are *slowly* putting you together, and there is healing in that, but in all honesty, I will not know you until heaven. The reality of that just sucks. Sometimes I wonder how I will even know it is you. And then I remember my heart is tethered to yours, and I'll know simply because *you are mine.* Your heart grew inside of me— how silly to think I would not recognize it. In the words of Nancy Tillman, "I'd know you anywhere, my love."

This evening an actual piece of you suddenly became clear to me. Almost as if God gave me a small and unexpected gift as the day came to a close. God built *Walk With Me* around *you.* He is a master designer who is intentional with His every move. Nothing is ever wasted or without reason. *Walk With Me* is a part of you, and pieces of you are mirrored throughout it. It's so obvious, in this moment, that I can't believe it took this long to realize.

You are a defender, an advocate, and a guardian.

It is echoed in the organization crafted all around you. You stand up for those who cannot stand on their own. Your heart hurts for the hurting. You, Logan, are my kid who *protects.* Finally, a *real* piece of you I can hold on to. Thank you, God, for this small and priceless gift. I definitely needed it today.

I asked Sullivan what he thought you did today. His response? "I think he blew me a kiss." You know what? I bet he was right. He also told me to tell you, "I love you so so much." Emersyn was more concerned with your birthday dessert selection, but she loves you too. She has actually been sleeping with your bear and carrying it around like a prize everywhere she goes.

Happy birthday, Logan—my protector and world-changing kid. You are the absolute delight of my heart.

Love you to the moon and back,
Mommy

You are about to dive into the second half of this book, and it's going to look a bit different. At this point, you know every layer and detail of my story. I left nothing out, because I wanted you to come to a place where you trust me with your heart *and* your sorrow. Sometimes we must hear things that are hard. But if that message is coming from a place of trust, where we feel safe, then we likely will be more receptive. That is where I hope and pray we find our relationship today. I hope you take my words to heart, and when I occasionally must touch on topics that are difficult, I hope you receive them, wrapped in the love and compassion with which they were written.

I certainly don't have all the answers. All I have is what I've learned from *my* journey. We are all different creations. We all have different stories, different wounds—different grief. There is no one-size-fits-all advice when it comes to winning the crappiest of lotteries ever. But I have been immersed in the pregnancy and infant loss world for nearly a decade now, and I have learned a thing or two. My hope and prayer for the second half of this book is to share that knowledge with *you*.

A fair warning for those of you who have *not* lost a child—the pages ahead are going to be hard for you too. Being a safe place for a loss-mom or loss-dad is no easy task, and your supportive role in this story will require some moments of self-reflection. Certain passages ahead will very possibly leave you feeling confused, frustrated, and at a complete loss of what to do. At certain times you may want to throw your hands in the air and this book in the trash.

Please don't. When those moments present themselves, push through. My intention is not to put a big red "wrong" stamp on everything you have done or hope to do. It is simply to provide insight into the tumultuous mind of a grieving parent. Sometimes the takeaway is simple, and sometimes it's anything but. The road ahead for you is absolutely walkable—as long as you pay close attention to where you step.

Andy and I often joke that "everyone needs a Kelley." Kelley is what I wish *every* family had after experiencing the death of their child. She was someone on the "outside" who felt a lot more like someone on the "inside." She was the epitome of wisdom, empathy, and grace. She is the friend everyone needs, but the friend not everyone has.

For that very reason, I've asked her to chime in at those places where some may begin to flounder. My hope is that her knowledge can counterbalance my experience—that she can take what I am trying to teach and make it simple and tangible for you. I promise she will equip you, if you just give her the chance. *Everyone* needs a Kelley—now you have one too.

If our experiences and the lessons God has taught us can help you in even the *tiniest* of ways—if we can spare you even a *fragment* of unnecessary pain—then I consider this a win. The chapters ahead are filled with the moments I have experienced and the lessons I have learned as I walk the road that will—one day—lead to Logan's arms. These next chapters are my life *in the waiting*.

THROUGH KELLEY'S EYES

Grief is messy. Life is messy. So it should be no surprise that life with grief is—you guessed it—totally messy. Supporting a grieving loved one as they learn to navigate life with loss isn't going to be a clean-cut process. If this happens to be your role in someone's story, please remember that as we embark on Part II of this book together. As we listen to grieving parents' pain expressed in raw ways, there are some realities you need to come to terms with. Loss sucks! It's tough and oh-so-overwhelming. So naturally, reading about it is also going to be all of those things for you too.

Sometimes we can make tweaks along the way that can prevent us from creating more damage. Sometimes we can't. That feeling of helplessness is uncomfortable. To be a support person will often mean that you have to *learn* to be comfortable in that space. Understand that you will not be able to be everything to everyone. Understand that you will not be able to fix this. Understand that at some point your feelings may be hurt and you may feel offended, and you may also hurt or offend someone you love. I once heard a pastor say that to be an effective lover of people, we have to have thick skin and soft hearts.

So that is my challenge to you. Be present, be patient, and have lots of grace for yourself and your loved one. Doing life together is hard . . . but it is also beautiful.

25 — THE "SICKNESS" CALLED GRIEF

Tears blur my eyes. My body and soul are withering away. I am dying from grief; my years are shortened by sadness. Sin has drained my strength; I am wasting away from within.

—Psalm 31:9–10 (NLT)

Photo by Jessica Fox

"They should be better by now. They should be over it at this point. They need to move on. This is starting to get unhealthy."

In my world, I hear comments like this far too often. I hear them echoed from defeated faces feeling shame and guilt, because according to the world swirling around them, they are doing this thing called grief "wrong." Careless and ignorant statements like this waken the mama bear within me, which somehow continues to grow bigger and more protective with each passing year. *Our society is broken.*

Our society is broken in the way it handles grief and those deep within its trenches. Our society is broken in the way it turns its back on the sorrowful because it's just too uncomfortable to look. A trend has set in where those in mourning are not only isolated but put on the clock. With a timer in one hand and a bouquet of flowers in the other, our culture looks down at the bereaved and says, "It's okay that you're not okay—*for now.*" And the clock starts ticking.

Our culture "accepts" grief to a point, but after that threshold is crossed, it is deemed excessive, over the top, or even *unhealthy.* There is a deep tension between what is seen as normal and what is not. The bereaved are lined up and categorized by how "well" they handle their loss. As if intensity and duration need to be put in a society-built box of what is considered "appropriate." And so, I'll say it again: *our society is broken.*

How can a broken society with broken norms and broken expectations properly care for *the broken?* Simply put, it can't and it doesn't. Certainly not in the way they deserve to be cradled, uplifted, and loved on. As a result, the grieving are left to live in a world that makes them feel isolated, judged, and downright crazy. They are expected to survive—and eventually thrive—in a world that is foreign, scary, and seemingly against them. Even in the most perfect of healing environments, the grief-stricken see the world as overwhelming and spinning far too fast. So what chance do they have to make it here, in a culture that teaches them (and everyone else) that what they carry is an illness?

A massive disservice has taken root in our society and continues to grow deeper and wider with each passing year. Along with it? The distance between the *real* process of grief and our culture's expectations. This disconnect has become nothing short of toxic.

And so, here I am—one tiny speck looking up at a very big world and speaking for all those who are too weak to speak, standing for all those who are too weak to stand. This is my cry to you, big world. If nothing else, please hear this.

Our grief is not something to cure.

It is not an illness. It is not a disease. We are not an epidemic, and we need for you to stop treating us as such. We are not sick—we are sad. Our sorrow is not something to get over; it is something we must go through. It's messy, and it's ugly, and it doesn't ever fully go away.

You see, we grieve intensely because we love intensely. If you have ever opened your heart to love, then you, too, are susceptible to this very grief. You may see my heart beating, and I may look okay, but what you don't see is that my heart aches with every beat. For the rest of my days, it is going to hurt, because it is forever changed and, now, incomplete.

So please put down your clock and stop looking for a treatment.

Stop trying to fix me. Stop trying to solve my problems. Don't cover your eyes. Don't look the other way. Instead, sit with me. Cry with me. Validate my pain. Be okay with my sorrow, and provide me a safe place to learn how to walk again.

And when your time of great sadness comes? I will do the same for you.

Change has to start somewhere. Too many generations have had to walk the road of grief alone and ashamed. It wasn't okay then and it's not okay now. It's time for the world to stop being uncomfortable with grief and shying away from the unknown. It's time to make grief *normal*.

Lastly, this is my whisper to you, broken friend, sitting all alone in that dark and messy place, with a heart seeping countless tears and a mind wondering if the pain will ever relent: *It's okay that you are not okay. Period.*

I know your grief feels claustrophobic, overwhelming, unending. But the heaviness will begin to lift one day. You are not alone. Your sadness is for a good reason, and your tears are *not* too many. Grief has no timeline. You are not doing this wrong. It hurts—and that's okay. The road you are on is long and difficult, but it can be traversed. You will learn to walk again, even if you must do so with a limp. Until then, one moment at a time, one day at a time, and one step at a time.

You still have so much life to live. Happier days are on the horizon, even if they are too far off to see now. Yes, you will always be broken, but even a broken crayon can color. The world doesn't know any better because it doesn't understand. So help it understand. Tell your story. Share your pain. Only then can we—the broken—break the stigma.

26 – LOSS SUPPORT 101

When someone is going through a storm, your silent presence is more powerful than a million, empty words.

—Thema Davis

Photo by Jessica Fox

I often get asked my advice for walking alongside and supporting someone who has lost a baby. I have received *countless* text messages, emails, and frantic calls from family members and friends desperately searching for answers and aid in their newfound chaos.

When we hear horrific news, most minds instantly shift into work mode. *What can I do? How can I help? A card? Flowers? Food? All of the above? Should I offer to watch their kids? Clean their house? Help with funeral arrangements?*

These are all great and necessary things; however, step one is acknowledgment, which should mirror your relationship (or lack thereof) with the family. Families who just endured a significant loss are in shock, *even if the loss was expected.* What they need is time to process. They need to be surrounded *only* by those closest to them—those who are a part of their inner circle. For me, that *only* included my immediate family. Mostly Kelley and my mom. For some, that may not include anyone. I know the inclination is to run over with open arms and a plate of food, but it is very important to give the family the time they need to stop spinning from the disorienting recoil of loss.

Outside our immediate family, Andy and I didn't talk to *anyone* for almost a week. We probably would have stayed secluded much longer had it not been for Logan's memorial service and the obvious need to interact. We received texts but didn't respond to them. We got cards but didn't open them. We appreciated all the love and support, but in no way were we ready to face *anyone.* It was too fresh a wound. I could hardly get out of bed, let alone care about seeing or responding to my community.

I am not advocating isolation by any means, so please don't misunderstand. Again, it's absolutely necessary to reach out in the manner that best reflects the depth of your relationship. If you are a close family member or a "2 a.m. friend" (the person you would call in a middle-of-the-night emergency), then you need to be available—*fully* available.

Kelley literally fed me grapes. Grapes! I wouldn't eat, but she knew her place and role in my life, and fed me when I didn't care to do it myself. If you are that person for a friend who has experienced pregnancy or infant loss, clean their house, watch their other kids, do some laundry, mow their lawn, feed them grapes. *Just be present.* Don't wait for them to ask for help, and don't ask them what they need—at this point they truly don't know. Just show up and do *something.* Even if that means sitting in their living room while they rest. They may just need to know you are there.

If you are a good friend (but not necessarily a "2 a.m. friend"), then reaching out through a call or text to offer your condolences is appropriate. If you aren't very close, a card in the mail is a great way to send the additional love and support they still desperately need.

But here's the kicker: don't be offended if you are met with silence. In fact, expect it. Have *zero* expectations for a response. Show your love and support, but always be aware of the family's need for privacy. Even at a distance, you can still be helpful in practical ways.

Coordinate with those closest to the family and set up or contribute to a meal train. Leave a cooler out front of the house so food can be dropped off in a "no contact" manner. That way, grievers can decide *if* they want to interact or not. Bringing a meal helps in two ways: it enables those on the outside to show their support *and* it is incredibly needed for the grieving family. In those early days, it requires way too much energy to meal-plan and cook, energy that is simply not there. Remember my grapes?

If you are close enough, and the family has small living children, offer to watch them for a few hours. Little people don't fully understand what is going on and why Mom and Dad are acting differently. However, that does not affect the amount of supervision and attention they need. So take the kids out to get some fresh air. Give the parents a few-hour break so they can take a nap, take a shower, or just have space to grieve completely uninhibited. If the family is going to hold a memorial service, offer to help coordinate. Flowers, food, venue, balloons, photos—find out where they could use some help from the person coordinating the service.

The extended family needs support, too, and while you may not be best friends with the parents, maybe you *are* best friends with a grandmother, an aunt, or an uncle. Use that extra energy you have to pour into *them*. After all, they are giving all they have and need to be refilled too. Be the person to *support* the supporters.

Above all else, just remember: what the family needs later on far exceeds what they need during the first days following a loss. If you want to be a support, and if you want to step up, then in the weeks, months, and years (yes, *years)* that follow, don't forget they are living life with a chunk of their hearts missing. If you really want to stand out, be the person who reaches out when everyone else has forgotten. Be the person who *remembers*.

—⁂—

I may know a lot when it comes to baby loss, but what I *don't* know is how it feels to *watch* someone you love endure it. Throughout our experience, Kelley was a near-flawless pillar of support. She has always had our mom's nursemaid heart, and it shone through effortlessly when her nephew died. My entire family was actually quite amazing, but unfortunately, I know that is not the experience everyone has.

In light of her innate ability to support, I asked Kelley to write a letter to all of you who are on the outside looking in. I hope and pray it can offer you a little insight on the best way to show your love to those who are broken.

Dear friends and family of grievers,

I know someone you love has lost something no one should ever have to lose, and you're just trying to hold it all together. I know all you are is being poured into that loved one right now, and it doesn't feel like enough—not even close. I know this isn't about you or me, but I want you to know I see how much you are hurting, I see how hard you are trying, and I know how helpless you feel. You, too, have lost so much. Please know you are not alone in this struggle. The following are some important things I have learned as I continue to do life alongside my sister and her husband since the loss of their son Logan in 2012. May this serve as a small guide to you as you embark on this journey with us. I am so sorry that you have found yourself here.

The first—and maybe *most*—important thing you need to know about this journey is that you get to choose whether or not to be on it. Please choose wisely! Once the dust clears, you quickly discover there are two types of friends and family: the ones who are going to grab on to their loved ones with a death grip, no matter how tough that proves to be, and the ones who are just too uncomfortable with someone else's grief and choose to turn their backs. Please don't run away. I promise you will regret it. Nothing about this is going to be easy, and I know you feel so inadequate in this situation. Guess what? We all do.

By sticking around, I guarantee you will probably do and say the wrong thing more than once. But I promise you, it is way better to stay and mess up than it is to abandon the ones you love. Please know, even if you *could* always say and do all the right things, you still would not be able to fix their brokenness. That is way above your pay grade—it's not your job to fix. *Your* job is to stick with the people you love, no matter what life throws at you. If you leave, not only will your loved one feel more alone, but so will you. Once again, I beg you, please choose wisely!

Another lesson I learned was the importance of sitting with your loved ones *in* their grief. I know our natural inclination is to try to encourage and uplift the ones we care about when they are feeling down, but when it comes to a grieving parent, you have to let them feel what they need to feel, for as long as they need to feel it. They need to know that you see them right where they are. Don't try to justify—just listen. Be with them in their sadness, their confusion, their anger, and their despair. It's okay to acknowledge that the loss of their precious child just really sucks and that it's totally unbearable. I've noticed that when encouragement is given by people solely because they are too uncomfortable being around someone's grief, it is usually more hurtful than helpful. Encourage the ones you love when you feel genuinely led to, but you also must be genuinely okay with their grief.

Talk about the baby who was lost—by name. Talk about how beautiful and perfect they are. How they have their mother's nose and their father's crooked toe. When something reminds you of the time you had with them, call or text their parents and tell them. When you gather together as a family for holidays or special occasions, acknowledge that their child is absent and deeply missed. Acknowledge all the things you wanted to do with their child and what you think they would have been like as they grew.

I know you are afraid you might make them sad or ruin their day by talking about their loss, but I guarantee they are always thinking about their child. When you speak up, they know you are too. I've heard, time and time again, that one of a bereaved parent's greatest fears is that one day their child will be forgotten. I know you will never forget the baby your loved ones lost; just make sure their parents know that too. Remember important dates—birthdays, the day their baby passed, their due date, etc.— and set reminders so you don't forget *those* days for the rest of *your* days. I know that may seem extreme, but grief *is* extreme and it lasts a *lifetime*.

Remember, once someone becomes a parent, they are a parent for life—no matter what. So please, refer to your loved ones as parents, even if they have no living children. *Always* acknowledge them on the toughest days, like Mother's Day, Father's Day, Christmas, etc.

Someday down the road, if your loved ones *do* have more children (or if they already do), make sure you always include the child they lost anytime you mention to others how many kids they have. The same goes for when discussing the number of grandchildren in the family or the number of nieces and nephews.

My sister always talks about how she isn't just grieving the day Logan died; she's grieving every birthday she doesn't get to spend with him, the day he would have graduated, his wedding day, and the ability to watch him holding his own children. Please understand, this loss is a loss for life.

I know it may feel overwhelming learning to stay on top of all the information I just gave you, but I promise you'll get the hang of it. A simple rule of thumb in most situations is to treat the baby who was lost like any of the other children in your family that you are blessed to be with on this side of heaven. Once you are given a child, they are yours forever, and even death cannot change that.

After Logan died, I remember feeling like my sister had died right along with him, and it was heart-wrenching. I was hurting and confused and missed my sister dearly. I'm sure many of you may feel like this too—like a precious young life wasn't all you lost that day. *Please don't give up hope.* The ones you love will never be the same after suffering a loss like this, but they will slowly start to get back pieces of who they once were. Your family will experience laughter again and know great joy. While you are waiting, please make sure you get the support *you* need. You matter too. I know nothing may feel further from the truth right now, but through it all, I still know God is good. He is kind, and He is always watching over us even when it doesn't feel like it. Be patient, and you will see Him at work.

Blessings,
Kelley

—∞—

At the end of this book, you will find the link to *Walk With Me*'s website and there you will find many other helpful resources. With the help of my team, we have compiled as much information as possible to educate anyone willing to dive deeper in. It's not a perfect or exhaustive list, but it's a start.

If you are watching someone you care about grieve, the best thing you can do is educate yourself. Learn as much as you can, and when you think you've learned enough, dive back in and learn some more. It's a *sacrifice of time* but an *act of love*. And loving someone *that* beautifully may even turn you into a "2 a.m. friend."

THROUGH KELLEY'S EYES

I want to share an incredible piece of wisdom with you all. We have shared this premise countless times, and will continue using it for years to come because it is just that good. It's called the "Ring Theory" and is a crisis model created by Dr. Susan Silk and Barry Goldman. When in a supportive role, it's simple, practical and memorable. We have come to call it "pouring in and dumping out."

Picture a target. The middle of the target represents the party who "owns" a loss more than any other. In this case, it's the parents of an infant who has passed away (or in general, the person facing the trauma). Every ring outside the middle represents individuals who are further removed from the loss. For example, ring number two might be family. Ring three, close friends; ring four, neighbors or coworkers; and so on.

The idea is simple. Anyone in an outer ring should pour their time, energy, and resources into the rings closer to the middle than theirs, with the *most* effort landing on the bull's-eye: the loss-parents themselves. That's the "pour in" section. The "dump out" idea works the exact opposite way. Any crappy, difficult, or messy feelings that are repercussions of the loss have to be *dumped out* or shared with people in rings *further out from your own.*

The "dump out" portion is equally important to the "pour in" portion. Varying degrees of collateral damage are inevitable for everyone when a trauma has been endured. If you are within one of the inner rings, there will come a point when you will need to "dump out" to someone. This doesn't make you a bad person; loss is just hard. Make sure the person you share your ugly with is a safe person who can make you feel seen and justified (without adding to the struggle of those in rings closer to the target). The takeaway is simple – support, love, and understanding go in, venting, complaining, and frustrations go out.

As helpful as this model is, there is one last thing I would add and it's something that should freely flow in and out of *all* the rings. That thing is *grace*. Patience and forgiveness are paramount in this system, because regardless of how hard we try, we are still human. And that means at some point, despite our good intentions, we will fail. But when grace like a lens covers that target, it creates ample space for both our grief and our humanity to exist in harmony.

27 — IN SICKNESS AND IN HEALTH

Therefore what God has joined together, let no one separate.
—Mark 10:9 (NIV)

Photo by Jessica Fox

M en and women are different creations. God designed us to do life with one another, but in so many capacities, we are completely separate beings. Just like the pieces of a puzzle that fit together only because they are opposites, the same is true with God's creation. We were made *uniquely* so we can fit together *perfectly.*

As God molded us, He gave each of us characteristics to complement one another. These pieces were designed to counterbalance each other. Where one is weak, the other is strong. God wove these things into our DNA, and while a woman may have been made *from* a man, women could not be more different than men.

I didn't fully realize the depth of *how* different men and women truly were until I started comparing my grief to Andy's. Grieving alongside him confirmed the difference between us wasn't just surface-level—it went all the way down to the core of who we were.

After Logan's death, our relationship evolved into something so different and unfamiliar, even compared to just months earlier, when we were a united front fighting for Logan's life.

Immediately following Logan's diagnosis, Andy and I made a stand for our marriage. We were not ignorant about the threat our situation posed to our relationship. We were already going to lose so much, so we made a promise to each other that our marriage would not be collateral. After all, what else could be more damaging to a couple than the death of a child? We vowed to be patient and understanding with each other, and when a slip occurred, we would try our best to recognize the source. Typically we weren't mad at each other—just frustrated, exhausted, and heartbroken at our situation.

We were in the middle of a battle, and if in the end Logan would only have a brief life, we would know we did all we could. Together we never quit fighting for Logan. Andy and I started praying and pursuing God with passion and earnestness we never had before. As we drew closer to Him, we drew closer to each other.

There is life in the Word of God, so we began speaking its truths over Logan as often as possible. We knew to the world it was a hopeless situation, but as God was quick to point out, while we were *in* the world, we were not *of* it. In a tension that could easily tear a couple apart, we instead grew closer together.

"In sickness and in health—" This promise was much easier when Logan was still alive. Together we were strong and united as we learned how to navigate carrying a dying child, but after he was gone, things began to change.

One of the many challenges about grief and trauma is their ability to boil all the ugly to the surface of a marriage. Emotions, after Logan died, were volatile and easily riled. Once the dust settled and the majority of the community around us had "moved on," Andy and I were left to face the ugly alone.

Separation was *never* on the table, but the threat was always lurking outside the door. Truth was, who we were had changed, and we needed to relearn how to navigate each other and become a healthy couple once again.

Circumstances prior to our loss that were never issues before, suddenly became issues. Logan's death had scraped off much of the patience, understanding, and trust on which our relationship had been built. It exposed explosive emotions that were hiding just below the surface, and they erupted without warning.

We both got set off by the littlest of things. The long fuse of respect and grace we once had for each other, the one that was able to burn slowly before an argument, had been cut down to mere centimeters. Our emotions were raw and unfiltered. We were angry. We were broken. We were bitter. And we took it out on each other. We were behaving in a way that was foreign to our normally strong relationship, yet we couldn't seem to pull ourselves out of it.

We saw a marriage counselor a few times, but the cost was too high to continue. We needed that third-party outlet. We needed that voice of reason to help us truly *understand* each other. We needed a set of eyes that was unbiased and could point out the red flags hidden in plain sight. But we didn't have that. I had lost my son and worried my marriage could one day be next.

—❦—

Over the lifetime of a marriage, who we are inevitably changes. It's easy to look back ten, fifteen, or twenty years and see just how much. It's natural for time and circumstance to make people different. In fact, it's almost impossible for it not to. But the pace of that change makes all the difference. When someone evolves slowly over the span of years (or a lifetime), it is easier for their spouse to adjust, adapt, and shift with them.

When a couple loses a child, something changes instantly and without warning. There is no time to adapt. Suddenly you find yourself married to a person you don't know as well as you once did. My husband looked the same. He wore the same clothes, enjoyed the same foods, watched the same shows—but he was different. And so was I. We needed to relearn each other, and that required energy—energy neither of us had.

It wouldn't be fair to put the deteriorating health of our marriage *fully* on the trauma of our situation. But it's almost as if Logan's death was a catalyst of sorts—a means to unearth and expose the weaknesses that existed in our marriage. Would these issues have eventually broken through the surface of our relationship on their own? Hard to say, but I guess we will never know.

To make matters worse, the focus and attention was almost entirely on me. Everyone was concerned about *my* well-being instead of *our* well-being. Andy was simply overlooked. It wasn't intentional, and it wasn't a lack of love for him; it just seems to be the knee-jerk reaction and norm in our culture. He was just as much Logan's parent, had endured just as painful a loss, yet he was left on the sidelines.

People asked him how I was doing (well, occasionally), but they rarely asked how *he* was doing. Just because he didn't show pain in the same way I did didn't mean he wasn't hurting. Grief is not "one size fits all." It comes in many shapes and sizes and looks different on everyone. He showed it in other ways, and I wish those around him, including myself, had done a better job picking up on that. Besides me, he had few with whom he could talk. He needed a male support system, but right after Logan's death, he didn't have one.

Women feel. It's just what we do. I cried. I talked. I prayed. I wrote. I cried some more. I talked some more. I wrote some more. I did some yelling from time to time, inevitably right before a breakdown, where, you guessed it, I would cry some more. I relied on those closest to me when I needed to vent or process. I talked to Andy, my mom, my sister, my closest friends. I had a group of loving people around me, helping to carry the burden of my sorrow. And still—I felt alone. It breaks my heart to think of how alone Andy must have felt.

Men are known for their desire to fix. But you can't fix losing your son. Andy was the man of the house, the strong one, the one expected to hold things together. He tried so hard to support and take care of me that he didn't do what was necessary to take care of himself. The burden was too much, as it would be for anyone, and it eventually broke him. He shut down and, in some ways, shut me out.

I rarely saw him cry, which sometimes made me question the severity of *my* grief compared to his. In my mind, grief equaled tears and conversations about our aching hearts. In my mind, if he wasn't crying or sharing that he was hurting, then maybe he wasn't still sad. I expected him to share his struggles in a way that felt natural and normal to *me*. But Andy wasn't built the same way I was, and to put that expectation on him was unrealistic and unfair. Again, he is an entirely different creation, and his grief manifested in a way that was also entirely different. Anger, anxiety, depression—those were some of his coping mechanisms, and for a long time, I completely missed them.

You may be thinking, "How in the world did you miss that, Jamie?" It makes me feel downright awful, if I'm being honest. Looking back, it is painfully obvious how much he was struggling, but in that season, I just couldn't see it. It's impossible to save someone from drowning when you, too, are fully underwater.

Right after Logan died, Andy buried himself in work. He was addicted to it and couldn't seem to focus his attention anywhere else. He seemed upset, frustrated, and depressed—but mostly about *work*. He was angry often and would come home on edge after a long day, but a lot of it seemed completely unrelated to Logan. He internalized all he was going through, and as a result, grief manifested as anger, anxiety, and, ultimately, depression. He buried himself in anything that could distract him or momentarily dull the pain, even if it meant a different struggle.

Andy felt alone in his grief, and I felt alone in mine. We somehow found ourselves isolated in our sorrow. It was like we were stranded on secluded islands of our own—yet in the very same house.

I believe—even though it's unintentional—our society fuels the disconnect. Our culture tells men they are supposed to be strong, resilient, and the fixers of all problems. It tells them emotion is a sign of weakness—something for the lesser, the timid, the meek. Our culture tells dads they aren't allowed to lament, that their hearts aren't allowed to be broken. *Their job* is to love and support their partner and hold things together until *her* heart is mended from *her* loss.

Gender roles have made it more difficult for men to grieve, simply because it is less acceptable for them to do so. But here is the truth: *dads grieve too*. Their grief just lives in the shadows, typically unseen, unknown, and unacknowledged by the world around them.

Our culture's current perception of what classifies a "strong" man is wrong, and it has caused irreparable damage. Strength isn't found in resiliency but in transparency. It's found when men surround each other, even when it feels uncomfortable. Strength is a man leaning in when it would be more comfortable to look away. Strength is a man who takes his grieving best friend to coffee and listens to what he has to say. Strength is a grieving man who *lets* his best friend take him to coffee and talks about his pain. Strength is a husband realizing the best way to help his wife's heart is by not neglecting his own. Strength is a man in the depths of sorrow standing up for what he needs. It's a man being vulnerable with those who deserve such an honor and having boundaries with those who don't.

Grieving dads have endured a massive disservice for far too long. If you are a bereaved father, I want to say to you, *I am sorry.* I am sorry you experienced a loss no parent should, and I am sorry you, more likely than not, had to (or are having to) walk much of that road alone. You deserve so much better.

Spouses, parents, siblings, and friends all play different roles and fill different voids for those on the road of loss. I felt helpless as Andy's wife because I was only capable of filling one of those gaps for him (and I was doing a poor job to boot). Andy had *some* support, but he didn't have what he needed and deserved.

Dear wives of grieving husbands,

> I would like to take a moment to be candid with you. I know you're hurting. I know you feel immobile, smothered by grief, and drained of all energy. I know, at times you probably feel alone in your marriage and in your sorrow. Maybe your husband doesn't cry around you, but that doesn't mean he isn't crying. Maybe he doesn't seem as affected by the loss, but that doesn't mean he is not affected. Maybe his grief manifests differently than yours, but that doesn't mean it hurts him any less. Even if you don't see it, he is broken too.

> Take the time to find out what your husband needs. Even in the middle of all your pain, and even when you don't have the energy, find a way to connect with him. If his family is being distant, arrange a time for you all to get together. If his friends aren't calling him on their own, then quietly reach out and ask them to. You know how hard it is for you to find people who are genuinely willing to sit in sorrow with you? Well, more than likely, it's ten times harder for your husband. It's easier for us to open up, but it is not typically so natural for a man. He needs an outlet. He needs someone other than you to talk to. Do your best to help him find that person. Protect him. Protect his heart in the same way he is likely trying to protect yours.

There is a good chance your husband feels it is his responsibility to fix you. I know he can't, and you know he can't, but he still will search endlessly for a way to take your pain away and put you back together. He will probably put so much focus on your healing and your heart that he will neglect his. Sometimes it's easier for him to focus on you and put his pain on the back burner rather than face his own grief. Please don't see his efforts as trying to rush your healing. He just wants you back and is fearful you may never return—that this sorrow will swallow you whole and he will lose you too. It's okay to gently remind him that it's not his job to fix you—that he cannot fix you. The best thing he can do to help you is find ways to help himself.

Pray for him—earnestly. Pray for God to comfort him, heal him, bring supportive people into his life, quicken you to his needs, and give you the strength you need even in the middle of your own pain to provide for him. Don't try to force him to open up in the same ways you do. Many times, it's not in his nature, but don't let that blind you to what he may be struggling with. Trust someone who has been there—someone who thought they were doing enough but maybe didn't realize their shortcomings until it was almost too late. Please trust me in this, sweet ladies. While blinded by my own struggles and grief, I could have lost the love of my life. I know you have already lost so much. So please, fight for your spouse.

Lastly, thank God every day for the man He gave you. God entrusted you to take care of his heart, and He will equip you with what you need to do so—you need only ask.

———⊗⊗⊗———

Dear husbands of grieving wives,

Now I would like to take a moment to be candid with you. I know you are in immense pain. You probably feel like you are stuck in a nightmare from which you cannot seem to wake. I know you feel lost and uncertain of the road ahead. I know you look at your wife and you want to fix her. I know you fear you have lost her, too, and wonder if she will ever return. I promise she will, one day, but you need to be patient. I know you want to be strong for her, but part of that strength is being able to share your weaknesses and pain with her.

She is going to cry—a lot. She is going to feel a need to talk about it—a lot. She is engulfed in sorrow. A bond is forged between a mother and child that is indescribable, and now she is trying to figure out how to continue when a piece of her is literally missing. She feels like she can't go on—like she can't breathe. So be patient with her. Don't rush her healing. Understand it is okay if she seems to grieve more intensely or deeply than you. It is because God designed her to have that passion and zeal in all capacities of her life. That is exactly why she is able to love and nurture you so well. Remember, she grieves fiercely because she loves fiercely.

Don't try to fix her, because even on your best day, you can't. But you can pray for her—earnestly. Pray for God to comfort her, heal her, bring supportive people into her life, quicken you to her needs, and give you the strength you need to provide for her.

Talk to her about your child, and do it often. Say their name—out loud. There are times when she will feel like everyone forgot except her. She may begin to believe that she is the only one who still thinks of them or says their name. Remind her it's not true. When your heart is hurting and your arms are longing to hold your baby, tell her. Let her share that moment with you. Share your feelings with her. If you don't let her see that you are hurting too, she will feel even more alone in her grief.

Tell her how proud you are of her and how perfectly she loved your beautiful child. Remind her it was not her fault. Even though deep down she knows the circumstances were out of her control, she is constantly fighting the thought that she is somehow to blame, that maybe, just maybe, she could have done something differently, and your child would still be here. If your child passed after birth, the same still applies. Maybe you are feeling responsible too. It's in our nature to question our past, and find every gap possible to fill with "what if" thoughts. Remember, neither of you chose this. You both loved (and still love) your child perfectly, and I know, had you been given the chance, you would have traded your life for theirs in an instant.

Take care of yourself. I know the world does not offer you much. I am deeply sorry if you have been overlooked. It's not right, and it's not okay. But believe me when I say your measure as a man is not lessened when you show your heart. In fact, I would argue it is the complete opposite. It takes a very strong man to share his weakness and his pain. Understand this—unless you find a healthy way to work through your grief, your marriage is left open and vulnerable. So please, take care of yourself so you may also take care of her.

Lastly, thank God every day for the woman He gave you. God entrusted you to take care of her heart, and He will equip you with what you need to do so—you need only ask.

———◦∞∞◦———

I would be lying to say our marriage is perfect, because it's not. We eventually learned how to cut each other a little slack when it came to unnecessary displays of emotion. One small step at a time, we began to pull ourselves out of the hole into which we had fallen (or more so, been pushed). Believe me, we have our moments, but we have learned how to better love each other. We still struggle to be patient with each other and still have moments where we should be quicker to forgive. The truth is, marriage, in general, is an ever-evolving process of learning how to navigate each other and stay in a healthy place.

We may have some scars from the ways we once treated each other, but I would still argue that we are more unbreakable today than ever. I know we can make it through anything. Not that I ever doubted it before, but what Satan intended for evil, God reworked for good. I am so grateful He gave me the man he did. For if I had to walk this path, there is no one on this earth with whom I would have rather walked.

Dear Heavenly Father,

Right now, I lift up the marriages Satan is attempting to break because he sees a sliver of opportunity. In the precious name of Jesus, I rebuke him and any stronghold he has on those relationships. Please, Father, do not let these families be torn apart. I pray confusion would be replaced with understanding, anger with love, and frustration with patience.

Remind them of the strong bond that is formed when they humble themselves together and come before you. Remind them today of the vow they made before you to love each other—in good times and in bad, in sickness and in health—and give them the strength and grace they need to follow through on that promise. Father, I ask that you would give them the endurance today to honor each other, protect each other, and persevere through even the darkest of times. I thank you, God, that above all else your love is perfect and will never fail. Reveal that very love to them today.

In Jesus's name, amen.

28 — UNNECESSARY WOUNDS

From the end of the earth I will cry to You, when my heart is overwhelmed; Lead me to the rock that is higher than I.
—Psalm 61:2 (NKJV)

Photo by Jessica Fox

The number of tears that have trickled down my cheeks and fallen onto my lap as I have poured my heart and soul into this book are too many to count. There have been times when the sound of my typing was accompanied by the sound of my sobs, and there have been times when I had to shut my computer and step away from the pain for a bit. This is one of the chapters where I know I will experience all of the above.

Even though this chapter is short, it's incredibly painful to write. But I share it regardless because I know how necessary it is. Although you are nestled in the middle of this book, this chapter is actually the last one I'm writing. The reason? Simply, I wanted to ignore it.

I almost did, in fact. I didn't want to talk about it, because I didn't want to hurt anyone. And yet, I know how incomplete this story would be if I intentionally ignored it altogether. My hope is that you can use my experience and the things I *should* have done differently to spare yourself some of the unnecessary pain Andy and I endured.

The truth is, no one knows what to do in a situation like ours. It's not black and white. There is so much gray area you could almost drown in it. Grief is as unique as a fingerprint. Everyone does it *differently*. Everyone gives love and receives love *differently*. Everyone feels support and neglect *differently*. If you have experienced a loss, it is nearly impossible to assume those around you would, by instinct alone, be able to understand your unique needs. In fact, it's an unfair expectation to put on them when half of the time we, the bereaved, don't even know what we need. Most people are not equipped to walk this road flawlessly with us, especially as we are just learning to navigate it ourselves.

It wasn't until I started getting used to life after loss that I was able to look back and decipher the places where I *should* have spoken up. At the time, it didn't feel clear. It was muddy and messy and confusing. I was broken, delicate, and scared. I had a voice, but it was still quiet. Now I look back and can almost see flashing red lights on the timeline of my life. I can see the *exact* places where I should have done the thing or said the thing—but didn't.

Currently, bereaved parents make up a huge part of my friend group, and one topic that always comes up in conversations are the wounds inflicted by our families or very close friends. These are the bruises you anticipate from the outside world but instead come from a place of trust.

I have wounds. Andy does too. Over the years, we have learned to push them down. Deep down, in fact. But they still reside within us, and from time to time we can feel frustration start to bubble up as those wounds unexpectedly open and bleed. There is pain from things that were said, things that were overlooked, and regret that we should have spoken up but didn't have the courage or understanding to do so.

Here's the thing—most people will *never* understand because they haven't experienced the same tragedy, and that includes those very close to us. Andy and I learned the hard way that it is no one's responsibility except ours to be candid with those closest to us about our needs, expectations, and boundaries.

If Grandma and Grandpa didn't include your child in the head count of how many grandchildren they have, and it upsets you—*tell them*. If your brother didn't say, "Happy Mother's Day" or "Happy Father's Day," to you, because you don't have any *living* children, and it hurt—*tell him*.

If your best friend forgot to acknowledge your child's birthday—*tell them*. If it's important for a certain someone in your life to *always* be available on difficult calendar days of the year—*tell them*. If someone said something completely out of line—*tell them*. If you need space—*tell them*. If you need attention, then, for the love, please, *just tell them*.

Are you catching on? While it may be hard to know what is truly helpful, it isn't hard to know what is *not*. Even in the early stages of loss, it's easy to distinguish what makes the pain worse. But it's impossible for your family or very close friends to know the things they have done that hurt you unless you make it clear to them. Chances are, the intentions were not malicious, just misguided.

It may be awkward. It may be uncomfortable. It may even lead to an argument. But I promise you, living with unspoken pain in your relationships and feeling like it's too late to speak up is far worse. It's like cancer that's invisible to the naked eye but wreaks absolute havoc inside. If it's not contained and stomped out, it will only grow and bleed into places of your life where it does not belong. Additional and unnecessary pain, in an already painful space, is the *last* thing your heart needs right now.

For those of you who are rolling your eyes and thinking something along the lines of, "Well, you don't know my family," you are probably right. Even a clearly painted picture will still appear blurry to some, but at least you can make peace with having done all that was within your power. Some people will never change or even try to. Sometimes that can include people tied to us by blood. Sometimes, as heartbreaking as it feels, it is something we must accept. But, yeah, it really sucks.

I encourage you to learn from our mistakes and speak up. You will never know the outcome if you don't at least try. But you must use your voice. It holds immeasurable power, which is rendered useless if you stay silent. Words give us the ability to sit with someone different from us and *learn*. They also give us the ability to sit with someone who doesn't understand and *teach*. Your voice has the ability to yield compassion, understanding, and sympathy. It allows us to admit our faults and forgive others for theirs.

Your voice has power, my friends, and so do you. For most of us, the long-lasting benefits of speaking up will far outweigh an uncomfortable moment.

THROUGH KELLEY'S EYES

"Thick skin, soft hearts, can't lose." Remember when I briefly mentioned this as we began Part II? If anyone here is a fan of the TV show *Friday Night Lights*, this saying will ring vaguely familiar. I've always told loss support families that one of the biggest things you can do to alleviate unnecessary damage is to establish an open dialogue with loss parents from day one, inviting them to come to you—at any time, with anything they need to discuss.

But there's a catch. This will only work if you are committed to having thick skin and a soft heart. If you are defensive or offended every time an issue is brought to your attention, then it's a complete waste of time. So let me make a suggestion. Consider setting up some ground rules in advance.

One such rule might be that when a loved one feels the need to "speak up" regarding an accidental wound you've inflicted, they should email or text it to you. I know to some of you this might sound crazy, as email or texts don't always translate properly, but for someone like me, this would help me to be able to read, reflect, and react on my own timeline. If my knee-jerk reaction would be defensive, this would give the chance to process and squash my initial hurt feelings and then truly receive their words.

This is different for all of us, but you know your triggers and tendencies. So figure out some boundaries, share them with the ones you're trying to support, thicken your skin, and soften your heart.

29 — THE HIERARCHY OF LOSS

Always be humble and gentle. Be patient with each other, making allowance for each other's faults because of your love.

—Ephesians 4:2 (NLT)

Photo by Jessica Fox

As bereaved parents, we stand and look at the landscape in front of us and often see treacherous mountains and deep valleys that appear impossible to traverse. Not only are the mountains high and the valleys low, but they are wrought with land mines. Every difficult step we take has the possibility of ending in disaster with unforeseen triggers just inches away from the soles of our feet. Most of the time, there is nothing we can do to diffuse what lies ahead. But sometimes *we* are the ones who have *unknowingly* made the road more difficult.

There is an unspoken hierarchy of grief that exists in the pregnancy and infant loss world that—let's be honest here—*no one* wants to acknowledge. Those who are confused as to what I am referring to have likely not experienced pregnancy or infant loss, and those who have are beginning to worry I am getting ready to address something we would never openly admit—to most people. But for the sake of complete transparency, let's air our dirty laundry.

Why, as humans, do we have such an innate desire to compete with one another? We are all guilty of it, myself included. We look around, rank those we see, line each other up on a scale, and then take a step back to examine where exactly we belong. Women (and I can say this because I am one) tend to be the worst.

We compare ourselves constantly. *Am I prettier? Better dressed? More successful? Is my house cleaner? Is my life more Pinterest-worthy? Is my Instagram page cuter? Do I look like I have it more together?* I wish we could instead use our energy to uplift and encourage each other, but that's a topic complicated enough to fill another book.

Unfortunately, this competitive and comparing spirit sometimes even seeps into our sorrow, our pain, our tragedies, and even the depths of our love.

Why do we rate the severity of each other's losses? Why must we compare the level of our grief to another's? Isn't pain, pain, and sorrow, sorrow? The road we took to find ourselves in this place may differ, but the destination remains the same: empty arms. Portions of our paths may have been more "difficult" to traverse. Some of us may have had a longer distance to travel. Some of us may have walked this road once, and some have walked it many times. But why, particularly within this community, do we innately compare the severity or trauma level of our stories? Why must we rate each other's losses on a scale of one to ten?

To compound the situation, we then sometimes compare the level of *love* left in the wake of that loss. Who did more, said more, shared more? Who has the 5K, the foundation, the fundraiser? Who honored their child the "best" or the "most"? Who has created the biggest legacy, the greatest memory, the most enduring love? Who parented their dead child the best?

Friends, can we recognize, just for a moment, how completely ridiculous that sounds? When we start to measure "how well" we honor our children's lives, or "how great" our love is compared to that of others, we are throwing land mines at our feet. We are inadvertently peppering the road ahead with more triggers and ultimately—more pain.

Stop comparing your grief, your love, and your loss. Stop making the road more perilous than it already is. Your sorrow and your love are *your own*—uniquely beautiful and as individual as the print on your finger. Our children's worth is not tied to a deed or the beauty of a social media page. It's not tied to how terrible your story was or how well your child is remembered through your actions. It is tied to your *heart*.

Our losses and the severity of our pain are not diminished, lessened, or threatened because someone, somewhere has what others would deem "a worse story." In the same sense, our losses and the severity of our pain are not more justified, affirmed, or appropriate because, compared to someone, somewhere, *we* have the "worse story."

Now that I have stepped down from my soapbox for a minute, I have to be frank with you about my walk through this comparison game. And let me insert a big *ugh* here. Sometimes I really hate my commitment to be totally honest and candid throughout these pages, but here goes . . .

As much as I hate to admit it, right after losing Logan, there was a season where I was guilty of the very thing that now breaks my heart. I didn't even realize my mind was capable of such thoughts, that what felt like such ugliness even lived in me, until someone told me she "understood" what we were enduring. An acquaintance was trying to empathize with my loss, and her intentions were pure. You see, she had suffered a miscarriage. A *really* early one. On her own, she grouped herself and her spouse with me and Andy. She felt our stories were equal. To be completely honest, it pissed me off.

Really?! Did you carry your child for seven months, part of the time knowing they were sick and dying? Did you spend three days in the hospital, go through two days of labor, deliver your baby, and ultimately watch that very child die in your husband's arms? Did you need a casket? No. So I'm pretty sure there is no way you could possibly—understand.

Double *ugh*. I could really use that emoji with the monkey covering its eyes right about now. I wish you could see the grimace on my face and the pull of my finger to hit the delete button on my keyboard about a hundred times. Thank goodness for the grace and forgiveness of our Heavenly Father.

To all of you who have suffered a miscarriage (or many), I *sincerely* apologize. I hate what ran through my mind at that moment, but I have a hunch—actually I happen to know for a fact—I am not the only one who has felt this way. I was so consumed with my own pain that I wasn't able to acknowledge another's, and I would not accept what she went through could even *remotely* compare to what I was going through. I would not accept that her pain matched mine. I believed she had suffered a loss, but not one as great.

Right now, it's very likely my "late loss" readers *and* my "early loss" readers are equally flustered—flustered and maybe even, dare I say, angry? The best thing to do in a moment like this is, once again, to embrace the tension, as unnatural as it may feel. This is where I hope that trust gained in the first half of this book will kick into gear and you will give me a moment to explain before you throw my book across the room. Too often, we innately lean *away* from what feels uncomfortable. Today, we are going to lean *in* and try to find some common ground.

The families who have suffered late losses are probably thinking something along the lines of what I said earlier: *A miscarriage cannot compare to what I've endured. I have an empty nursery. I have an empty car seat. I have clothes, toys, and supplies. My milk came in and I had no baby to feed.* That is 100 percent accurate and totally valid.

In contrast, the families who have suffered early losses are probably thinking: *Just because my loss was early doesn't mean it was any less a loss. I didn't love my baby any less just because I wasn't able to carry it as long and it didn't weigh a full six pounds. I still planned a life with this child. I still have a hole in my heart. I still have empty arms.* That is also 100 percent accurate and totally valid.

This is where empathy needs to fill the gap, but the process of allowing your heart to grow and empathize can be messy. It doesn't always feel good. It stretches us beyond our comfort level and sometimes it's downright painful. Compassion is a beautiful thing, but in the delicate garden that is our hearts, it needs tending. Due to circumstance and experience, its presence, or lack thereof, ebbs and flows throughout our lives. But we must learn, in time, not to allow our stories and our pain to harden our hearts and rob us of one of the most beautiful things God designed them to do. And that, my friends, is to love one another.

When it comes down to it, we are *all* looking to be validated in our pain and the magnitude of our sorrow. Feeling like the world thinks our grief is greater than our loss is never easy. Feeling like our children didn't count in the world's eyes only exacerbates the tension. Does it actually matter what the world believes? No, of course not. But if we are being honest, we *all* seek affirmation that someone out there agrees we have been through hell. Bereaved parents are unified in many capacities, and regardless of age or gestation of loss, this is one of those areas that tie us together. This is a piece of common ground.

By this point, you all know I lost Logan shortly after he was born. What you don't know is that six years later, I lost another baby to a miscarriage. Guess what? *They both hurt.*

Full transparency here: my miscarriage was not nearly as difficult as Logan's death—not even close—but it was still painful. I happen to have the unique perspective of having endured both, which gives me permission to make such a statement, but it's unique to *my* story. Unless you, too, have endured both types of losses, then you have no right to compare the two. It would be like saying a broken arm is more painful than a broken leg, when you have broken your arm but never your leg.

If I had never lost Logan and had never known the trauma that accompanied his diagnosis and death, my miscarriage would have been one of the most awful experiences of my life. And in many ways, it still was. Were it not for the pain I walked through with Logan's death, it would have *easily* been a ten on my life's trauma scale. My miscarriage did not carry the trauma that Logan's death did, but it *still* was painful and it *still* was traumatic. It wasn't a ten for *me*, but for many people it is.

My early loss was a very lonely sorrow. When Logan died, our story was blaringly public. People didn't understand, but they *knew*. I remember sitting in a meeting at Starbucks for a Walk With Me fundraiser and having to excuse myself several times because I was bleeding so badly. I remember bawling my eyes out on the way to the meeting because I had stopped at the store to grab *just one more* pregnancy test to see if the line was continuing to fade. Well, it was. And to boot, the bleeding and pain were only continuing to increase. As I pulled into the parking lot, I remember trying to fix my makeup and pretend all was okay. I was knee-deep in planning a gala to raise money for people whose babies had died, while at the same time, I was losing another of my own.

My beloved dad was also dying of cancer at the time (again, that's another book), and that pregnancy, as brief as it may have been, was a ray of light and hope. It was something for him to fight for—an unplanned but welcomed little blessing our family desperately needed. When I lost that baby, as tiny as it was, it felt like consuming darkness and death had taken over my life *once again.*

I remember the sadness—it reached my core, yet stayed deep within me, never coming to the surface. Just because miscarriages happen early and often doesn't make them *any* less important (and if you *have* endured one, or many, hang tight—there is a chapter coming up just for you).

If you are one of the few who have experienced both early and late losses, we can probably agree that each was different and uniquely painful. Circumstance intensifies and changes the pain, but no loss is ever the same. I cannot and *should* not compare the pain of the bones I've broken to the bones you've broken, because my pain is not yours, nor is your pain mine. Sorrow is many things, and if you only take a few things away from these pages, let one be to *never* compare yours.

I wish I had understood this lesson earlier in my walk. It took time (to the tune of many years) for God to do a work on me in this area, but His tender hands eventually remolded me. He slowly chiseled away the tough outer shell that had grown around my heart. It was a process, but as I got further down the road, I could feel my thoughts begin to soften and my heart's callousness begin to fade. Eventually, I was able to stop comparing my pain to the pain of those around me. Eventually, I realized the power in allowing my heart to be broken *alongside* another's. Compassion yields love. Comparison yields division. God has taught me that the loss of a child in *any* capacity is *still* the loss of a child. It's that simple.

I lost my littlest life at home, and it was awful, but I can only imagine a couple going in for an ultrasound—just like the day Andy and I had with Logan—only to be told there was no heartbeat, no life. I can't imagine staring at that painfully still image. I can't imagine those further along than I was, going through what can feel like full-blown labor—very possibly *at home*. Delivering what is left of their baby—*at home*, maybe alone, afraid, and with no medical staff to assist, help, or guide the next steps. I can't imagine going into a procedure room pregnant and then leaving hours later—no longer pregnant. Even after having a miscarriage of my own, there are still journeys of pain I will never understand.

I am so sorry to those of you who have experienced any type of baby loss. Just like I had pictured a lifetime with Logan, you too, pictured a full life with your child. You too, looked forward with great anticipation to your future as parents, and you too, found yourself "minus one" in the end. All of us will live the rest of our lives grieving what could have been, what *should* have been. Grieving all the memories we hoped we would have the opportunity to make, grieving the moments that slipped through our fingers. Our stories may be different, but our broken hearts are, in many ways, very similar.

Pain is not objective. It is not something you can put in a box and measure. Just because someone may *feel* like their box is fuller and heavier, doesn't make another's less substantial or easier to carry. *Stop trying to measure something that cannot be measured. All* of us who have lost a little life—whether it was in the first trimester or the third, in-utero or out— have children waiting for us in heaven. *That* is a heavy box whatever way you choose to look at it.

The truth is, there will *always* be someone with a more tragic story. There will *always* be someone who has been dealt a "more difficult" card, but that does not lessen what each of us has endured. We cannot and should not compare our scales. My ten was watching my son die and later watching my father die. Your ten might be a miscarriage, infertility, a divorce, or something else. My point is this—it is still your ten, and that makes it valid.

My hope and prayer is that, as a community of loss parents, we can learn to carry this weight *together*, and if we must continue the comparison game, let's stick with who has the cutest shoes and the greenest lawns.

30 — ANTICIPATED GOOD-BYES

Now is your time of grief, but I will see you again and you will rejoice,
and no one will take away your joy.

—John 16:22 (NIV)

Photo by Chesney Midcap

"At least you had time to prepare." If only I had a dollar for every time someone belittled the intensity of my loss because, for a time, I knew heartbreak was headed my way.

We all do it, even if we don't realize we are doing it. We hear a story of loss—a friend's friend, a coworker's husband, somebody's somebody—and we automatically hold our breath in anticipation of hearing the circumstances surrounding the death. It's not until the reason is shared that we either exhale or continue to grimace in discomfort. In particular, when we hear about someone whose death was anticipated, we feel a weight lift and justify the surviving family's pain by saying things that give *us* comfort. "At least they got to say good-bye." "At least they knew it was coming." "At least they could prepare."

We just wrapped up a chapter discussing why our personal losses cannot and should not be compared to another's, and here we find ourselves once again lining up on a scale, not our own pain, but the pain and stories of others.

The root of it isn't malicious. I innately do it too. Before I lost Logan, I remember feeling strangely more at peace knowing a family had a "heads-up" when there was a death. It took away a bit of the sting and knocked the trauma of it all down a few notches in my mind. In contrast, let's pretend the loss was instantaneous. A heart attack. A car accident. Something quick and unexpected. Now, *those* losses shake us to the core because no one saw them coming and they cannot be justified.

We can all agree that some tragedies feel more horrific and cause more of a visceral reaction. We get rattled by these stories, pull our families tight, cower back into a corner, and wrap ourselves up in the *false* comfort that something like that could never happen to *us*. Rightfully so, our bodies shudder and our hearts break for families in the midst of such awful stories.

However, and here is the big takeaway, none of that negates or lessens the feelings of sorrow produced by what society seems to consider a less "justifiable" or "acceptable" loss. I wonder why our knee-jerk reaction to tragic news is the need to take a story and place it somewhere on a scale between "not too bad" and "awful." Why do we have the need to judge tragedies this way?

When it came to Logan, my pain was often minimized by those around me because his life was brief and his loss anticipated. Because of my profession in a salon, I interacted daily with numerous people and heard things like this more often than not: "What you went through was *sad,* but oh my gosh, listen to *this* story . . . *this* woman *suddenly* lost her six-month-old. Now *her* story is *awful.* At least that didn't happen to you."

Stories like that are terrible and bring a sick feeling to my stomach. However, a story like *that* was irrelevant to *my* pain. I think in many situations, the justifying is solely for the comfort of the justifier. It did nothing to help my bruised and bleeding heart. *Absolutely nothing.*

Waiting for Logan to die was like having the foresight of an imminent car crash that I knew would take the life of my child sometime in the next few months. Now, did anticipating this horrible event make it any less horrible? Was I at peace anytime I was driving, or was I looking around every corner for the semi that was going to destroy my family?

Which side will it hit? Will we see it coming? With every close call, I lost a bit of myself as my anxiety and fear continued to grow. *Is this it? Am I about to watch him die? How bad is it going to hurt? Oh thank goodness . . . just a close call. Deep breath, Jamie. All is okay . . . for now.* I obeyed all traffic laws and tried my best to be as careful as humanly possible. I drove slowly. I looked in every direction before moving forward. But none of it mattered. None of it stopped the inevitable. *None* of it saved him.

Were there still beautiful moments? Yes, of course. Sometimes as we drove we couldn't help but notice the incredible sunset. In those moments, I knew God was in the car *with* me. But did I "enjoy" the ride? Take advantage of the time we had together? Or was I so afraid about what was to come that I felt paralyzed? Tense? Having to brace for impact at any moment but having *no idea* when that moment would be?

The dance went on and on for weeks, and as more time passed, my anticipation, my dread, only grew. But *at least* I knew it was coming, right? *At least* I had time to say good-bye, right? *At least* I had time to prepare, right?

Wrong.

That doesn't even take into account the suffering endured *in* the car on the way to a "planned death." It doesn't take into account the trauma of watching someone you love truly suffer, and still the logic is absurd. I don't know anyone who would *choose* to get in that car.

<hr>

How does someone anticipate and prepare to say good-bye to a loved one, let alone to their child? I had never heard the term *anticipatory grief* until years after Logan died. I had experienced it, of course, but I had no idea what I endured carried a title. Out of frustration for the conversations I had over the years with people hinting that my grief was *at least* easier because I could *prepare* for it, I decided to do a little research. Here is what I found regarding the definition of *anticipatory grief*:

> The normal mourning that occurs when a patient or family is expecting a death. Anticipatory grief gives family and friends more time to slowly get used to the reality of the loss. Grief that follows an unplanned death is different from anticipatory grief. Unplanned loss may overwhelm the coping abilities of a person, making normal functioning impossible. Mourners may not be

able to realize the total impact of their loss. He or she may not be able to accept the loss mentally and emotionally . . . Following an unexpected death, the mourner may feel the world no longer has order and does not make sense.[1]

On the surface, it sounded valid, clinical, and accurate. And it was—but about grief *in general* (with all circumstances surrounding that grief removed). To assume the addition of the word *anticipatory* has the power to make the aftermath any less traumatic is misleading and false. To assume one little word could "get [someone ready for] the reality of loss" is ridiculous. Putting *anyone's* grief in a circumstantial box is unfair and unnecessary.

The same article eventually went on to say this: "Grief experienced before a death does not make the grief after the death last a shorter amount of time."[2] This part is true; however, it only acknowledges that the *duration* of grief after a loss is not minimized by anticipation, whereas the author had implied that the *intensity* and *ability to cope* are different. So overall, this article still misses the mark. An expected loss has equal ability to cause all of the above reactions. There is absolutely no ability to anticipate the coming death of a loved one and no amount of preparation that can make the grieving process any easier.

People unintentionally treat those with stories like mine as if we got a "head start" or some sort of advantage on the journey of grief ahead—like we were *lucky* enough to "Pass Go" in Monopoly before everyone else. We are often treated as though our hearts aren't as badly wounded as those whose losses were unexpected.

I can tell you after two full rounds of anticipatory grief, the second being my father's death, that the perception that *anyone* could get ready for a shattered heart is a load of crap. Sorry. That was a bit blunt. Not sorry actually—because it's the truth.

Just days after learning the beautiful boy growing in me would never have the chance to grow in this world, I told myself over and over that *at least* it would be easier for me because I knew it was coming. I could get

---

[1] Charles Patrick Davis, ed., "Medical Definition of Anticipatory Grief," MedicineNet.com, reviewed March 29, 2021, https://www.medicinenet.com/anticipatory_grief/definition.htm.

[2] Charles Patrick Davis, ed., "Medical Definition of Anticipatory Grief."

ready for what was on the way. It became even more ingrained in me as I would hear the theme repeatedly confirmed from the lips of others.

I shake my head as I look back at that much younger and more inexperienced version of myself. What I would give for the opportunity to look into her puffy eyes and gently tell her, "I'm sorry but there is no way to prepare for what you are about to endure. This isn't going to be easier because you know." Would that have been immensely helpful to Jamie, circa 2012? No, most likely not. But it would have squashed the false and misleading premise that I was one step further along in the process of grief—that I, unlike many, was lucky to have a head start. That lie was something I held on to with a white-knuckled grip in those days. The problem was, at the time I didn't know it was a lie.

When my dad passed from a three-year cancer battle in 2020, I had to relive all the same sentiments again. "At least you got to say good-bye." What was so often overlooked was the three years my family had to *watch him die* in order to have that cherished good-bye. For three years I watched my dad *suffer,* and I can't help but think how much pain he could have been spared if his death had been earlier and sudden. Living without him is unbearably difficult regardless of how he left this world. And yet, I'm sure if he *had* died suddenly, in my mind I would have preferred the latter. Three additional years would have felt like a gift.

So here's my point. Planned or unplanned, expected or unexpected— it really doesn't matter. *Death sucks.* Death sucks when you know it's walking behind you. Death sucks when it jumps out in front of you. The aftermath is always the same. Grief is grief, and all of it sucks. *Period*.

The next time you hear a sad story, stop the narrative that so often begins to play automatically in our minds. Once you know it is there, it becomes easy to identify. To what end and for what person is the comparison of pain *helpful?* Once again, my friends, let's stick to comparing shoes and lawns.

31 — YOU DID NOT "MISS" CARRY

The LORD is close to the brokenhearted and saves those who are crushed in spirit.

—Psalm 34:18 (NIV)

T he dynamic of this book is complicated and multilayered because it was written over such a long period of time. For years, it really bothered me that my book was taking *forever* to complete. I fervently wanted to finish my labor of love for Logan (and for you), and I continually beat myself up that it was dragging on for so long.

Then one day, as I sat across from a dear friend (and fellow writer), it suddenly made sense. We were deep in conversation about sharing our pain and the lessons learned through our written words. I had just shared with her the guilt I felt in still being so far off from finishing, but before I had even completed my sentence, God suddenly revealed to me why it had to be written so slowly. I felt Him whisper, "You still have more to learn. This will not be complete until I'm done teaching."

If I had thrown in the towel and expedited this process, simply for the sake of checking it off my list, many chapters of this book, like the one you are about to read, would be absent. A couple of chapters ago, I promised I would take a moment to focus on those who knew the ache of miscarriage. Before I had one, I thought I understood them simply because I had experienced loss too. I sympathized for the women who endured them, but I didn't—and couldn't—*empathize* with them.

The following words poured out of my heart in 2018 (six years after Logan's death), as I unexpectedly found myself, yet again, in a place I never intended to be. The experience opened my eyes in many ways. It gave me a new compassion for the miscarriage community that I did not have before. Why you might ask? Because, suddenly I was a member. To everyone who has ever had a miscarriage—this one is just for you.

Misspoke. Misunderstood. Misplaced. Each of these words has a common denominator: one way or another, they are the result of an "operator error." *Misspoke*, for instance—I said something I shouldn't have; I expressed myself insufficiently. *Misunderstood*—I did not grasp the thoughts or words of another; I failed to interpret well. *Misplaced*—I lost and cannot find; I positioned something incorrectly. Here's another one for you . . .

Miscarried. In keeping consistent with this trend, this would mean I did not carry well; I failed to attain; I failed to hold on to. I have a *big* problem with that way of thinking. Why would it be appropriate to put that blame on a woman's body?

Anyone who has suffered a pregnancy loss of *any* kind already feels responsible in some way. To use that word and label such a loss as my "inability to carry" is just cruel. I have never liked that word, but right now, I am finding it insulting on a whole new level. Maybe that's because, right now, I am sitting in the middle of one.

As I stand in the shower trying to dull the horrific pain in my stomach and back, I am continually reminded how "well" I did *not* carry. Every couple minutes, there is an unwelcome contrast in the tub, as I see my hopes and dreams literally go down the drain. The shower is usually my safe place. It's where I go to hide. Tonight, though, I feel betrayed by it. My refuge has momentarily turned into a harsh reminder of just how fragile life is.

I don't share for sympathy. I know that might sound weird. Of course, sympathy is welcome, but to be honest, I didn't want the world to know. Not because I'm ashamed or feel like my sadness is not okay. It's just that a resounding majority of my mind and heart says, *No, Jamie, not this time. You have done your part in this world. You have and continue to share enough of your pain. This piece? This time? This is just for you.*

But there is this tiny whisper I can't ignore. This little tinge in my heart that says, *She needs to hear this. She needs to know that she is not going through this alone.* So tonight, as I write, I share only because there is someone out there for whom that little whisper spoke. To that woman—I see you. I see you *much clearer* than before, when I thought I already saw you.

I see how sad you feel over the potential of what could have been, and in the very same breath, I see you question the intensity of that very sadness.

I see the only evidence you now have—the only proof that life existed—is an ultrasound picture or a positive pregnancy test that now seems to mock you. Well, let's be honest. You initially took more than one, just to be sure, right? Personally, I have five.

I see the confusion in your eyes and how your brain is trying *so* hard to process something that it just can't. *Yesterday I was pregnant, and today I am not.*

I see you close your eyes and clench your teeth every few minutes, as yet another commercial or show has a new baby or pregnant woman front and center. They have always been there. You just didn't notice when you weren't looking.

I see how lonely you feel in this place—a speck surrounded by a world that says, "This is not a big deal, and your sadness is excessive." Grief is hard enough. I am very familiar with that, unfortunately. But it's even harder to endure alone.

I see you question God and His timing once more. *Why? What was the point? Don't you know what I was already in the middle of? The heaviness that was already in my world? Why would you add more?* (Those last ones may just be mine). But I assure you, sweet girl, He is still good. And you still are the delight of *His* heart regardless of the words that may occasionally bleed from *yours*.

I don't know the reasons why. I'm sure you don't either. It's okay to question His plan. I know I do right now. Yet while I cannot understand

His ways, I know I can trust His heart. He is with me even in this, and one day it *will* be okay.

It seems God gives me words when my heart hurts. As uncomfortable as it makes me at times (like now), it would be a disservice to Him not to share those words with you. I refuse to stand in the way of Him using my story. My pastor once said, "Your testimony is a weapon." Those are words I try my best to live by (although sometimes I do much better than other times).

I would be a hypocrite tonight if I kept this to myself. It goes against everything I stand for in the pregnancy and infant loss community—transparency, vulnerability, and authenticity. The strength to say "me too" in a world that is simply more comfortable covering its ears and closing its eyes. So tonight, I am merely standing up and saying "me too" once more.

And to that sweet mama holding a pregnancy test in her hand and a heating pad on her tummy—I see you. I am you. Your tears are not misplaced, and your broken heart is validated. You did *not* "miss" carry. You actually carried *very well*, and this is not your fault.

32 — THE SHORE

But mightier than the violent raging of the seas, mightier than the breakers on the shore—the LORD above is mightier than these.
—Psalm 93:4 (NLT)

Photo by Jessica Fox

Grief is unpredictable. It's like standing in the ocean but facing the shore. I'm not standing there admiring the beautiful coastline, as one would imagine. I am standing there, soaking wet, water dripping into my eyes, fists clenched, body shaking and tense. A permanent grimace is on my face. My knee and elbow are cut open and a pink mixture of water and blood dissipate into the ocean surrounding me.

I am standing there, *waiting*. I am waiting for the next impact, the next wave to hit. In anticipation, I do my best to ground my feet by digging them deeper into the sand below me. I try my hardest to steady my body and brace for what I know is coming. It's a futile effort at best.

I have no idea when it will hit or how big it will be. It might simply make me stumble or cause me to lose my footing for a moment. It might be tall enough to hit me square in the back—its impact causing me to break the surface of the water and go under for an instant. It could also be, however, one of those rogue waves that are big and strong enough to fully consume me—one of those violent and ominous-looking waves, where more white is visible than blue. This type of wave ruthlessly knocks the wind out of me and sucks me under to tumble uncontrollably in its core. It slams me violently against the rough ocean floor, causing my body to tear and bleed. Once the water retreats, I find myself on all fours, gasping for air, trying desperately to find the energy to stand and face the shore once again.

As I am buying my groceries, the cashier casually asks, "Do you have any children?" *WAVE.*

Just needed to get one thing at Target. It's right next to the baby section. *WAVE.*

I get an email saying, "Congrats! Your baby is one week old today." *WAVE.*

A baby shower invite arrives in the mail. *WAVE.*

My favorite show, and normally a safe place, just had a woman's baby die. *WAVE.*

I see a social media announcement that a good friend of mine is pregnant. *WAVE.*

We receive a massive bill for my son's "Time in the Nursery." He died in my husband's arms and never even made it to the nursery. *WAVE.*

Someone tells me, "It's okay. At least you didn't have time to get attached." *BIG WAVE.*

We lower a tiny casket into the ground. *ROGUE WAVE.*

Sometimes the sets are on top of each other, and sometimes they are more spread out. But one thing is always constant: the promise of the *next* wave. It's a brutal cycle where the only predictable part is its unpredictability. As time goes on, the waves will most likely get further apart and give us more room in between to dry off a bit and maybe catch our breath. Eventually, we will have time to admire the beautiful coastline before the next one hits. But for a season, they are right on top of each other.

I am thankful there are two lifelines in these waters. The first is quite obvious: the love and support of our family, friends, and community. As a family, we are in these waters together. Some waves knock us all down, and some take us out one at a time. But we do our best to have our arms linked, which makes us stronger and able to help each other stand. Our community may not be *in* the water with us, but they certainly can and have thrown things our way to make the process more bearable.

The second lifeline is not obvious to all, but it is more important than the others. This lifeline is hope, and grief without hope is far too dark and desolate a place for anyone to exist. My heart is heavy because I know everyone is staring at a shore of their own in some capacity or another, but not everyone has hope to ground them.

Right now, my family and I are facing the shore. We are bruised, beaten, cold, and tired. We may tumble, gasp for air, and bleed, but regardless how aggressive the wave is, we will always find the water's surface. How? Because we are wearing life jackets. Jesus is our life jacket. He is our hope. We are held up by the hope that this isn't the end of our story. We *will* see Logan again, and our every tear will be wiped away.

This season feels so dark, *even with* the promise of heaven. But in my core, I know this is not the end. Not even close. I know this life is temporary, and we were built for eternity. I know we will all be together and whole in the end. In the end, Jesus wins, and so do we. Until that day, equipped with the grace of God, I will continue to stand . . . and face the shore.

33 — SIX PLATES

I pray that from his glorious, unlimited resources he will empower you with inner strength through his Spirit. Then Christ will make his home in your hearts as you trust in him. Your roots will grow down into God's love and keep you strong. And may you have the power to understand, as all God's people should, how wide, how long, how high, and how deep his love is. May you experience the love of Christ, though it is too great to understand fully. Then you will be made complete with all the fullness of life and power that comes from God.
—Ephesians 3:16–19 (NLT)

Photo by Jessica Fox

Immediately following Logan's death, grief crept into every nook and cranny of my life. My entire world was overflowing with sorrow, and there was no avoiding or escaping it. No matter which way I turned, it was in front of me, and every time I looked behind me, it was right there. It followed me just like the relentless nature of a shadow. It never tired in its pursuit and seemed to consume everything around me.

As the days, months, and years eventually passed, my life began to grow *outside* my grief. The size of my grief never changed. It didn't get bigger, and it didn't get smaller, but as time continued, I began to have more and more space to move around without touching it. Early on, I bumped into it often, because I had nowhere else to go, but as my life continued to expand, I didn't run into it quite as much. However, in the moments when I did, it was as overwhelming and messy as it was on the day we first met.

Someone once explained grief to me in that way, and it paints a perfect picture of its nature. I have always been a visual person, and this description of grief is something my brain has been able to hold on to and understand. It clarifies why, when those moments of grief emerge, they feel just as bad as the day we first lost Logan. This is why we can be fine one moment and blindsided by the intensity of our grief the next.

I wanted to share one of these blindsiding moments because from time to time, they can, and *will,* knock you over. I am years out from Logan's death, and while I don't bump into my grief as often these days, every once in a while, I still have a head-on collision. One of these collisions happened when I made lunch for Logan. Yup, you read that right. I made lunch for my dead son.

It was the middle of summer, and Kelley and her kids came over to hang out for the day. Eventually, hunger grumbles started to emerge from the horde of children, so I began making lunch like I have hundreds of times over. Without a second thought, I set out six tiny, brightly colored plates and made six tiny ham sandwiches. At one point, I even double-checked my count to make sure I wasn't a meal short. I added grapes and chips and then started calling kids to the table. I didn't even notice my error until there was one plate left, sitting alone on the counter. It took me a moment to realize that all the little people in my house had their lunch, and there was still one plate remaining.

Then I pieced it together. There *should* be six plates. I have three kids, and Kelley has three kids, and there *should be six plates.* And yet, we only need five. *ROGUE WAVE.*

244

I was a bit surprised how choked up it made me. I stood in the kitchen staring at that lone plate, trying to hide my tears. I was mad that I was crying over something that seemed so ridiculous, *and* that I could still be so caught off guard by my grief.

After a moment, Kelley delicately asked me if I had just accidentally miscounted. I was so upset, because I knew in my heart *I didn't.* I am always very aware of what is missing. I still think about Logan *every single day.* There is a piece of me that is aware of his absence constantly. I have lived that way for many years. Until that day, however, I didn't realize there was a dormant part of me (albeit small and very deeply hidden) that carries on like he is here.

That day, as I watched my kids and their cousins run around in the backyard, I was *tangibly* reminded that someone was missing and always will be on this side. I was reminded, as I personalized each kid's sandwich, that I will never know if Logan would have wanted mustard and mayo or if he would have liked sandwiches at all. That one always kills me.

Moments like these are fewer these days but still bring me right back to the day Logan died. It had been nearly six years at the time. *Six years!* Up until that day, I had never experienced anything remotely close to that, which is exactly why I wanted to share it with you. There are always new and unexpected hurdles on this journey, regardless of how many years you have been on it.

And so, the grief journey goes: mountains and valleys, good days, bad days, straight-up sad days, days I just need to sit in the sorrow, and days where, by God's grace alone, I can keep walking.

My pastor once said, "In the end, it will be okay, and if it's not okay, then it's not the end." It indeed is not the end. On that day, I went ahead and put a check in the "sad" box. The next day, I dusted off my knees, stood up, and tried to start walking again.

34 — PROOF OF LIFE

You have searched me, LORD, and you know me.
—Psalm 139:1 (NIV)

Photo by Jessica Fox

I have little proof of Logan's life. The weight of that statement and the reality that, in many eyes, he never was, sometimes feels heavy enough to crush me. I cling to and cherish any piece of him I can find, and although I know the effort is futile, I often find myself desperately searching for something else to put in the keepsake box that represents his life. It's a box that sits mostly empty in my basement, and regardless of the passage of time, will always remain— mostly empty.

Footprints from the hospital—in the box. A Bible with his name etched on the cover—in the box. A stack of sympathy cards—in the box. The dress I wore when I buried him—in the box. The candle I burned for three straight days after he died—in the box (the smell of it still hits me square in the chest each time I lift its lid). A plastic fork tenderly wrapped in a sunflower napkin that we used for a picnic on his eighth birthday— in the box.

Then there is "Logan Bear"—a stuffed animal with a weight matching Logan's, and an item with enough importance that its permanent home is right next to my bed. This bear is the placeholder for him in our family. My living children *love* it. I often find it hidden throughout the house, lovingly stolen from its safe place on my dresser. I find it covered in lipstick kisses, tucked into bed, or in their arms during story time.

As much as these items are proof that Logan existed, they are also a painful reminder that he is gone. A constant tug-of-war plays out in my heart where I both love and hate these things. The truth is, I cherish that painfully empty box *and* that bear. But the greater truth is, I don't want a box, and I don't want a bear. *I want my son.* I want my daughter to give her brother *actual* kisses. I want my son to *actually* read a book with his big brother next to him. But that will never be our story.

So, until I pass from this world, I will hold on to that box and this bear with a death grip. I will love, remember, and honor Logan as best as I can. And one beautiful day, as my life on earth fades, I will gladly relinquish my grip on those things to run into his arms.

———— ∞ ————

I was working on a project in 2020 where I was asked to share what my "special space" was with Logan. It seemed simple enough, but as I sat down to write, something unexpected happened. In full transparency, I stared blankly at my computer for a full twenty minutes.

What started off as mere frustration shifted to something that felt a lot more like anger. *It's not supposed to be this way. He should be here. We should have a special place together.* Those thoughts played on repeat in my mind as I took a much-needed moment to step away from my computer. Suddenly, as I stood in my kitchen clutching a warm coffee cup, my anger gave way to sorrow.

Maybe I was reading into it too much. Perhaps my mind was thinking of the special spaces I have with Sullivan and Emersyn and the automatic slew of pictures that follow. Perhaps I was subconsciously and frantically looking to match one of those pictures or one of those places to Logan's face. As you know too well, I can't.

Sure, we have the graveyard and the spot that marks his name, but I can't pretend it's a place that brings me peace. There are days my heart longs to be where his body rests, but often it feels like a place that was thrust upon us—a place that only holds value by default.

We also have his tree planted in a park on the other side of town. Maybe *that's* our special place? Once again, I realized it's not. If it truly was sacred to me, surely I would visit it more than once a year. Then it hit me. *There is simply more proof in my life that Logan is gone than evidence that he was ever here.* There are no words to describe how much I hated this newfound realization.

Then God opened my eyes to something so obvious and so simple that it made me laugh out loud. Grief surely can cloud our vision and confuse our hearts sometimes. My special place with him is *here*. The place I feel most connected with Logan is in the comfort of *words*. It's where I find him, it's where he is alive to me on this side. And when I am missing him most, it's where my heart longs to be. What you are holding in your hands *is* our special space.

<hr />

Strangely enough, I think sometimes my heart's search for evidence of Logan is not just because *I* need it but because I want *the world* to have it. A part of me still seems to desire affirmation of my loss. A part of me still wants to prove that he lived, even though I know it shouldn't (and doesn't) matter. It doesn't matter if the world knows, agrees with, or believes what I do. What matters is what *I* know, and I know *he was here*.

The proof of Logan's life and the evidence that he once existed in this world will always fall short of what my heart desires. For the rest of my days, I will continue to search for him everywhere I look, and I will always yearn for more. But in the midst of that struggle, I will continue to thank God for the pieces of Logan I do have and the places where I can *still* find him.

THROUGH KELLEY'S EYES

There is nothing we can do to fill the permanent and untouchable void a child's death creates in a parent's heart. However, there are some ways we can fill *other* places in their life that will inevitably begin to feel empty too.

Picture your hurting loved one holding an empty box. That box represents love, support, acknowledgment, remembrance, understanding, empathy, and a slew of other things bereaved parents desperately need. Now you may not have the power to fill the hole in their heart, but you *do* have the power to fill that box. "Filling the box" will not replace that which was lost, but it will give them one thing I have come to learn all bereaved parents fear—their child being forgotten.

I know there is no way this could possibly ever happen with Logan. He is my little man! I will love him with every fiber of myself until the day I personally get to squeeze him for all eternity. But how are Jamie and Andy supposed to know that unless I make it my business to remind them? You are probably thinking, *Okay, Kelley, point made. But how exactly do we "fill the box"?*

Physically speaking, "filling the box" simply means keeping your eyes peeled for significant memorial gifts. For this, I would like to offer a practical suggestion and introduce you to one of my favorite friends: Etsy. Etsy, or any other similar online store, is a support person's wingman when it comes to finding incredibly meaningful remembrance gifts. You can find everything from birthstone jewelry, to ultrasound art and all kinds of things in between. Consider meandering through these types of offerings for Christmas, Mother's or Father's Day, baby's first birthday, or "just because I was thinking of you today."

Also consider tapping into your own personal craftiness. For the first year of Logan's life, I made him cards for special occasions and sometimes wrote him letters just because I missed him. I would laminate them and add them to a book that I left by his grave. This was a way for me to grieve what I had lost *and* for Jamie and Andy to have insight into my heart's love for their boy.

"Filling the box" emotionally is equally important. This is the idea of keeping a baby's memory alive and well simply by talking about them. Noting their absence instead of shying away from it. Talking about what your hopes were for a relationship with them. Questioning as the years go by who you think they would have looked more like, what you think they would have enjoyed doing, if they would have been a cake or ice cream kind of person. Would they have loved or hated watching *Sponge Bob Square Pants*? Logan would have hated that show, by the way, out of loyalty to his Auntie Kelley. All of these incredibly important, intricate things make a person, a person. Things that we agonizingly don't get to know on this side of heaven if an infant has died.

Just remember—that precious box is constantly being emptied by this world and *constantly* needs refilling. On this side of eternity, a loss-family has to carry the heaviness of their loss with them wherever they go. It is our job to let them *also* feel the weight of your love.

35 — STICKS AND STONES

Let no corrupting talk come out of your mouths, but only such as is good for building up, as fits the occasion, that it may give grace to those who hear.

—Ephesians 4:29 (ESV)

Photo by Jessica Fox

I had forgotten the feeling of a giant sucker punch to my core. And no, I'm not talking about being physically hit in the stomach, but rather, emotionally having the wind knocked out of me—hunched over, hands on my knees, gasping for air, tears at capacity and ready to spill from eye to cheek.

I scan my surroundings, looking for what just hit me. Nothing is there. A mixture of frustration, sadness, anger, and pain run rampant through my body. They aggressively bounce around, competing for who will win the inner battle of what I am truly feeling.

I start to shake. The tremors are apparent in my hands, which I cannot calm no matter how hard I try. Eventually, the world swirling around me starts to slow back to a tolerable level, and I realize I am clenching my teeth and taking in deep, intentional breaths. My chest expands as large as it is able and exhales heavily. It looks—for the moment, at least—like *anger* is the first to win. *How can they be so naive? So blind?* The anger eventually subsides but shifts to an immense *sadness*. Tears no longer trickle down my face. They pour. *Will I always feel so alone? Will they ever understand?*

Another moment is gone and my bipolar emotions continue the fight for who will be first in line. Sadness has now taken a backseat and *frustration* has set in. *How long will I fight this battle? Will people ever change?* The intensity of the moment finally passes, and I am left with an old and familiar "friend"—sorrow. It's always present, often hidden under layers of other emotions, but dig down deep enough and it will be there.

At this point, you are probably wondering what could derail me so badly. How is it possible to have such a physical reaction when nothing actually touched me? What wields such power? What has the ability to inflict that kind of instant distress? *Words*—words hold such power.

Opinions. Naive statements. Ignorance. Stigmas. Misguided, misused, and misinformed ways of thinking. An email. A text. A social media post. A seemingly innocent statement from a friend. All of these things hold power, because words can hurt. They are capable of causing damage that, although unseen, can be as painful as an open and gushing wound. They are sharp enough to pierce through the skin, the bone, and the marrow, all the way to the core of us, with little to no resistance at all.

"Sticks and stones may break my bones, but . . . words will never hurt me." I cannot think of a more ill-advised and inaccurate statement.

In the years following Logan's passing, I was the recipient of *endless words*. The spectrum ranged from kind and compassionate to naive and ignorant. Some words instantly made my blood boil, some made my eyes roll, some made me feel loved, some made me feel seen, and a rare few made me feel understood.

The comments full of grace, the ones that didn't instantly cause my heart to put up its defenses, never made my pain subside, but offered the support and validation I desperately craved. In contrast, the comments that made my heart race and my face flush, caused me to walk away from conversations feeling even more misunderstood, isolated, and hurt. Words didn't have the power to soothe my heartache, but they certainly had the power to make it ache even more.

I was shocked in the weeks and months after Logan's death to hear the colorful variety of comments that would often spew out of people's mouths. They loved to rationalize my pain with every "at least" statement their minds could conjure, with a genuine belief that their words actually had the power to heal.

After a while, there were certain sayings that would make me *physically* cringe. "You will come out of this a stronger person." "At least it was early." "At least he wasn't a *real* baby." "At least you didn't have time to get attached." At least. At least. At least. My all-time favorite? "At least you can always have another child." When that frequent comment surfaced, I had a very hard time not asking the individual which of *their* children they would be okay no longer having.

I remember one of my clients asking to see a picture of Logan during her appointment. I thought it was a strange request, and maybe a tad out of line considering I hardly knew her, but I awkwardly obliged. When she saw the picture, her eyes widened. "Wait! He looks like a *real* baby?!" *Put the shears down, Jamie, and step away from her head, before you do something that's going to get you fired. Or put in jail.* "Well, yes." *Deep breath.* "That's because he *was* a real baby." Some people were even surprised to find out I had to go through a *full* delivery—that there was a body, an *actual* child, to bury. It was ignorance—plain and simple.

Soon after, I had another client tell me, "It's hard to see now, but eventually you will be happy your baby died." That one was a doozy. I know, it's hard to even imagine, and I appreciate your anger brewing on my behalf. She was a mother of two and tried to explain how "lucky" I was, because *now* I could sleep as much as I wanted to. As she got up from my chair, she added, "I hope that didn't offend you." "Offend" was an understatement. No joke, I wanted to punch her in the face. Shockingly, she wasn't even the worst, but for everyone's sake, I'm going to stop right there.

On second thought—*no*. Ha, shocker! I have shared everything else, so why stop now? I heard *a lot* in those days, but this was the worst. A year after Logan died, while on the topic of in-utero terminal diagnosis, I had a client say, "Well, *my* daughter chose to abort. She couldn't let her baby suffocate, like you let yours." Mic drop. I know. Told you it was bad. And no, she is no longer a client of mine.

I can fully understand not knowing what to say and feeling the need to fill an awkward or silent moment with *something*. But if one of the gems above is about to fall out of your mouth, or if you are on the verge of any sentence that starts with "at least" or "but," I would suggest embracing the silence.

As a whole, we are uneasy in the midst of silence and the pockets of the grieving process where our mere presence speaks louder than our words ever could. Sometimes (many times), our willingness just to be present is enough. There were so many days when all I wanted was someone to sit with me. Not helplessly try to fix me—just quietly sit with me.

Those words above were spoken from ignorant lips, and if you have experienced a loss, you will unfortunately hear ones like them too. Oh my goodness, how I wish I could put all bereaved parents in a bubble that automatically filters out every pain-inducing comment that inevitably finds its way to their ears. Or even a machine that could evaluate each and every thing people are about to say to grieving moms and dads and put a big, fat "Return to Sender" stamp on certain painful . . . words.

Then there are words that, if you are a believer in Christ, come from a trusted source, like the Bible, and may even pass-through trusted lips, like those of a pastor or mentor. The problem is, sometimes even *those* words can be misguided.

These are the *interpretations* of Scripture or the religious platitudes (which sometimes have zero biblical backing) that so often circulate in religious circles upon the event of a tragedy. "God won't put more on you than you can handle." "God just needed another angel." "He only takes the best." "Just have some faith." "He has a plan."

I wish all these platitudes would disappear altogether. They are well-meaning, but most times, anger inducing. I realize that sounds confusing, considering I believe the Bible to be the spoken Word of God—a God to whom I have fully given my life. Nevertheless, even the Bible can be used the wrong way. Here are two examples:

"And we know that in all things God works for the good of those who love him, who have been called according to his purpose" (Romans 8:28 NIV). This verse, it seemed, often led to comments like, "At least God will use this for good. At least He has a plan."

"The LORD is close to the brokenhearted and saves those who are crushed in spirit" (Psalm 34:18 NIV). Verses like this would create comments like, "It's okay, God is with you. You are not alone."

Both verses are great, but they have a time and a place. I fully believed God's Word, but right after Logan died, I didn't want to hear it. *Especially* not from the lips of someone who wasn't going through it personally. *Of course* God would use my pain. But did that make it subside? No. Was I okay with my son's death just because someone tried to remind me the Bible said there was a silver lining? Absolutely not.

Yes, it's true—sometimes in life we can't see the forest for the trees. But that expression does not apply here. The "big picture" was meaningless when I was merely fighting to survive. So someone trying to use the Bible to drag me out of the trees and into a clearing where my vantage point could change, did nothing but hurt me more. Nothing, and I mean *nothing*, could justify my kid dying.

THROUGH KELLEY'S EYES

Shhhh. Do you hear that? As I grow older, it has become one of my favorite sounds. It is the sound of silence. It's calming, refreshing, and rewarding. Unfortunately, it is often incredibly fleeting in the craziness of life.

As a society, it's not something we often put much stock into, which is perplexing considering the abundance of advice we have been given regarding its worth. Here are a few gems I stumbled across regarding silence that I would like you to ponder.

"Silence is the sleep that nourishes wisdom" (Francis Bacon). "A meaningful silence is always better than meaningless words" (Unknown). "Wise souls speak loudly in silence" (Unknown). "Silence is sometimes the best answer. It can actually be one of the most meaningful replies you give someone." (Dalai Lama XIV). My personal favorite is pulled from the Bible in the book of Psalms: "Be still, and know that I am God" (Ps. 46:10).

If silence is so beneficial in sensitive situations, why do we feel the need to fill it? Especially when we find ourselves doing so not out of a need to share hard-earned wisdom, but rather the panic of avoiding personal discomfort. In the infant loss world, filling the silence with platitudes doesn't make someone feel comforted; instead, it makes them feel isolated. Think about that—platitudes prevent solidarity. Admitting that "there are no words to fix this" in a horrific situation affirms three things. One, you have fully thought about their situation. Two, you have fully considered what they have lost. Three, you have done your best to wrap your head around what it must feel like. We may not be able to make them feel understood, but we can make them feel *seen*.

But what does sitting in solidarity or silence actually look like? It's literally just letting someone sit in their pain without trying to make them feel better or justify what has happened. I'm telling you, it's really freaking hard to do. Between our inability to shut our traps and our need to rescue everyone, silence feels very counterintuitive. But trust me, it's one of the greatest kindnesses you can show a grieving heart.

Practically this might look like sitting on a loved one's bed and crying with them, agreeing that this is crap and not okay. Or it might mean binge watching an ungodly amount of *Grey's Anatomy* together because they aren't ready to peel themselves up off the sofa just yet. Or it may be *not* voicing your concern that it's been several days since they have taken their last shower, knowing they will get there when they are ready. Silence and solidarity involve taking ourselves out of the equation, reading the room, and trusting that healing can be found in quiet places.

36 — FEAR AND ANGER

No one ever told me that grief felt so like fear.

—C.S. Lewis.

Photo by Jessica Fox

The death of a child can *instantly* remove the barrier of protection many of us find (or found) great comfort in. Before I became a loss-mom, I lived in a bubble where terrible things *did* happen—but to *other* people. Then I lowered my son into the ground and along with him any naïveté that my family was immune to loss. I suddenly lived in a world where the people I loved were no longer safe.

After Logan died, I was immersed in grief and, to top it off, terrified another great loss would soon come my way. A haunting "What if . . . ?" accompanied *every* good-bye. I tried feverishly to shove it down and pretend I couldn't hear its whispers, but I could. Every single day, I could. It consumed my thoughts. Logan's death unearthed a heart that was broken—but also *afraid*.

Nearly a decade later, I wish I could say it has subsided, but it hasn't. Sorry if that is bad news to any of you whose heart is in a similar place mine was. Just because it's the reality of *my* story, however, doesn't mean it will be the reality of yours. The fearful thoughts may not be quite as loud as they used to be, but they are still there—every day. Fear is a relentless enemy and one I battle often.

But why do I find myself so afraid, when God didn't give us a spirit of fear? Why does the thought of another one of my children dying sometimes consume, overwhelm, and paralyze me? Why do I hate any time my family leaves the house without me? Why do I constantly feel in imminent danger of another one of those thick black lines being drawn on the calendar of my life?

In all honesty, I'm tired of living as if I'm simply between lines. I'm tired of wondering which good-bye will be the last with someone I love. *I'm tired of fear stealing my joy.* As a person who is supposed to mentor those on the grief journey, it's hard for me to admit I still struggle so much in certain areas. It is no way to live, but it's where I find myself. If nothing else, let this be an example of how long-lasting and far-stretching grief's hand can be.

I hope and pray that someday I will be freed from the grip fear has on me. I hope and pray that for you as well. Until that day comes, I will do my best to fight for peace.

"Why do bad things happen to good people?" It's a question I field often. Why does the family that did *everything* right—the family desperately wanting a child—have to watch theirs die? Why does the loving and kind couple dreaming of a child to call their own find themselves, year after year, after year, unable to bear one? Meanwhile, horrible things happen to healthy but "unwanted" children every day. Perfect, beautiful, and deserving children are subject to drugs, abuse, neglect, and sometimes even *death*. How is that okay? How is that fair?

I wanted my son. I took all the prenatal vitamins and carefully monitored what I did (and did not) allow into my body. For the love . . . I stopped eating cold-cut Italian sandwiches. And if you know me, that is a *huge* deal. I went to every doctor appointment, took medications that made me feel awful and stopped other medications I had used for years on the off chance they could cause complications. I tried my best to get good sleep and drink lots of water. I prayed every day for the child growing within me. *I did everything right.* And still—he died.

I wish I could wordsmith something clever here, but I just can't. The truth is, we don't have the answer. Even if we had one, I'm not sure it would help us feel better about the countless injustices life hands out. It just seems so unfair, wrong, and cruel.

We live in a broken world, a sin-filled world that is light-years away from its original design. That is my only response to this question. Bad things happen to good people because we live in a world not bound by the laws of what is fair. Thank goodness for the hope and redemption that lies at the foot of the cross. Thank goodness we will one day trade this fallen world for one without flaw.

⸙

"I sat with my anger long enough until she told me her real name was grief." This quote has circulated around my world for a long time now. I often wonder what the unknown author endured to transcribe such words full of so much truth.

Shortly after Logan died, I didn't think I was angry. Sorrow, anxiety, and fear seemed to take charge more than anything else. I had never been an angry person, and even after Logan's diagnosis, I never would have put myself in that category. Then he died—and I *was* angry. It just took time to recognize its presence hidden in the messy pile of emotions making a home in my heart. But as the clock continued to tick, and as I spent more and more time in the world, the more the world seemed to piss me off. If you read Part I of this book, *some* of these stories should sound familiar . . .

A pregnant teen rolling her eyes at her mom as she dug through racks of baby clothes at Target. A lady at the grocery store looking like she would deliver any day—with five *additional* children. Overhearing a conversation between two expecting women, one crying because she was having a (healthy) boy instead of a girl. A brand-new baby being put in my arms without asking because an acquaintance thought it would "help."

A story at church with a family sharing a scary diagnosis of their unborn child, but the wife prayed "really hard and never gave up," and so, their baby lived. Driving by Babies"R"Us, walking past any baby clothing section in a store, getting invitations to baby showers, seeing social media posts of happy families, feeling abandoned by friends, and sometimes even God. Trigger, trigger, trigger—anger, anger, anger.

Yeah . . . I guess you could say I was angry. And all it did was make me feel like a horrible person. But here's the thing—anger is natural. It's a human response, and I am human. So are you. God created all our emotions—and yes, that includes anger.

So, maybe you're angry at Him, your family, your friends—the world. Maybe you're angry at the crappy card you were dealt (possibly more than once) and how unfair it is to watch others receive what your heart desperately craves. Maybe you're angry at *everyone* and *everything*.

Just know, it's okay. It's normal. And it doesn't make you a lesser version of who you used to be. Scream it out, go for a long run, go outside and throw some dishes against a wall—just do *something* (safe) to release the energy. If not, it will build and inevitably rupture and bleed all over everything. Then call your sister, your mom, your dad, or your bestie. Call the person who will be angry *with* you. Not the person who will tell you it's wrong. Then go get some yummy food or a cup of hot coffee, and have a good cry with good company. That's what I did.

THROUGH KELLEY'S EYES

For a really long time I hated Babies"R"Us. I remember thinking it was a horrific, evil store packed to the brim with disgustingly cute and cuddly items. Every time I drove past it, I gave it the bird, and not just a single bird but a two-handed, incredibly passionate display of my birds. I was quite possibly putting every driver around me in grave danger, because I was no longer navigating my car. But it was worth it.

I remember my blood boiling whenever I saw cute little pregnant ladies that seemed to be *everywhere* I went. They just waddled around, uncomfortable, yet beaming at the same time. And don't get me started on the emotions sweet, tiny babies would trigger. Unexpectedly bumping into one of those precious bundles of joy during my day was very possibly the worst thing that could happen. Down with Babies"R"Us, cute pregnant women, and tiny babies. Who's with me?!

Sound crazy? Well, that is literally how it felt in a world absent of Logan. I was a mix of rage, sorrow, and irrational emotions. All around were reminders of what could have, should have, and would have been *if* Logan hadn't been sick. Painful superstores reminded me of all the things we didn't need, and healthy, tiny humans reminded me of all the things we wanted but were missing.

I couldn't seem to avoid the triggers regardless of where I went—that made me mad too.

When I first finished this chapter, I looked back at the long list of things that triggered my anger *just* to make sure I hadn't left out anything obvious. At the end of *every* chapter, I read and reread, to make sure I am confident in what I have written. I felt good at the end of this chapter and felt assured that I had made my point. I was about to put a big check mark on chapter 36 and move on to the next when I realized I had overlooked what was possibly one of my biggest anger triggers.

I was a bit shocked at the realization and thankful God had brought it to my attention. After all, it was something I struggled with *every day*. I'm not sure how in the world I came so close to overlooking it. To some this may sound confusing, and to others it may be more relatable than you would like to admit.

But in hindsight, and out of all the things I was mad at, the greatest of all was *myself*. My body had failed me and, more importantly, failed Logan.

Yes, he was sick, and that was out of my control, but *my* water broke early, and it was nearly impossible not to wonder what could have been if he'd just had more time. Maybe if I hadn't worked such long days. Maybe if I had paid better attention to my body's signals. Maybe if I hadn't been so stressed. Maybe if Logan had made it as long as baby Megan. Maybe if my body had only done what it was supposed to do. Maybe if my body hadn't failed him from the start. Maybe . . . maybe . . . maybe.

Since the beginning days of Walk With Me, I have yet to meet a loss-mom who doesn't feel like she somehow was to blame. In our conversations, a point in time always presents itself where I am able to look right into her sweet eyes and tell her it was not her fault. Even if she doesn't believe my words, the tears that instantly follow only confirm the guilt she has been holding, which seems to feel absolute in *many* of our minds—for we are the holders of life, but also the keepers of death.

If this book is in your hands because you have held life and lost it, I want to tell you the same thing I have told countless moms. From one loss-mama to another, I hope you can receive and accept these words today—*it was not your fault.*

It took years for me to forgive my body and stop blaming myself and my shortcomings for Logan's death. It took many more years to gain the wisdom to finally realize the truth. *I didn't need forgiving.* And neither do you. Let that sink in for a minute. Forgiveness is a by-product of wrong-doings. Atonement is an outcome of transgressions. *You did not choose this. You did not want this. You did not do this. You do not need forgiveness from this.*

You have too much to carry, sweet friend. So today, my prayer is not that you would finally forgive yourself, but that you would realize there is nothing to forgive. Until you can believe it for yourself, I will believe it for you and stand in that gap *with* you. If there was a point in this book where I *really* could give you a ten-second hug, this would be it.

37 — WEEDS AND
WILDFLOWERS

*[He will] bestow on them a crown of beauty instead of ashes, the
oil of joy instead of mourning, and a garment of praise instead of
a spirit of despair.*

—Isaiah 61:3 (NIV)

W e recently spent an entire chapter discussing the way people over-
complicate and oftentimes completely butcher what bereaved
hearts need to hear in the wake of significant loss. We talked about the
innate desire of others to put our story in a box wrapped with a silver-lining
bow. Prior to my loss, I did the same thing, so I am by no means innocent
here. I surely offered well-meaning but shallow condolences that sounded
great on the surface but, once deconstructed, were without substance. I
know I tried to fill the space of others' grief and put an unrealistic responsibility on myself to come up with the "perfect" thing to say, when no such
thing existed. At the time, I just didn't know I was doing it.

At dinner one night, with good friends who lost their full-term daughter in 2019, we started talking about this very thing. We shared countless instances where well-meaning individuals unknowingly poured a gallon of salt in the open and bleeding space where our once-complete hearts used to reside. By night's end, we all agreed the safest and most loving thing a broken heart can hear is, "I'm sorry," and *nothing* after. We agreed that a heart, delicate and freshly laden with grief, does not need to hear countless rationalizations and justifications on what caused that grief in the first place. We agreed searching for the silver lining is something that can wait.

"I'm sorry," and nothing after. Could it really be that simple? Is it possible that fewer words could actually equal better understanding and empathy? Is it possible we have misunderstood what support actually looks like? Maybe we have made it too complicated. Maybe that box we built, and the definition we passed from generation to generation, needs to be deconstructed, rethought, and then—very carefully—rebuilt.

In the wake of great pain, tragedy, and loss, our hearts and minds naturally gravitate to the good in a bad situation. *Look at the way the community gathered. Look at the love that was displayed. Look at the nonprofit that was born.*

It's much more comfortable to focus on the positives and have the "glass half full" mentality. Instinctively, we turn our eyes away from the portion of the glass that is still *half empty*. It's *those* truths that make our faces grimace and our hearts bristle. *Look at the children who are now without a father. Look at the family that is now torn apart. Look at the parents who buried their child.* Is the price of the good worth the cost of the bad? If you ask the hurting, the answer is a resounding *no*.

To search for beauty in painful seasons can be profoundly healing. But *sometimes* we lean so far into whatever good was brought forth that we completely neglect the pain that is still being endured behind closed doors. When appropriate, why can't the two coexist?

In one hand, we hold up and admire the transformation of darkness to light. In the other hand, we hold that which was lost, but we keep *that* hand low and hidden behind our backs, where it's out of eyesight and earshot. We don't want to see the uncomfortable, so we keep our eyes fixed in the opposite (and much more comfortable) direction.

If only both hands could be held at eye level and equally balanced. Our eyes could then track from left to right, thanking God for His faithfulness in the darkness, while *also* remembering those still in the middle of that very darkness.

I believe wholeheartedly that God has the power to take the worst situations and bring forth light. I believe He is the Master Storywriter and can turn rubble into riches. The painful parts of our stories can be redeemed in this life. However, I also know our full redemptive stories aren't found on this side of eternity.

As believers, we use certain verses as blanket responses for every sorrow or difficulty we could ever endure. Take the one we touched on earlier, "In all things God works for the good of those who love him" (Romans 8:28 NIV). I believe the words but think we sometimes misappropriate their meaning when using them as a means to comfort others.

God says He will work *all* things for good to those who love Him and are called according to His purpose. He never promised we would get to witness it firsthand. He never said it would be a soothing balm to our broken hearts. He never said it would make the pain go away. Sometimes we are able to experience beauty growing from the tragedies of our lives, and sometimes that beauty grows out of sight.

What if we lose pieces of our hearts and don't see that pain redeemed, restored, soothed, or tempered in this life? Only in heaven will our eyes see the full tapestry, not the mess of knots underneath that created it. Only there will we truly understand how the shredded and torn pieces of our lives can translate into such a seamless and perfectly designed masterpiece. Only in heaven will we be able to see the full manifestation of "all things working for good."

I love my life and owe so much of its beauty to Logan. I can look around at almost every piece of my world and trace it back to him. I can see so many things that never would have been. I know my life would look so different if my eldest had been born healthy (and I think that version would have been absolutely wonderful as well).

But that wasn't my story. My eldest died, and my world was flipped upside down. In hindsight, I can look back and thank Logan for his life and for being responsible for so much of the beauty I now find in mine. I thank God for allowing us to see the beauty only He could create.

The majority of our dearest friends—the ones we do life with and couldn't imagine our life without—are because of Logan. That is both immensely beautiful and profoundly heartbreaking. Our nonprofit's birth, the calling on my life to write, my living children—so much of my everything is a direct offshoot of his passing. Because of Logan, I can see parts of the tapestry, and it's exquisite. Logan is proof to me that broken is still beautiful.

But try not to let those words deceive you, for the presence of beauty does not dispel the existence of pain. My sorrow has not dissipated because a field once full of ashes is now covered in wildflowers. For if I were to kneel in that field and dig my fingers into the soil, it would take minimal effort to find proof of the past. You see, no amount of beauty can make those ashes disappear.

The year 2020 (the one we would *all* like to forget) is the year I lost my dad to cancer. He was the second great loss in my life, and it was *his* death that truly opened my eyes to the reality that beauty birthed from loss isn't always found on this side of heaven.

I wish more than anything my dad's field was full of wildflowers too. But as I kneel there, all that covers my hands is still just ash and soot. The remains of smoldering memories expand as far as I can see. This field is desolate and burnt. Maybe there hasn't been enough time for life to grow. Maybe the smoke is still too heavy, and my eyes burn too badly to truly look at my surroundings. Or maybe, life is just hard and we will all inevitably lose people we love.

Outside of the fact that my dad is finally whole and with his Creator, there isn't as much beauty to be cultivated on this side. He has gained redemption from all the hurts he faced in his life, which is cause for celebration, but outside of eternity, I am struggling to find a silver lining from where I'm sitting. I know God will use it on this side—I'm just wondering if I will ever see it.

I think *sometimes* our hearts are trying so hard to squeeze some good out of a heartbreaking situation that we twist, bend, and contort it with all of our might, yet in the end, we yield nothing. Right now, I don't see the death of my dad producing much fruit in my life. Right now, it's just a big, gaping hole.

Right now, that is exactly where some of you find yourselves. Your baby died, and there is a big, gaping hole in the center of your life. Your knees rest in a burnt field, you are covered from head to toe in ashes, and you are wondering if the smoke will *ever* settle.

My words are not meant to be covered in a rain cloud. I hope by now you know my heart and understand how fiercely I cling to hope, but I also believe it's okay (and appropriate) at times for loss to be solely sad. No strings attached. No justification. No platitudes. Sadness unaccompanied. Plain and simple.

I've learned there are times in this life where I need to stop digging through the thistles of sorrow, searching for traces of something beautiful. Many times, it has only left my hands bruised and bloodied. I am learning to be still in certain seasons and accept those thistles for what they are—weeds. We live in a fallen world *full* of them.

I've realized sometimes the lessons I learn about grief and try to teach others are ones I *first* need to apply to myself and my own life. Today, as I finish up this chapter, I miss my dad and my son almost too much to bear. Today I simply tell my heart, "I'm sorry," and nothing after. Today I am telling *your* heart the same.

I also know God made a promise. He *will* use our sorrow even if we never see it on this side. Even sitting in the midst of those weeds or in that desolate, burnt field, I can still hear Him whisper, "Redemption is coming." He then reminds me of the most stunning "beauty from ashes" story of all time: His son and the cross. Jesus—the ultimate wildflower.

38 — BATTLE WOUNDS

Be anxious for nothing, but in everything by prayer and supplication,
with thanksgiving, let your requests be made known to God; and
the peace of God, which surpasses all understanding, will guard
your hearts and minds through Christ Jesus.
— Philippians 4:6–7 (NKJV)

Photo by Jessica Fox

M y eyes are shut, and the headphones I'm wearing are sending buzzing
tones to my ears. Each side is taking its turn in a tag team fashion—
left, right, left, right, left, right. In my hands I hold two sensors. They send
corresponding vibrations and are apparently in cahoots with the headphones, because they, too, are dancing back and forth—left, right, left,
right, left, right. It seems to make my eyes flicker and is supposed to do
something to my brain—rework, rewire, or redistribute my thoughts, I

guess. I'm actually not quite sure what exactly it does, but I have heard from good authority it helps with trauma. I'm asked to go back to a very painful memory.

I relive a diagnosis and a room where my life changed forever. I see the tech remove her gloves and walk out of our room. I can feel my heart pounding in my chest. I see my husband trying hard to hide his panic. Then images of the following months start to flash before me, as if in a sped-up slideshow: the doctor with kind eyes looking down at me saying, "Your son is going to die"; standing in the shower holding my belly and screaming in agony; falling to my knees and sobbing on the living room floor; dancing in the kitchen surrounded by my husband's embrace; early mornings sitting in a ball on the couch with my Bible by my side and tears streaming down my cheeks. In those scenes, I am praying and begging God for a miracle.

The next scene comes, and I am at work fumbling for keys with shaking hands. This is where my water broke, and with it all hope I had been so desperately holding. A cold hospital room, doctors everywhere I look, lying on a hard bed, looking up at my sister and husband, noticing their glistening eyes and clenched jaws. Everything is crumbling.

Finally, I see my son. He is as beautiful as I remember, and he is wiggling. Moments later, he is no longer wiggling. He has gone from our arms to the arms of his Creator. A bruise emerges on his chest where the nurse pushed to listen for his heart.

The next scene emerges, and I am walking behind my husband as he carries a tiny casket. A deep hole I'm jealous of because it gets to hold my son. Amazing grace. Doves. The horrific sound of a truckload of dirt collapsing on the place where his body was just placed. Dead flowers with muted colors now cover his grave. I drape my body over where I laid my son's days earlier, and sob. My world has shattered, and the world around me is still spinning, unfazed and at a relentless speed. Then it goes dark.

Tears spill from my eyes, and I hold my breath trying to fight the release of emotion. Refusing to give in, I squeeze my eyes even tighter and cover my face with my hands. The effort is futile, and I am drenched from head to toe in sorrow. I finally succumb and let the tears flow freely. I pull the headphones off my ears, drop the sensors in my lap, and look up at another set of kind eyes. "Tell me what you saw."

Those kind eyes belong to my counselor. She is trying a process known as EMDR, because *something* has to give, and I refuse to continue living in this place much longer. Logan died many years ago, but I still have wounds. I will always have a broken heart. That wound will never fully heal, but I am learning to tolerate the feeling (well, most of the time, at least). But that's not the wound my counselor has her focus on. What we are working on is a very ugly byproduct of the trauma I endured many years ago. It still plagues me and somehow continues to grow bigger and more deeply rooted with each passing year.

Anxiety. No one ever told me grief manifested in ways other than sadness. Fear, anger, anxiety, depression—the list goes on and on. I had to learn that on my own, unfortunately.

It started off small and without threat—a lone brick sitting at my feet. Initially, I didn't know it was there, even though I would trip on it from time to time. It was constructed by sorrow, fear, exhaustion, and the work environment I had to face every day. Slowly, one brick at a time, a prison was being constructed around me.

My first anxiety attack happened at work while cutting the hair of a new client. Out of nowhere, the pace of my heart began to quicken. Within moments its beats were pulsating through my entire body and taking over all my ears could hear. I started to feel a flutter in my stomach, and no, not the good flutter you are thinking of, but the one that makes you nauseous and cuts your breath short. Heat began to crawl up my neck and eventually consumed my face. That's when the shakes started. It began low in my legs and quickly made its way up through my body and out my hands. I thought I was having a heart attack. I excused myself and ran to the break room, not understanding what was causing the very aggressive assault. It took me some time, but I eventually figured it out. I had just experienced my very first panic attack.

For weeks following Logan's passing, I started to dread new clients in my chair. There were too many questions, too much of that small talk I had grown to hate. All innocent and well-meaning—*unless* you had just buried a child. I would slap a big and welcoming smile on my face, but on the inside, I was pleading with them to change the direction the conversation was heading. Inevitably, the question would find its way to the surface.

"Do you have any kids?" It was that same question we talked about earlier, the one I told you caused me great anxiety and, eventually, anxiety attacks. Each time it came up, the tension surrounding me was clear as day. Those in earshot would bristle and grimace, as they waited to see how I was going to field the question—yet again. Every time, I stumbled.

Do I say yes? Do I say no? I don't want to make them uncomfortable, but if I lie, am I doing my son a disservice? Dishonoring him? I don't want to talk about it, but I feel like I must. Forget it, I'm just going to say no this time.

"No I don't, do you?"

Nice job, Jamie. Way to pretend like he didn't even exist so you could avoid an awkward moment. If you lost a sibling, would you deny their existence too? You failed. You let him down. You are a terrible mother, and Logan is so disappointed in you.

The next time around, I would try the other route. "Well, I have a son, but he died shortly after birth." Instantly, a once casual and surface-level conversation would turn heavy and difficult.

Awesome, Jamie. Now you scared them. Now you are going to have to watch them squirm and see how fast they can change the subject. Or you might have to answer all the questions they are going to ask without shedding a tear. Why do you feel the need to share him? The girls you work with are going to get tired of you always bringing up your dead kid. This client doesn't want to hear it either. It's okay. Just act like you are fine and redirect the conversation.

This back-and-forth struggle became part of my daily routine. My work had slowly turned into a battleground. It was invisible to those around me, yet consumed my mind, slowly taking me apart one piece at a time.

The anxiety attacks that initially only hit with new clients started to rear their ugly heads with old clients as well, clients I felt safe with. It made no sense, and now I had no refuge. Somehow work had become my trigger, the epicenter of all my trauma surrounding Logan. The prison that had slowly started to build itself around me was complete.

The anxiety ebbed and flowed. Some months, I was 99 percent okay. Others, I was crippled. I would wake every morning with a pounding heart and sob on my way to work. It got so unbearable that I wanted to quit hair entirely. A couple of times, I almost did.

The attacks evolved over the years from a fear of talking about Logan to a fear of anxiety itself. Yup, you read that right. I have anxiety about having anxiety. The second the thought enters my brain, the battle is lost. Sometimes, it is on my brain constantly. Eventually, I am able to claw and fight my way out of the valley. But then, without warning, the land gives way beneath my feet, and I find myself looking up at another insurmountable mountain.

That's where I found myself the day I tried EMDR for the first time—looking up at a mountain with a summit I couldn't see, shaking my head and saying, "I'll never make it to the top." The prison of anxiety I was trapped in was closing in on me, and the bars seemed to grow thicker and more impossible to break with each passing day.

That day, my counselor casually asked me where I physically felt the anxiety most. A strange question, but I played along. My response was instant. "My hands." She leaned back in her chair and gave me the type of nod only a wise person knows how to give. She grinned as if she was privy to something I was not and responded, "Wow. It means you are a healer. They *always* feel it in their hands."

I gave a doubtful and nervous chuckle. I actually probably even raised an eyebrow, as the thought *I assure you I am no healer* ran across my mind. As she explained further, I began to understand a bit more, and once again, tears flooded my eyes.

Don't romanticize it. I'm not calling myself a healer. Not even close. But what she did confirm to me—probably unknowingly—is the willingness God gave me to share my struggles and the ugly in my life for the sake of others, and the ability not to care what it might cost my image.

Sharing this part of my journey is really painful, which I'm sure doesn't make much sense. But sharing my anxiety struggle makes me feel fully exposed. I still struggle with anxiety attacks, and at times I feel ashamed, weak, pathetic, and embarrassed that I haven't found a way to rid them from my life.

Then, somewhere in the midst of writing this chapter, and *only* because God continues to cover my vulnerability with His grace, I realized I am not what is being exposed. As humans, we innately want to take that which afflicts us and hide it—put it in a dark and secret place and try our best to camouflage it from the world. But it is in that dark and secret place where the environment is ideal for growth. Darkness loves darkness.

What I've needed to do all along is to expose it. Shine a bright light and belittle it, because that is exactly what it is—*little* compared to the greatness and authority of my King. Our burdens are not quite so big and scary when they are not kept so secret. That thing you can't make out in the corner of your room at night is no longer as threatening once the lights are turned on.

So today, with you by my side, I am calling out an old and *far* too friendly foe. I am calling it out of hiding and into the open. Today I declare, "Anxiety, you have no authority here."

I still have a long way to go and many steep mountains to climb. I am still on the frontlines of my battle, but at least now I know I am not alone. For those of you who struggle with anxiety, and even those of you who struggle with depression, please believe this for yourself too. I know it feels consuming, claustrophobic, and never-ending. So . . . call it out into the light. Name it, rebuke it, seek *all* the help you can to combat it. Call your doctor, find a counselor, join a support group, read a book—press into your faith. It won't happen overnight, but slowly those bricks will begin to crumble. Eventually, they will no longer surround you, but instead, will be dust beneath your feet.

———✥———

We live in a culture where therapy often feels taboo. A sense of shame seems to go hand in hand with those who use it as a tool to navigate the difficulties life brings. But do we not go to the doctor when our bodies are sick? Do we not go to the dentist if we have a cracked tooth? When our vision is blurred, whom do we call? In addition, we get *countless* physicals and check-ups *every year* just to ensure we are in good health. Yet, I could begin a conversation with, "My counselor said . . . ," and instantly feel the recoil.

Why is there such a stigma to seeing a counselor when our hearts and minds are hurting? Why is it any different from the various ways we tend to the rest of our body? There is no shame in seeking help, and seeking help does *not* make you weak or inept. It actually is a sign of strength.

The war for our mental health is a gruesome one. I'm right there with you. Even now, as I think about my next day in the salon, I can begin to feel a tremble in my hands. But I am choosing to believe I am on the verge of a breakthrough. I am choosing to believe I don't have to *climb* to the top of that mountain, because God has made a promise to *carry* me.

We sometimes speak of our burdens as the "cross we must carry." Almost as though we believe that was God's plan for our lives all along. We act like we must drag around this heavy piece of wood, have it tear into our backs, knock us down, and make us bleed, all because Jesus asked us to. But we have that so wrong.

When He said, "Take up your cross and follow Me," He was speaking more along the lines of dying to one's self and surrendering to Him, *not* carrying the very things He died to save us from. *Jesus carried the cross so we don't have to.* Before He died, the cross did represent sin and death, but now it looks much different. Now it is symbolic of life, forgiveness, and freedom. So yes, carry your cross—just realize what it is you are actually supposed to be carrying.

39 — SYMPATHY CARDS AND WHAT NOT TO SAY

For the LORD grants wisdom; from his mouth come knowledge and understanding.

—Proverbs 2:6 (NLT)

Photo by Jessica Fox

My cart was full to the brim. Emersyn was barely visible sitting in the middle of the shopping cart with her little head emerging from all the newfound, but necessary, Target bounty. Luckily, she didn't seem to care about her surroundings due to the strategic placement of my iPhone in her tiny hands. In all fairness, she had already put up with a full morning of errands with minimal complaining, and in an effort to buy myself a few more minutes of peace, I caved to technology.

I love Target. It's just the best—or the worst, depending on how you look at it or who you ask. However, during every trip there comes a time when "I just love this place" suddenly turns to "Oh my gosh, get me out!" That threshold had been crossed. Target had officially done me in, and I suddenly found myself on a mission to exit, find my car, and free my daughter from the shopping cart she had lived in for the past hour.

As I walked briskly to the front of the store, my cart screeched to a halt—enough so to get a grumble out of Emersyn from down below. To my right sat the card section, the reason my cart had stopped so abruptly. I found myself frozen in the middle of the aisle with a suddenly heavy heart. An old friend of mine had just experienced a loss, and I needed to send her a card. In that moment, I had to make peace with the fact that, while I may be done with Target, Target was not done with me.

I stood there staring at the sea of cards and did what we all do—judge them by the inch visible to the naked eye and inevitably play a game of Sympathy Card Roulette.

No. No. Nope. Definitely no. Seriously? Have any of these writers ever actually lost someone they loved?

Prior to losing Logan, I could have plucked one out effortlessly, thinking it was top notch in the sympathy card department. Beautiful picture? Check. Religious encouragement? Check. Pretty envelope color? Bonus check.

It's amazing how certain veils in life can be torn down, instantly revealing so much that was previously unseen. Circumstance and experience seem to have a way of changing not only our hearts but our eyes.

I crouched down low, so I was level with the sympathy section and scanned card after card after card, but now through the set of eyes I was given after Logan died. I can't imagine sympathy cards have changed much over the years, so it quickly became apparent that *I* was the one who had changed.

Almost every single card rubbed me the wrong way. They may have been well intended, but they were poorly executed. Some of the cards did have good words of encouragement, but the timing would have been terrible for someone whose wound was still fresh. The *when* is equally as important as the *what*. There is a time and a place for certain things to be said, and absolutely *no* time and place for others.

Here's the proof:

"You are stronger than you know."

False. In the wake of the death of a loved one, you don't feel strong, and more importantly, you don't need the pressure from those around you to feel strong. In the months after Logan died, the thought of taking a shower often felt overwhelming. I was anything but strong, and that was okay. I was weak and broken, and that was okay too.

"May the memories of sunshine chase away the clouds."

Nothing can chase away these "clouds." And on that note, grief needs to stop being viewed as something that needs to be "chased away." It's a process, and it has a purpose. The bereaved need to lean into their grief, not attempt to scare it away. Grief needs to be faced head-on. Otherwise, it comes back bigger and uglier and messier than before. Chasing it, burying it, or attempting to outrun it is futile at best—not to mention *incredibly* unhealthy.

"Nothing can ever replace a loved one's presence in your life."

Absence. Absence most certainly can. Death *stole* the presence of Logan in my life. Yes, I will always carry him in my heart, but that is nothing close to what I desired and what I deserved as his mother. God may gift me moments where I feel more connected to him or more clearly see his delicate footprints in my life, but that is not the same as him living *with* me. Feeling an essence of him when I see a sunflower or hear a certain song is something I will, of course, gladly take, but it's nothing close to his *physical* presence. I can't hug an essence. I can't tickle an essence.

Creating flowery statements by stringing together pretty words and then finishing them off with a dusting of sugar does zero good. Sure, they may sound poetic on the surface, but once deconstructed, they have the truth and depth of a half-full kiddie pool sitting in a backyard on a blistering hot summer day. These words simply evaporate the moment they are read.

"You are never alone when you have the love and support of those around you."

Support fades. At first, the floodgates are open, and support is rushing in, but as time carries on, that once raging river slows to a trickling stream (if you are lucky). For some, it dries up entirely.

Even when support *is* present, it does not have the power to eliminate loneliness. No amount of love could have filled the lonely void left in my son's absence. No amount of support could have filled the painfully empty nursery-to-be that I sat in every day. No one was with me as I broke down in the shower every night. No one was sitting by my side as tears fell off my cheeks on the way to and from work for well over a year. I may have been loved by many, but I never felt more alone in my entire life.

"You and your family are held close in our hearts and wished comfort in the days to come."

Days? The path of grief cannot be traversed in days or weeks or even months. It's a *lifelong* journey. The road changes and evolves, and as time goes on, it can (hopefully) be better navigated and tolerated, but it never fully ends. It is anything but a weekend road trip gone bad. Offering support in the *days* ahead is appropriate for someone recovering from a minor surgery, not for someone with a chronically broken heart. After a significant loss, life gets split into two parts: before and after. There's the life I lived before Logan died, and then there's the life I live now that he's gone. Offering me comfort only in the "days to come" overlooks the *lifelong* comfort I actually need.

"They say bad things in life happen in threes. Hopefully, that doesn't happen. But if it does, I'll be by your side for all three."

Oh my ever-loving goodness. No, this is not a joke. This card was available for the bargain price of $4.99. "Heads up—you might have two more tragedies heading your way." Completely speechless on this one. *Completely speechless.*

I could go on and on with countless examples, but I have probably *more* than made my point. I'm confident my bereaved parent community is standing behind me sounding a unanimous "Amen." Meanwhile, everyone else is possibly feeling irritated by my *maybe* too abrasive or too blunt of an opinion.

Please know, my heart is not to come across as cynical or skeptical of human sincerity. I actually think tragedy is one of the greatest catalysts of the beauty that can be found in humanity. Nothing else spurs a heart into action more than the suffering of others. Nothing else makes a human heart look and act more like Jesus. So, if you are reading this and "Oh no" is echoing in the back of your mind, please do not overanalyze every sympathy card you have ever sent. Acknowledging a loss *is* necessary, the thought *does* count, and support *is* appreciated.

The takeaway here is quite simple—stop and think. Take the extra five minutes. Actually *read* the card *before* you purchase it. Absorb the message it is sending. Acknowledge your loved one's loss without attempting to justify, fix, or minimize it. Were all those cards filled with the intent to love? Of course. Were the words meant to offend or hurt or cause a grieving heart to roll its eyes? Of course not. Luckily, more often than not these "word misfires" are born out of a genuine desire to support.

That tells me there is still *hope* for change. I just can't help but think how a slight recalculation or couple-degree shift in the compass of our culture could truly change everything. I can't help but dream of a world that one day accepts even that which it does not understand.

Just to clear up any lingering apprehension, please rest assured in this—we got countless cards after Logan died, and I kept *every single one*. I don't recall their words or feeling any anger when I read them just because *some* of those words may have been misplaced. I actually felt very loved. In all honesty, I don't remember a single one. The stack of those cards lives in that little box that contains every piece of what remains of Logan's life. Those cards are proof Logan existed, and I will hold on to them until the day I leave this world (and that box) behind.

Just in case you are wondering what card I picked after twenty additional grueling minutes in Target: "It's Just Not Fair." Yup. It was that simple, and it was perfect.

THROUGH KELLEY'S EYES

Hallmark's stock in greeting cards is plummeting as we speak. I'm assuming you are probably thinking two things right now. One, "Well, crap. I have for sure sent sympathy cards that sounded just like that." Thing two, "Double crap. What the heck am I supposed to do now?" I think the lesson to be learned here isn't that sympathy cards are the epitome of all evil, but more so that when dealing with the brokenhearted, we should choose cards that avoid empty platitudes and keep the message simple.

Remember, this isn't about fixing something—because that's impossible. It's simply about acknowledging it.

Join me in making our next sympathy card endeavors simple and direct. Try to find cards that say something along the lines of, "I am so sorry. This isn't ok. I love you!" This will feel genuine. This will feel like love.

Now, here comes the real challenge. Consider sending one of these little gems every few weeks for the foreseeable future. "I'm *still* sorry. This *still* isn't okay. I will always love you and the baby you've lost. I'm *still* thinking of you." And so on and so forth. Anyone can send a card and move on with their day (by the way, these gestures are still totally appreciated). Only a select few will engage for the long run, and that can make all the difference. Together let's start a sympathy card revolution.

40 — IF NOT US,
THEN WHO?

*Start children off on the way they should go, and even when they
are old they will not turn from it.*

—Proverbs 22:6 (NIV)

Photo by Jessica Fox

"I feel like I have been such a downer mom lately. I don't want my kids
to see me like this. I need to snap out of it." Let those words sink in,
and I'll circle back to them in a moment.

As parents, we have an innate desire to protect our children from
all things. We try our best to shield them from the scary, unpredictable,
and unforgiving world around them. However, we very quickly learn how
not in control we are. Sometimes, as a result, we overcompensate in areas
where we may have a sliver of control. With a white-knuckled grip, we
hold tight to what we can, but occasionally, in the name of protection and
with good intentions, we miss the mark entirely.

In this world of so many opinions, where a parent's every move is scru-
tinized and put under a microscope, how do we find a healthy balance?
How do we know the areas to press in and the areas to pull back? How
do we know what is too much or not enough? Too strict or too lenient?
Too transparent or too opaque?

All in all, my goal as a mom is quite simple. I want my kids to have a heart for Jesus, be a light in this dark world, and ultimately live a long and full life. In hindsight, that is anything but simple and is much easier said than done.

I am a helicopter mom. Those who know me would agree. It's a constant struggle trying to find a healthy balance of being responsible and proactive versus overbearing and overprotective. I live in tension—an internal and constant tug-of-war where I am trying to embrace the independence of maturing children *and* the mama bear that rages within me. I'll be honest, my kids are still relatively small and don't have much freedom . . . yet. But I know that will change in the blink of an eye. I doubt, however, the mama bear within me will.

Having already buried a child only exacerbates the issue. When the unimaginable touches your life, you change. My history with loss, coupled with my lifelong propensity to worry, was the perfect recipe to turn me into an overprotective parent. I can't say I love how protective I have grown to be, but what's a mom to do?

I just want to keep my kids safe—spiritually, physically, mentally, and emotionally. Spiritually, it's quite simple—I want them to know Jesus. I want them to believe God loved them *so much* that He moved heaven and earth to find a way to be with them forever. I want them to know there is nowhere they can go that He cannot follow. I want them to open their hearts to His great sacrifice. I want their love for Him and His people to be overflowing.

The physical component is obvious. Wear your seat belt. Don't talk to strangers. Don't run with scissors. Wash your hands. Don't do drugs. Exercise. Limit screen time. Don't lick the bottom of your boot (that one is specific to Emersyn). Eat your vegetables, and so forth.

The mental and emotional pieces are a bit harder to dissect and hold ample space for gray areas, because they are ever evolving and vary from kid to kid. Every child is a unique creation who needs to be loved and supported in ways unique to them. Mental and emotional health is not a one-size-fits-all deal. This is the one I struggle with the most, *because* it's not black and white.

As parents, we don't want to expose our children to the parts of this life that are hard to navigate, even as adults. We don't want them to see us fighting. We don't want them to see us scared. We don't want them to see us sad. In an attempt to protect, we sometimes shield them from the very things they will surely experience in their lifetimes, instead of showing them *how* to navigate those things in a healthy way. Yet someone *must* teach our children how to do these things. My question to you is this: if not us, then who?

As parents, it is our job to teach. Just as we teach them how to ride a bike and how to share, we also must teach them how to manage big emotions and difficult life events. Children are sponges. They mimic. They copy. They often grow into unique versions of what they are repeatedly exposed to. *They watch our every move.* Yes, they pick up on our bad habits. The upside, however, is they also will pick up on our good ones.

With that in mind, let me ask you another question. What about grief? Sorrow? The process of lamentation? Whose job is it to teach the young generation these things? Could this possibly be the reason why, as a culture, we often feel unequipped to handle grief and its collateral? Could it simply be that we were never taught?

"I feel like I have been such a downer mom lately. I don't want my kids to see me like this. I need to snap out of it and get over this."

I have heard these words pour out from loving hearts that genuinely want to protect in the wake of great loss. Grief somehow *feels wrong*. It feels like something we need to hide, something we don't want our children to see, and thus, something from which we must shield them. But if not us, then who will teach them how to grieve?

How will they ever know how to grieve if we, their parents, never show them? Remember, children mimic what they see. They watch our every move, and it is *our* responsibility to show them the reality of sorrow. I'm not saying we need to expose our children to *all* the ugly. Just like all things in life, we need to temper and adjust according to what is age-appropriate. But they must be exposed to it, or when their time comes, they, too, will be completely lost.

If I had living children when Logan died, I wouldn't have let them see the moments where I was on my knees and screaming at the top of my lungs in anguish. I wouldn't have let them see the moments of searing pain that produced reactions in me that would have scared them. I broke things. I yelled obscenities. I did things that were out of character. I would, however, have let them see me cry.

I would have told them my heart was broken, and it made Mommy's energy low. I would have explained that low energy made me very sleepy. I would have told them I was going to a "doctor" or "counselor" to talk about my broken heart. I would have reminded them it's good to talk about the things that make us sad and even the things that may make us uncomfortable. I would have openly talked to them about their brother being in heaven and given them space to share their feelings too. I would have let them see me write and would have told them how it helped me handle the emotions I was feeling. I would have explained to them that, just like a wound we can see on the outside that needs to be cleaned, bandaged, and given time to heal, wounds on the inside, though not visible to the naked eye, need to be cared for in the same way.

I would have *still* tried my best to be the mom they deserved. I would have *still* loved and cared for them to the best of my ability. I would have forced smiles, built forts, and engaged in tickle battles. I would have cooked dinner, gone on bike rides, read bedtime stories, and then . . . I would have cried in front of them some more. I would have shown them grief is not something to avoid or ignore, rather something we must embrace. I would have protected them, to the best of my ability, from things children should not have to carry, but at the same time, I would have *taught* them it's okay to be sad—that grief is a *normal* part of life. And because of that, they would have grown up with an understanding many adults today do not possess.

Now I am going to turn all of that upside down. For the sake of transparency, do you want to know the truth? I would have done almost *none* of those things.

I, like so many, would have hidden my grief in an *attempt* to protect my children. I would have thought it was the right thing to do. And do you know what? It wouldn't have been my fault, for I was never taught otherwise. My parents were never taught otherwise. My grandparents were never taught otherwise. And now, we have a silent epidemic.

I would have done all those things *only* if someone who had walked the road before me had instructed me to do so. But had I been in that situation with no guidance, my grief would have been private and kept at a safe distance from my children in the name of protection. And my children would have grown up unequipped—not understanding grief and believing it was a road to walk in silence. When a time of great sadness entered their lives, grief would have barged through their front doors unannounced. Its presence would have been threatening, unfamiliar, and overwhelming.

It's impossible to be prepared for the magnitude and all-consuming nature of grief. It is possible, however, to be equipped with the knowledge, tools, and community necessary to help a brutally difficult journey be navigated in a healthier way.

The posture of our society toward grief, and the belief that grief is only for a season, breaks my heart. It is so deeply rooted in our culture that it makes me question how we will ever find a force great enough to choke it out. For a long time, that question was on repeat in my mind. *What force could make a difference? What force could sever those toxic roots?* Then it hit me—*it's our children.*

It's the next generation. It's one family at a time leaning into their grief, showing their kids it's okay to hurt, and being open to discussing the uncomfortable. It's one child at a time growing up learning the difference between healthy and unhealthy coping mechanisms. It's training our kids in trying times to have knee-jerk reactions that are life-giving, not life-stealing. It's counseling no longer feeling taboo or something only for the weak. It's mental health being discussed openly. It's change taking place in one home at a time.

It's *our* responsibility as parents to make these things second nature to our children. Do something often enough and it becomes a habit. An automatic response. Reinforce it. Practice it. Allow it to become deeply rooted in them.

Logan was my first great loss, but unfortunately, he was not my last. When immense sadness covered me again after the death of my father, I tried my best not to live those words out in rhetoric alone, but to walk a road, step by step, that mimicked them. And guess what? *My kids watched my every move.*

Our children are the path to change. Slowly the tide will begin to shift, and what once felt foreign, unknown, and uncomfortable will grow into something familiar, understood, and entirely normal. These beautiful roots, the ones our children are capable of growing, *will* choke out that which for so long has made the very ground we walk on toxic.

Young generations *will* rewrite the habits of our society. One day, as they dig their toes into the fertile soil they unknowingly helped cultivate, they will look back at us puzzled, shaking their heads and wondering how we had it so wrong. I may not like it, but I am okay being a part of the world that *had* it wrong. You see, *had* is past tense. If something *used to be* wrong, that means it *no longer is.* What a beautiful day that will be.

41 — LOVE REMAINS

*And now these three remain: faith, hope and love. But the greatest
of these is love.*

—1 Corinthians 13:13 (NIV)

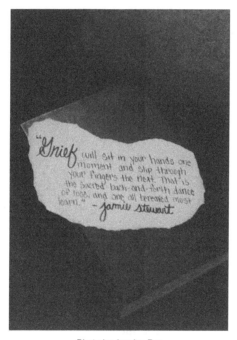

Photo by Jessica Fox

We are, once again, at a chapter where my words may cause your pulse
to quicken. So, once again, I am asking you to put down your guard
and be open to receive what I am about to share. This doesn't apply to all.
This is a message more for those of you whose losses are not recent (and yes,
I'm aware *recent* is a relative term), but pieces of it still can apply to everyone.
This is a chapter that was birthed from observing and interacting with hundreds of bereaved parents over the span of many years. The topic is something I never would have understood if I hadn't seen it unfold firsthand.

"Healing doesn't mean the damage never existed—it means it doesn't control you." I heard someone say that once, and it really stuck with me. *Control, consume, define*—pick a word appropriate to you, but the sentiment remains the same. This can be a hard one for many of us.

For a long time, sorrow *controlled* my every thought and every decision. Grief *consumed* my world. Being "the girl with the dead son" *defined* me. It took years for these things to adjust in my life, and when they did, it left me feeling conflicted.

Was my love for Logan less because my thoughts would drift to other places? Was my love for Logan less because my eyes learned to see things other than just him? Was my love for Logan less because my title began to shift?

Healing and learning how to live with pain does not erase the past. Moving through sorrow and embracing its different seasons does not lessen love. Being seen as more than just a bereaved parent doesn't belittle the loss of a child.

Whatever your definition of healing may be, it does not, could not, and never will erase your love and what you have endured. It just means your life has grown to a place where it has room for more than just a broken heart, and even though it may feel like a betrayal, it's not a bad thing.

Grief has a process and a purpose. You've by now heard me say it many times. It can't be rushed, and it never should be pushed away, but over time and often without notice, it can *sometimes* shift into something far outside its original design. *Sometimes*, we can slowly begin to see our grief as a badge of honor or a sign of respect to those we have lost. *Sometimes*, we think our sorrow must remain paramount in all things and at all times for the level of our loyalty to remain unchanged and intact.

Grief has *many* purposes, but it was never meant to have the duty and responsibility of gauging the amount of love that still exists in the wake of great loss.

In the early days, months, and even years of sorrow, we grieve intensely because we love intensely. But as time continues, we sometimes get stuck thinking that if the intensity, duration, or frequency of grief's visits minimize, then our love must as well. When we find ourselves years out from our losses, we sometimes make an intentional decision to *live* in grief rather than *visit* it, to prove to ourselves (and those around us) the magnitude and severity of our loss. We think we honor the dead in body by refusing to live, forgetting they are very much alive in spirit. We see any shred of joy beginning to take root in our lives as some form of a betrayal, as if moving forward in life is the same as moving on. We think by digging our heels in and pushing away hope that we somehow better uphold the memory of those our hearts miss so intensely. We believe the daily level of our sorrow and the rate at which it fluctuates indicates the level at which our hearts are still connected to those we have lost.

Yes, grief *is* the cost of love, but grief cannot exist where love did not first abound. Grief is *dependent*—it's a byproduct of love. Love was designed differently. It is far greater, much stronger, endures forever, and can stand on its own. Love can and always will exist, even with grief's fluctuations.

Once sorrow has touched your life, it will forever ebb and flow throughout it. It will weave in and out as it needs. Sometimes its visits will seem extended, and sometimes they will be brief. Grief will sit in your hands one moment and slip through your fingers the next. That is the sacred back-and-forth dance of loss, and one all who grieve must learn.

Give yourself permission today to trust your heart when it gives you moments (or seasons) of peace. Let go of your sorrow for a minute, an hour, or—dare I say it—even a day. Let yourself take a deep breath and release the grip you have on its significance and the misconception that its absence somehow has the power to alter the magnitude of your love. Letting go of your grief, if even for a moment, is in no way letting go of your loss. Love remains—and it always will.

42 — AN UNFATHOMABLE GIFT

For God so loved the world that he gave his one and only Son, that whoever believes in him shall not perish but have eternal life.
—John 3:16 (NIV)

Photo by Jessica Fox

Before I lost Logan, I can't honestly say I fully understood the gravity of what it meant for God to sacrifice His son, Jesus, for my sake. Growing up in church, *sacrifice* was a common word—one toward which I unintentionally became desensitized and callous. *Jesus died for me.* Because of that sacrifice, I have everlasting life. It seemed pretty simple back then, but I naively skimmed over the details and only grasped the end result: my salvation.

After watching Logan die, the idea of sacrifice instantly looked dramatically different to me. God sacrificed His son. *He sacrificed His son.* The weight of those four little words seems obvious now. But before I had a child of my own, I did not, and I could not, understand the magnitude of what actually took place that day at Calvary.

When Logan died, I had no choice in the matter. In the end, I knew and wholeheartedly believed God would use Logan's little life to save lost souls. I saw it firsthand. I heard about it in letters and emails and in conversations with strangers who were full of tears and appreciation of what Logan's life had done for them. I was so grateful to see God using our story, but . . . *I had no choice*. After I knew Logan was going to die, and especially after he was gone, it was easier to accept that his death brought life to others. The pain Andy and I were experiencing had a purpose. I knew it was true. I fully believed it. *But I had no choice.*

What if God had given me a say in the matter? What if He had said, "Jamie, you can have a full and happy life with your son *or* you can give his life and ensure one more person will spend eternity in heaven"? To my everlasting shame, even knowing full well the gravity of what that meant for a lost soul, I would have chosen Logan—without hesitation. I would have responded, "No. Absolutely not. Not my son. Not this life. Find another way." Just goes to show how far away my heart is from that of my Savior's.

Before you are quick to judge, I want you to think about *your* child— your son, your daughter, your niece, your nephew, your cousin, *your* baby. Would you give *their* life to save another's? Would you be willing to watch them suffer and die for the sake of someone else? Possibly a stranger? Possibly someone who might reject the salvation your sacrifice would offer? It's a heavy question full of more repercussions than I would like to admit. Maybe you are a better person than I am, or maybe, just maybe, we are human, and even if we tried for a million years, we could never understand the depth of love our God has for us. It is truly extravagant and beautifully reckless.

God *willingly* sacrificed His son so we could live. Sometimes I need to repeat that to myself, to let it sink in. He *willingly* sacrificed His son so we could live. He allowed Jesus to endure the most excruciating pain this world has to offer to give us the *opportunity* to choose Him. He knew many would still reject Him, and yet, He still made a choice I believe none of us could make.

Some of us understand what it's like to watch your child die. Some of us understand how it feels to see your child's body lifeless and cold. Despair. Helplessness. Agony. There are no adequate words to describe it. Having Logan, and then watching his life fade in front of me, opened my eyes to see God in a way that was never possible before. For the first time,

I could actually empathize, albeit in an incredibly minute way, with the weight of His decision to send Jesus to the cross.

———⊗⊗⊗———

Even knowing the priceless gift I had been given, even knowing what God had *already* done for me, I still couldn't help but sometimes question the *why* behind Logan's death. At times, certain thoughts ran uncontrolled in my mind. *Why would God give Logan to me if He was just going to take him away? He knew Logan would die, so why did he even let me get pregnant in the first place? Why would He intentionally put me through such pain? What was the point of it all?*

I asked these questions to Him for years—yes, *years*. And then, one day, very likely as I became more concerned with listening rather than talking, God finally gave me an answer.

He began to remind me how this earth, our home, is temporary. He reminded me that we were created for eternity. I was made to be with Him in heaven forever. Because of our human nature, it's almost impossible not to see only the here and now. This life feels like everything to us. It feels like it's all we have. Right there is the root of the problem, because *this* life is just the beginning. It's the first chapter in a book that will never end.

In this first chapter, it's easy to feel angry or bitter after loss. It's easy to feel like "God took my child." It seems like such a cruel thing for a loving God to do, and we're left feeling conflicted and confused about who He really is. But God, in response to my questions, softly began to tell me, "I didn't *take* your son, Jamie. I *gave* him to you for all eternity."

Such a simple shift. In a single moment, I learned to adjust my focus on God *giving* me a son rather than *taking* him—and it completely changed my perspective. It's hard to think about forever in the midst of such grief. But God *is* thinking of our forever. Heaven is real, and if you have lost a child (or children), that is exactly where they wait for us. One day, we will never have to say good-bye again. In no way does that belittle or diminish the hell we have to walk through before that time comes, but if I must go through the pain of losing Logan here in order to have him for eternity there—*I'm all in.*

43 — FORSAKEN?

He will wipe every tear from their eyes. There will be no more death or mourning or crying or pain, for the old order of things has passed away.

—Revelation 21:4 (NIV)

Photo by Jessica Fox

Looking back at the storm I once endured, the storm I still occasionally see looming above my head, I have realized more than ever the need for God as the backbone of my life. Although I have gone through some very dark places and experienced sorrow that many times took away my desire to continue, I know that without God it would have been worse. I write those words with a heavy heart, because I cannot imagine the level of pain one would endure in a similar situation if they didn't know God and His promises.

In the midst of tragedy, those who believe in Jesus and His sacrifice have an immeasurable advantage over someone who doesn't—we have *hope.* The Bible tells us we can grieve with hope (1 Thessalonians 4:13). In Christ we can grieve *differently* than the rest of the world because we know death is not the end. We can cling to the promise that heaven is real,

Jesus is the bridge to get there, and we *will* see our loved ones again. We have hope in the promise that one day our tears will be wiped away and will forever be no more. I cannot imagine burying my son and believing that was the end. What a dark and scary place that would be. Even when I am overwhelmed with sorrow, I know when I enter the gates of heaven one day, my little boy is going to run into my arms once again and together we will run into my dad's. I anticipate these moments with great joy.

Faith doesn't make life easy. *Not even close.* As Christians we often put on our "church face" out of obligation. We try to hide behind the image we've painted in our minds of what we *should* look like to our community. We want to appear to be strong, obedient, and upstanding Christians. We raise our hands in worship, throw some cash in the offering basket, slap on a smile, and pretend like we have it all together. Rarely do we let down the facade and admit our struggles. We feel the need to hide who we really are to the very group of people with whom we *should* be the most transparent.

What would happen if we stopped the act? Would we realize *all* Christians are messed-up, imperfect people who are together pursuing a perfect God?

I am mad at God. I am struggling in my walk with Him. I feel unworthy. I feel abandoned. I haven't read my Bible in a year. I am in the middle of an ugly divorce. I struggle with depression and anxiety. I'm trying to get sober. I'm addicted to pornography. I'm having an affair.

It can be really hard to admit those types of thoughts and truths around other Christians for fear of being judged. And unfortunately, given the behaviors of many and the reputation of "organized religion," we are justified in such fears. My pastors always say, "Our church isn't a country club for saints, but a hospital for sinners." We owe it to ourselves *and* our church family to be transparent in our struggles. Just think of the new ways God could use us *if only* we would just drop the perfect-Christian facade we try so hard to maintain. I believe God wants us to share our pain, our struggles, and our disappointments so that others don't feel alone.

What if that which afflicts you is the very thing you were meant to help heal in others' lives? What if your willingness to be open with your difficulties has the power to be the survival guide one day for another? Some of the most meaningful relationships in my life have come from people who have walked the same path I am walking and been willing to share it with me.

A big part of Logan's legacy for me is being able to be that person to someone else. Sharing his story and my struggles are a huge piece of my healing process. My heart is broken—a part of it always will be on this side—but I fully believe God's glory is able to shine even brighter *because* of my brokenness and my willingness to put it in the spotlight. Had I not decided to take off my "church face" while sharing this journey with you, my story would be surface level and ineffective. I'm not perfect, but for the sake of community and authenticity, I'm perfectly okay admitting it. The truth is, there is only one human who was ever perfect, and His name is Jesus.

If you struggle with the idea of complete authenticity with God and transparency with His followers, just look to Jesus as the example. On the cross, He took our guilt, our shame, and the judgment we deserved. He literally had the weight of the world's sin—the weight of *my* sin and *your* sin—placed on his shoulders. *Jesus became sin for us.* As a result, God had to separate Himself fully from His Son for the first time ever. In complete anguish, Jesus cried out on the cross, "My God, my God, why have you forsaken me?" (Matthew 27:46 NIV).

Is it possible, in that heartbreaking moment, that Jesus felt abandoned by his Father? He *knew* what was to come. He *knew* the separation was only temporary, and that God would never truly look away from Him, but His cry to God was an honest one, from a desperate, hurting, and *human* heart. Jesus was fully God, but we often overlook that He was also *fully man*. Everything Jesus did was with intention. I believe He was suffering in a way we cannot comprehend but also giving us permission to cry out with honesty to our Father. I believe he was setting a precedent for an authentic relationship with God.

You, too, may be asking if God has forsaken you. You may be in the middle of a season where it feels like He has turned his back on you. But here is the good news in all of this for us: Christ became sin and, thus, experienced the separation we deserved. God said, "Never will I leave you; never will I forsake you" (Hebrews 13:5 NIV). Now we can live with that promise in the forefront of our minds. Jesus endured it so we wouldn't have to.

God never promised life would be easy. In fact, he actually guaranteed trials and tribulations. "When you go through deep waters, I will be with you. When you go through rivers of difficulty, you will not drown. When you walk through the fire of oppression, you will not be burned up; the flames will not consume you" (Isa. 43:2 NLT). Notice in this verse the very intentional use of the word *when*. God did not say *if* you go through deep waters—He said *when*.

———⊗⊗⊗———

When I first found out Logan was sick, I experienced an incredible surge in my spirit to pray and read the Word. The storm around me was raging, but I kept my eyes on Him. I felt great comfort in being in His Word. It was like I was sitting in the middle of a hurricane, but in those private moments with Him, I was safely protected within its eye. I wish I could say that endurance and sense of protection continued after Logan died, but it didn't. I felt defeated, broken, exhausted—*abandoned*. I no longer had Logan to fight for. He was gone, and to be completely honest, I no longer cared about anything. I was too tired to pray, and I practically stopped reading my Bible. I still felt like I was in that raging hurricane, but had left the protection of its eye. I had nowhere to go where I could escape its wrath.

Much of the time I did spend with God was questioning Him and His ways—telling Him how much my heart hurt and begging Him to fix it. Sometimes I would even pray for Him to take me home too. I didn't *want* to die, but I didn't care to live either. It wasn't that I had lost faith in Him. Who God was to me had not changed. I just went into a spiritual hibernation of sorts. The months continued to pass, and it took me a very long time to regain the strength to pray again. Almost a year later, I still felt emotionally exhausted and had to make it a point daily to spend time with Him. But God's grace and forgiveness, like the never-ending tide, continued to come. Every time I turned around, another wave of His grace was right there about to completely wash over me.

God wants a *relationship* with you. In a relationship, we owe it to each other to speak up when we have been hurt. The takeaway here is quite simple. If you are upset, *tell Him*. If you feel betrayed, *tell Him*. Run to Him mad, crying, or screaming—*just run to Him*. God loves you. There is nothing you could say or do to change that. His love is overwhelming, never-failing, and never-ending. He will never give up on you.

———⊗⊗⊗———

There is a tension one must choose to embrace or deny when it comes to the discomfort this life inevitably inflicts and God's sovereignty in the midst of it all. It's hard not to wonder how an all-powerful and loving God could allow so much suffering in this world and *still* be good and trustworthy. I believe it's one of mankind's greatest inner battles and one many of us struggle with—*especially* after loss.

Maybe that is why so many hearts deny Him and the hope that lies openly in His hands. Maybe the strain of the question alone, and our inability to answer it, is the perfect breeding ground for doubt and resentment to grow.

God could have saved my son—but didn't. That truth was profoundly difficult to accept. But God was much bigger than the emotions I threw at His feet. It took time for our relationship to heal, but I knew He was my only hope, even in the midst of my questions and anger. I knew *my* story did not change the integrity of *His* heart.

I didn't have the answers then, and I don't have them now—not even close. But I know Him, and I know this: He is good. Having a relationship with God means knowing He is sovereign over everything that happens *and* still believing He is loving and kind. It's trusting His heart, even when you cannot trace His hand. It's accepting that He could have healed my son but, for reasons I may never understand, chose not to. And despite how painful life can be, it's believing that no piece of Him is cruel, even when everything around you screams the opposite.

For me, my faith was the only avenue to peace. It was knowing and believing without fully understanding. It was the ability for polar-opposite emotions (like joy and sorrow) to coexist in one moment, even when it didn't seem possible. It's God being wholly good, even when His decisions sometimes make us feel incredibly bad. It was realizing that, without the promise only He could provide, I would never see Logan again. It was faith, plain and simple, and I will choose that even on the darkest days.

44 — CHOOSE HOPE

But those who hope in the LORD will renew their strength. They will soar on wings like eagles; they will run and not grow weary, they will walk and not be faint.

—Isaiah 40:31 (NIV)

Photo by Jessica Fox

"How did you survive?" In the first few years after Logan's death, my response was instant and steadfast: "We had no choice. We were placed on a path, and our only option was to walk it."

In the early days of grieving, I believed those words with *every* fiber within me, but they were only partially true. Of course we didn't choose for our son to have a deadly condition. Of course we didn't choose the path that was *forced* upon us. However—we *did* choose to keep living.

I now see tragedy constantly. Babies dying has become some sort of a very messed-up normal in my life. I have seen families grow stronger and families fall apart. I have seen faith grow and faith die. I have seen marriages survive and marriages crumble. I have seen individuals consumed by anger and individuals trying their best to cling to any tiny shards of joy that still remain. I have seen the good, the bad, the ugly—and sometimes, the *very* ugly.

If it hadn't been for Walk With Me and watching others walk the same path we did, I would still believe (with complete conviction) that we had no say in the journey that followed our son's death. But now I have watched countless families' journeys, and the vantage point has made one thing very clear—we had a say. And so do you.

I realize those words may be upsetting. Especially to those who are still very much in the thick of their grief. They surely would have been upsetting for me. For those in that place, it's okay if you are feeling defensive toward what you just read. I want to be a safe place for you, a sort of refuge, and a friend who understands. Right now, you may feel a bit betrayed by that statement, like I *almost* got it right. Embrace it and then let it subside, because I have something important I must share with you.

We absolutely *never* chose to be put on this horrific path. But we absolutely have a choice in *how* we walk it. I had a choice to get up every morning. I had a choice to keep living, to keep breathing, to keep taking life on, one micro step at a time. It wasn't easy. There were days when I was lucky if I even got dressed. There were days when the weight of my grief made it physically hard even to get out of bed. There were days when making dinner was near impossible and washing week-old hair a huge victory.

Often, I felt like a shell, but nevertheless, when I was able, I tried to walk. I forced myself to continue, because I truly didn't think there was another option. It did not look the way I wanted it to, and many times I hardly even wanted the pieces of my life that remained. I was bruised and battered and moved slowly with an obvious limp, but I kept moving. I wish someone would have told me during that season that I was making progress, even when I felt so incredibly stagnant.

I have seen loss-parents press forward to the best of their ability through immense pain, and I have seen individuals so consumed with their sorrow that, years after their loss, they haven't moved an inch. They refuse to take a step away from their grief, not realizing you can always come back to it when needed.

It is not sustainable to fully immerse yourself in sorrow and never come up for air. "Sit in the pit" for as long as you need, but when the day comes that you are brave enough, crawl out of that pit for a few minutes, breathe in some fresh air, and take a step—or several, if you dare. Then, if you can, start walking. Go back to that pit as often as you need. Allow yourself time to embrace the ugly, the messy, and the painful parts of this path. Remember, they are necessary and serve a purpose. So sit in that sorrow, and then, when you can, crawl out and start walking again. As time goes on, you will make it further down the road and find that you return to the pit less and less often.

You see, sitting in your grief is not the problem. Grieving is *not* the problem. Grieving is vital to the healing process. The problem, however, is the *conscious* decision, the *refusal*, to move forward. The problem is when we, the bereaved, decide to *live* in the pit rather than *visit* it.

Sweet friend, there is still life to live. There are still good days ahead. Hope is on the horizon. Sometimes it's just hard to see when there is so much rain. As much as this book was written to hold your hand in the sadness and to sit in that rain *with* you, it was also written to cheer you on and tell you that someday the happy days *will* begin to outnumber the sad. Hold tightly to this hope. Fight for it with all that is left in you. And if you can't believe those words right now, then just know I am fighting for hope on your behalf. I am going to fight for you, pray for you and help you stand until, one day, you believe it to be true.

Losing a child is a defining part of your life, but it does *not* define you. You are so much more. For so long, I thought I would forever be seen as the girl whose baby died. I wish so badly there had been someone around to tell me I was more than that. Yes, I was Logan's mom, but I was also Sullivan and Emersyn's mom, a wife, a sister, a daughter, a friend, a business owner, a writer, a lover of good food, good movies, spring skiing, and warm summer days. The list goes on and on. I needed someone to tell me I had more work to do in this life, that Logan was not my *only* purpose, and that I shouldn't feel guilty when, eventually, other pieces of my life would become important once again. So today, make a choice, right now. Amidst the pain, amidst the sorrow, even when it feels impossible— choose life. *Choose hope.*

45 — EARTH HAS NO SORROW HEAVEN CAN'T HEAL

Now if we are children, then we are heirs—heirs of God and co-heirs with Christ, if indeed we share in his sufferings in order that we may also share in his glory. I consider that our present sufferings are not worth comparing with the glory that will be revealed in us.
—Romans 8:17–18 (NIV)

Photo by Jessica Fox

Many times along this journey, I have gone over and over the list of things I would like God to explain to me one day when I am finally face-to-face with Him. It's absurd to assume the Creator of the universe owes *me* any explanation, but I'm sure I'm not the only one who has questions I'd like answered.

How did you . . . ? Why didn't you . . . ? Where were you . . . ? But the more and more I try to comprehend the reality of one day being in the physical presence of my King, the more and more I realize, when that time comes, I will no longer need the answers. *I will be home.* My soul will be at peace and quenched in a way not possible before, *solely* because of the grace of the God before me. In my heart, I know being surrounded by the purest form of love possible will trump each and every question I ever had. I will be on my knees, and that list of mine? Gone without a trace.

If for some reason I do get the privilege to learn why certain struggles in my life took place and why He allowed certain things to happen, then I hope I *also* have the privilege to learn of the countless times He intervened on my behalf and all the potential pain He spared me. All the times the scary doctor appointments turned out to be okay, all the close calls on the road where there should have been a serious accident, all the moments where I barely missed being in the wrong place at the wrong time. I have a suspicion these events would outweigh my list of "grievances" tenfold.

I don't understand why we have to go through so much pain in this life. I don't know why Logan had to die. I don't understand why you had to endure the pain that led you to these pages. I *do* understand, however, that we live in a sin-filled and fallen world, full of sin-filled and fallen people, and because of that, blame does not fall on God. His original intent was not for His people to live in such a painful and scary place. This is *not* the world He designed for us, but He gave us free will—and we chose sin instead of Him.

Yes, He has the authority to repair any situation, and I don't understand why, on many occasions, He chooses not to. I don't understand how He decides who does and does not get the miracle. But this is His tapestry, not mine. I am simply the creation, and as I near my late thirties, it is something with which I have *finally* made peace. "'For my thoughts are not your thoughts, neither are your ways my ways,' declares the LORD. 'As the heavens are higher than the earth, so are my ways higher than your ways and my thoughts than your thoughts'" (Isa. 55:8–9 NIV).

The truth is we were never meant to understand. We are not capable of understanding. It's a gap that can only be filled by faith. In the midst of the pain and the noise this life throws at us, there are a few things I will choose to hold on to with everything that is in me. He is good. He loves me. In the end *it will be okay*.

If I believe God's Word, if I believe Jesus truly is the Messiah, then with the same conviction I must believe Him when He says He will never leave me—even if at certain moments in my life it may feel the opposite. It's simple really. Either *all* of it is true or *none* of it is. It's all written in the very same book that professes Christ, and I cannot pick and choose only parts of the Bible to follow or believe. This can be a hard pill to swallow, but His Word and His truth will *always* trump my feelings.

God has already given us the greatest gift imaginable. He has already given all of us a miracle, and that is His Son and our salvation. It is a priceless gift with endless value, because there is nothing we could ever do to earn, deserve, or pay Him back for it. That doesn't negate or lessen the fact that life inevitably brings seasons of consuming pain.

If you find yourself in such a season today, my heart is with you. I'm still very much in the middle of my own struggles—life doesn't relent in its challenges, but I still believe the things to come for Christ's followers *after* this life will be so wonderfully unimaginable that the pain and suffering we feel down here will pale in comparison.

Thomas Moore, an Irish songwriter, once eloquently said, "Earth has no sorrow that heaven cannot heal." With every fiber within me, I believe that statement to be true.

———❧———

I could never have understood the depth or capacity of love that was possible between a parent and their child until I had one of my own. The truth is, having Logan opened my eyes to a love I never knew existed and never thought possible. On the surface, it seemed like no greater love could possibly exist. Life would eventually teach me I couldn't have been more wrong. You see, when I take a step back, there is a love that trumps all others.

As you read through these pages, you probably assumed the "love story" I spoke of at the very beginning of this book was between me and my son. Sure, that was a beautiful byproduct, but the love story I spoke of was actually between God and you. Yup—*you*.

God's love for *you* surpasses all others. *You* are His beloved, His child, and the absolute delight of His heart. The greatest of all loves exists between the Creator and His creation—the people He formed in His image, the people He willingly sacrificed His Son for, and the people He loves so perfectly that it could never be fully comprehended.

It is the honest desire of my heart that God has used my family's story—the ashes of my family's life—to grow something beautiful out of you. You, sweet friend, are my *wildflower*.

I hope, as you find yourself coming to the end of these pages, that they have brought you comfort. I pray you no longer feel alone, and that in some measurable way, your hope has been renewed. I pray my beautiful little boy has impacted you in a way that helps you view life a little differently. But most of all, I pray Logan's story has brought you closer to Christ.

Throughout these pages, I have been asking God to speak to you. For *ten* years, I have been asking God to prepare you for this very moment, praying that you would realize the quickening of your heartbeat is not coincidental but your spirit beginning to celebrate in anticipation of the union it craves. I pray you will not let this moment pass.

If you have never known Him, I am delighted to tell you it is an easy fix. There is no exact prayer. Just ask Jesus to forgive you of your sins and welcome Him into your heart. *It's that simple.* Say yes to Christ now, and you will have Him and His love for all of eternity. "If you confess with your mouth that Jesus is Lord and believe in your heart that God raised him from the dead, you will be saved" (Rom. 10:9 ESV).

In the end, Jesus wins. If He is in your heart, then in the end, you win too. Regardless of every other chapter of our book, even the messy and painful ones, our *last* chapter ends in victory. Our last chapter ends with our families whole.

I used to wish I had a testimony. Funny thing was, even prior to my journey with Logan, I already did. Jesus was and *still* is my testimony. There is really no need to complicate it—it's just Him. I am the one who deserved death but in return was given life. I believe God looks down on us much like I looked down on Logan the day he was born—madly in love, heart seeping tears over our brokenness, and desperately wanting to help. If you haven't already, I hope and pray that today would be the day you would finally let Him.

May the Lord bless you and keep you; may His face shine down upon you and be gracious to you; may He turn His face toward you and give you His peace (Num. 6:24–26).

Much Love,
Jamie

A SPECIAL THANK-YOU

Photo by Jessica Fox

This book could never have reached the depth and vulnerability its readers deserved without the help of my sister.

Kelley, your words are drenched in wisdom, and I am honored the world gets to hear your voice within the pages of this book. Thank you for being so beautifully you. I could never repay you for the ways you showed up in my life all those years ago and continue to show up today. Thank you for not running away. Thank you for loving my boy with zeal, protecting him with fierceness, and upholding his memory with passion. I could not have told this story without you by my side.

I love you so much, big sis.
JME

ABOUT THE AUTHOR

J amie Stewart is the youngest of three children, was raised in a loving Christian home, and grew up in the beautiful state of Colorado. Jamie has been married to her wonderful husband, Andy, since 2009, and together they have three beautiful children: their firstborn, Logan, his little brother, Sullivan, and their youngest, Emersyn Grace. Her children are her life's greatest gifts, and being their mom is her greatest title. It is the most beautifully challenging thing she has ever experienced but by far the most rewarding.

Jamie has been a follower of Christ as long as she can remember, and she strives every day to be more and more like Him. He is her Creator, her Savior, and hands down, her foundation. Jamie is the Co-Founder and Director of the nonprofit Walk With Me, which devotes its time and resources to help families through the death of a baby in utero or shortly after birth. It is undoubtedly not a ministry she would have ever dreamed of being a part of but, nonetheless, something she feels called to do.

Jamie's life and identity are woven together by many loves, strengths, weaknesses, dreams, and fears. However, considering the long list of what makes her who she is, she would never have placed writing under "strengths." Never in a million years would she have considered herself a writer or spent any amount of her free time writing. And yet, thanks to the life of an amazing little boy, she fell in love with words and spent countless hours in the last ten years of her life using them as part of her healing process.

To learn more please visit our website at
WWW.WALKWITHME-NONPROFIT.ORG

Follow us on Instagram
@WALKWITHMEDOTORG

CPSIA information can be obtained
at www.ICGtesting.com
Printed in the USA
BVHW051554111022
648966BV00005B/8